Mastering Go Programming

From Basics to Expert Proficiency

Contents

Introduction

Go, also known as Golang, is a statically-typed, compiled programming language designed for simplicity, efficiency, and reliability. Developed by Robert Griesemer, Rob Pike, and Ken Thompson at Google, Go was created to address the challenges faced by developers in large-scale software development. It aims to balance the ease of programming and performance, making it a powerful tool for both beginners and seasoned developers.

The primary goal of this book, "Mastering Go Programming: From Basics to Expert Proficiency," is to provide a comprehensive guide to learning Go, starting from the fundamental concepts and extending to advanced techniques and practical applications. As you progress through the chapters, you will gain a thorough understanding of Go's syntax, features, and best practices, enabling you to develop robust and efficient software solutions.

Go stands out among programming languages due to its concurrency model, which is based on goroutines and channels. This model allows developers to write highly concurrent programs efficiently without the complexity associated with traditional multithreading. Additionally, Go's garbage collector, powerful standard library, and strong community support make it an attractive choice for modern software development.

Throughout this book, we will explore various aspects of Go programming, including setting up the Go environment, understanding basic syntax and data types, mastering control structures, working with functions, and utilizing composite data types such as arrays, slices, and maps. We will delve into more advanced topics like structs and methods, concurrency, error handling, and leveraging the extensive capabilities of the Go standard library.

Testing and quality assurance are crucial components of the software development process. In the later chapters, we will cover testing practices in Go, including writing test cases, benchmarking, and mock testing to ensure that your programs are reliable and perform well under various conditions.

To provide a practical learning experience, this book includes numerous examples, exercises, and projects. These practical applications will help solidify your understanding of Go concepts and demonstrate how to apply them in real-world scenarios. Whether you are building web servers, developing RESTful APIs, working with databases, or implementing concurrent data processing, you will find valuable insights and techniques to enhance your skills.

By the end of this book, you will be equipped with the knowledge and tools necessary to tackle complex programming challenges using Go. You will have a deep appreciation for Go's design principles and an understanding of how to leverage its unique features to build scalable and maintainable software.

We invite you to immerse yourself in the world of Go programming and to approach each chapter with curiosity and focus. With dedication and practice, you will master the language and be well-prepared to create innovative and efficient software solutions in today's rapidly evolving technological landscape.

Chapter 1

Introduction to Go Programming

This chapter provides an overview of the Go programming language, covering its history, philosophy, and unique features. It draws comparisons with other languages to highlight Go's strengths and modern uses. Key benefits and common applications are discussed, followed by a basic introduction to Go's workflow with a simple "Hello World" program. Community resources and support channels are also introduced to assist beginners in their learning journey.

1.1 Overview of Go

Go, also known as Golang, is an open-source programming language designed for simplicity, efficiency, and reliability. Created by engineers at Google and released publicly in 2009, Go combines the performance and security benefits of statically-compiled languages with the ease and productivity of dynamically-typed, interpreted languages. Its design caters primarily to systems programming through a robust standard library, concurrency mechanisms, and cross-platform support.

One of the most notable features of Go is its clean syntax, which facilitates readability and maintainability of code. This language embraces a minimalist approach without sacrificing power, making it appealing to both new and experienced programmers. Key features include garbage collection, concurrent programming capabilities, and modern networked applications' deployment capabilities.

Go's type system is both flexible and expressive, allowing developers to write comprehensible and error-free code. A balance between explicit declaration and inferred typing fosters both precision and brevity. For instance, the var keyword allows for explicit type declarations, while the := operator supports concise variable declaration with automatic type inference:

```
var x int = 10 // Explicit type declaration
y := 42 // Type inference
```

Go's focus on simplicity extends to its package management. The language utilizes a modular structure where programs are organized into packages. Each package has a well-defined path and scope, aiding in code organization and preventing namespace collision. The import statement is used to include packages:

```
import "fmt"
import "math/rand"
```

Concurrency in Go is handled with elegance through goroutines and channels. Goroutines are lightweight threads managed by the Go runtime, allowing thousands of concurrent tasks to be executed efficiently. Channels enable communication between goroutines, facilitating synchronized data exchange:

```
go func() {
    fmt.Println("Hello from a goroutine")
}()

ch := make(chan int)
go func() {
    ch <- 42
}()
fmt.Println(<-ch)
```

Error handling in Go is explicit, eschewing exceptions in favor of multiple return values, separating normal and exceptional paths clearly. This reduces the likelihood of ignoring errors and enhances program reliability:

```
file, err := os.Open("example.txt")
if err != nil {
    log.Fatal(err)
}
defer file.Close()
```

The Go standard library is a key strength, providing comprehensive packages for tasks such as I/O, cryptography, and HTTP server implementation. The libraries are designed with the same attention to simplicity and performance that typifies Go:

```
func main() {
    http.HandleFunc("/", func(w http.ResponseWriter, r *http.Request) {
        fmt.Fprintln(w, "Hello, Go!")
    })
    http.ListenAndServe(":8080", nil)
}
```

Go's tooling ecosystem is robust and includes tools for formatting (gofmt), testing (go test), and dependency management (go mod). These tools promote best practices and streamline the development process. The gofmt tool, for example, enforces a coding style, making code consistent across projects:

```
$ gofmt -w yourcode.go
```

Go supports cross-compilation, allowing developers to build binaries for different operating systems and architectures from a single codebase. This feature is particularly valuable for deploying applications across diverse environments:

```
$ GOOS=linux GOARCH=amd64 go build -o myapp
```

Overall, Go's design emphasizes code simplicity, performance, and developer productivity. These principles are ingrained in the language and tooling, making Go an excellent choice for modern software development. Whether developing scalable server software, data pipelines, or cloud services, Go provides the features and performance characteristics needed to succeed.

1.2 History and Philosophy of Go

The Go programming language, often referred to as Golang, was conceived at Google in 2007 by Robert Griesemer, Rob Pike, and Ken Thompson. It was created in response to the growing complexity and concurrency challenges faced in large-scale software development. While Go drew inspiration from several languages, including C, it was designed to be more efficient and simpler to use. This synthesis resulted in a robust language that balances simplicity, performance, and reliability.

Go's development was publicly announced in November 2009, and its first stable release, version 1.0, was launched in March 2012. From its inception, the language's development process has emphasized transparency and community involvement, ensuring a well-supported and continuously evolving ecosystem.

The philosophy behind Go centers on several key principles: simplicity, concurrency, efficiency, and strong support for modern hardware architectures. These principles guided the design of Go's syntax and features, which aim to facilitate clean and efficient coding practices while maintaining readability and productivity.

Simplicity in Go is achieved through a minimalistic but expressive syntax. The language eliminates unnecessary complexities present in other programming languages, such as C++ and Java. For instance, Go avoids the convoluted type inheritance of object-oriented programming, favoring a more straightforward composition approach. This design choice leads to clearer and more maintainable code, which is particularly beneficial in large-scale projects.

Concurrency is a core aspect of Go's design. Given the increasing prevalence of multicore processors, Go provides first-class support for concurrent programming via goroutines and channels. Goroutines are lightweight threads managed by the Go runtime, enabling scalable and efficient execution of concurrent tasks. Channels allow goroutines to communicate and synchronize with each other seamlessly. This model simplifies the development of concurrent programs, ensuring that they are both performant and easy to reason about.

The efficiency of Go stems from its statically typed nature and the use of a garbage collector that manages memory automatically. The garbage collector in Go is designed to operate with low latency, minimizing its impact on program performance. Additionally, Go's compiler produces fast, native code that can be executed directly on the target architecture, further enhancing runtime efficiency.

Go's language design also pays close attention to modern hardware architectures. The language and its standard library are optimized for performance on multicore processors, which are now ubiquitous in computing devices. This optimization ensures that Go programs can leverage the full potential of contemporary hardware, making it a preferred choice for performance-critical systems.

An essential part of Go's philosophy is its embrace of open-source principles. The language has been open-source since its public release, fostering a vibrant community of contributors and users. This community-driven development model has accelerated the language's growth and adoption, with a rich ecosystem of tools, libraries, and frameworks emerging to support developers.

To illustrate Go's concurrency model, consider a simple example where we create multiple goroutines to compute the sum of an array concurrently. Here is a Go program demonstrating this concept:

```
// Concurrent sum computation using goroutines
package main

import (
    "fmt"
    "sync"
)

func sumPart(arr []int, resultChan chan<- int, wg *sync.WaitGroup) {
    defer wg.Done()
    sum := 0
    for _, v := range arr {
        sum += v
    }
    resultChan <- sum
}

func main() {
    arr := []int{1, 2, 3, 4, 5, 6, 7, 8, 9, 10}
    resultChan := make(chan int, 2)
    var wg sync.WaitGroup

    // Divide array into two parts and process them concurrently
    wg.Add(2)
    go sumPart(arr[:len(arr)/2], resultChan, &wg)
    go sumPart(arr[len(arr)/2:], resultChan, &wg)

    // Wait for both goroutines to complete
    wg.Wait()
    close(resultChan)

    // Sum partial results
    totalSum := 0
    for partialSum := range resultChan {
        totalSum += partialSum
    }

    fmt.Printf("Total Sum: %d\n", totalSum)
}
```

In the above program, sumPart function computes the sum of part of an array. This function is run in two separate goroutines, which are synchronized using a sync.WaitGroup. The results of the partial sums are communicated back to the main goroutine through a channel resultChan. Finally, the partial sums are aggregated to produce the total sum.

The historical context and philosophical underpinnings of Go demonstrate its intentional design to address contemporary software development challenges. By focusing on simplicity, concurrency, efficiency, and suitability for modern hardware, Go provides developers with a powerful tool to build robust, scalable, and maintainable software systems.

1.3 Comparing Go with Other Languages

When contrasting Go (often referred to as Golang) with other prominent programming languages, several factors come to the forefront. These include simplicity, performance, concurrency model, compilation speed, and the standard library's comprehensiveness. This section explores how Go relates to languages like C, C++, Java, Python, and JavaScript in these key areas.

Simplicity: Go is designed with simplicity as a core tenet, prioritizing clear and maintainable code. Unlike languages such as C++ or Java, which have extensive feature sets and syntactic complexity, Go intentionally omits features like inheritance, polymorphism, and generics (though it is being considered for future releases). This simplicity reduces the learning curve for new programmers and minimizes the potential for complicated and unreadable code.

Performance: Go is a statically typed, compiled language, akin to C and C++, enabling it to deliver high performance. While Go might not match the fine-grained optimization potential of C or C++ in some scenarios, it performs significantly better than interpreted languages like Python and JavaScript. The ability to compile to native machine code provides an edge in execution speed over Java, especially in programs requiring low-latency solutions.

Concurrency Model: One of the standout features of Go is its concurrency model, anchored by goroutines and channels. Goroutines are lightweight threads managed by the Go runtime, which provides efficient concurrency without the overhead seen in traditional threading models, such as those in Java or C++. Channels facilitate safe communication between goroutines, fostering a CSP (Communicating

Sequential Processes) style of concurrent programming. This is in contrast to Python's GIL (Global Interpreter Lock), which hampers true parallel execution of threads.

```
package main

import (
    "fmt"
    "time"
)

func say(s string) {
    for i := 0; i < 5; i++ {
        time.Sleep(100 * time.Millisecond)
        fmt.Println(s)
    }
}

func main() {
    go say("world")
    say("hello")
}
```

Listing 1.1: Example of Concurrency in Go using Goroutines

Output of above program execution:

```
hello
world
hello
world
hello
world
hello
world
hello
```

Compilation Speed: Go's compilation speed is another notable advantage. The compiler is designed to be fast, often compiling large projects within seconds. This is a stark contrast to languages like C++ or Java, where long compilation times can impede development productivity. Go achieves this speed by employing a single-pass compilation system and efficient dependency tracking.

Standard Library: Go offers a rich standard library that includes packages for web servers, cryptography, and file I/O, among many others. This built-in functionality reduces the need for third-party libraries, in contrast to languages like JavaScript, which relies heavily on external packages from npm. The comprehensive nature of Go's standard library streamlines the development process and ensures a higher level of code reliability and security.

Additionally, Go's philosophy of "batteries-included" mirrors Python's design, albeit with a focus on network and system programming, where Go excels due to its origins in building highly scalable systems at Google.

Memory Management: Go employs automatic garbage collection to manage memory. This is similar to Java and in stark contrast to C and C++, which require manual memory management. However, Go's garbage collector is designed to have minimal impact on performance, making it suitable for systems programming where predictable latency and performance are critical.

The language choices affect applications differently. For instance, Go's garbage collection and goroutines make it ideal for backend systems, microservices, and network tools, where its performance and concurrency features are best utilized. Conversely, languages like Python and JavaScript are favored for web development and scripting due to their vast ecosystems and dynamic typing features.

Error Handling: A unique aspect of Go is its approach to error handling, emphasizing explicit error checking over exceptions. This is a departure from languages like Java or Python, which handle errors through try-catch mechanisms. Go developers handle errors by inspecting returned error values, promoting a clear and predictable error management style.

```
package main

import (
    "errors"
    "fmt"
)

func divide(a, b float64) (float64, error) {
    if b == 0 {
        return 0, errors.New("cannot divide by zero")
    }
    return a / b, nil
}

func main() {
    result, err := divide(4, 0)
    if err != nil {
        fmt.Println("Error:", err)
    } else {
        fmt.Println("Result:", result)
    }
}
```

Listing 1.2: Example of Error Handling in Go

Output of above program execution:

```
Error: cannot divide by zero
```

In conclusion, Go's distinct features and design choices reflect its goals of simplicity, performance, and efficient concurrency. By examining these attributes in comparison to other languages, it becomes evident why Go has been adopted widely for systems programming, cloud computing, and backend development. These comparisons underscore Go's strategic advantages and illustrate its appropriate application contexts.

1.4 Go's Place in Modern Software Development

Go has firmly established itself as a significant player in modern software development. Among its many attributes, the language's simplicity, efficiency, and concurrent programming capabilities stand out as critical components contributing to its widespread adoption and success.

One of the central reasons for Go's relevance in contemporary software development is its concurrency model, which employs goroutines and channels. This model allows developers to efficiently manage multiple tasks simultaneously, which is particularly beneficial in the era of multicore processors.

To demonstrate the concept of goroutines and channels in Go, consider the following example:

```
package main

import (
    "fmt"
    "time"
)

func worker(id int, jobs <-chan int, results chan<- int) {
    for j := range jobs {
        fmt.Printf("worker %d started job %d\n", id, j)
        time.Sleep(time.Second) // simulate work
```

```
        fmt.Printf("worker %d finished job %d\n", id, j)
        results <- j * 2
    }
}

func main() {
    const numJobs = 5
    jobs := make(chan int, numJobs)
    results := make(chan int, numJobs)

    for w := 1; w <= 3; w++ {
        go worker(w, jobs, results)
    }

    for j := 1; j <= numJobs; j++ {
        jobs <- j
    }
    close(jobs)

    for a := 1; a <= numJobs; a++ {
        <-results
    }
}
```

When executed, the program will produce an output similar to:

```
worker 1 started job 1
worker 2 started job 2
worker 3 started job 3
worker 1 finished job 1
worker 1 started job 4
worker 2 finished job 2
worker 2 started job 5
...
```

Another critical factor is Go's comprehensive standard library, which provides robust tools for various tasks such as text processing, web development, and cryptography. This extensive collection of packages simplifies common programming tasks, allowing developers to create efficient and secure applications without relying heavily on external libraries.

For example, Go's net/http package enables rapid development of efficient web servers:

```
package main

import (
    "fmt"
    "net/http"
)
```

```
func handler(w http.ResponseWriter, r *http.Request) {
    fmt.Fprintf(w, "Hello, World!")
}

func main() {
    http.HandleFunc("/", handler)
    http.ListenAndServe(":8080", nil)
}
```

Running this server allows users to access http://localhost:8080 and see "Hello, World!" displayed on their browser, demonstrating the ease of setting up a web server with minimal code.

In modern software ecosystems, Go is extensively used in cloud services and infrastructure projects. Kubernetes, Docker, and Terraform are notable examples of critical infrastructure projects built with Go. These projects benefit from Go's statically linked binaries, which are easy to deploy and have minimal runtime dependencies.

Furthermore, Go's strong type system and garbage collection contribute to its reliability and efficiency. The language features, such as slices, interfaces, and garbage-collected heap allocation, reduce the likelihood of memory leaks and runtime errors, which are crucial in long-running server applications.

The introduction of generics in Go 1.18 has further strengthened its position by providing more flexibility and type safety. Generics allow developers to write reusable and efficient code without compromising performance:

```
package main

import "fmt"

func Map[T any](s []T, f func(T) T) []T {
    r := make([]T, len(s))
    for i, v := range s {
        r[i] = f(v)
    }
    return r
}

func main() {
    nums := []int{1, 2, 3, 4}
    squares := Map(nums, func(n int) int { return n * n })
    fmt.Println(squares)
}
```

This example showcases how generics can simplify the creation of a function that applies a given operation to each element of a slice, producing a new slice with the transformed elements.

Finally, the active and growing Go community, along with strong support from Google and many other corporations, ensures the continuous development and evolution of the language. Regular releases and an expansive set of tools, such as the Go Playground, facilitate learning and experimentation, further cementing Go's digital footprint in modern software development.

Overall, its efficient concurrency model, powerful standard library, widespread use in critical projects, type safety, and active community involvement highlight Go's crucial role and effectiveness in modern software development contexts.

1.5 Key Features and Benefits of Go

Go, often referred to as Golang, is a statically typed, compiled language designed for modern software engineering needs. Its simplicity and efficiency have resulted in a growing adoption in various domains. This section elucidates the key features of the Go programming language and expounds on the benefits derived from these features.

1. Concurrency Support

Go's native concurrency model, based on goroutines and channels, is a standout feature. Goroutines are functions or methods that run concurrently with other goroutines. They are lightweight, managed by the Go runtime, and can efficiently handle thousands of concurrent operations.

```
package main

import (
    "fmt"
    "time"
)

func hello() {
    fmt.Println("Hello from a goroutine!")
}

func main() {
    go hello()
    time.Sleep(1 * time.Second)
}
```

The above code demonstrates launching a goroutine with the go keyword. The time.Sleep function ensures that the main function does not exit before the goroutine prints its message.

Channels facilitate safe and efficient communication between goroutines, enhancing concurrency.

```
package main

import "fmt"

func main() {
    messages := make(chan string)

    go func() { messages <- "ping" }()

    msg := <-messages
    fmt.Println(msg)
}
```

Channels in Go ensure that data exchange between goroutines is synchronized without explicit locking mechanisms, reducing the likelihood of concurrency bugs.

2. Simplicity and Syntax

Go's syntax is designed to be straightforward and readable, encouraging clarity and productivity. It avoids complex inheritance hierarchies, templates, and operator overloading that can obfuscate code in other languages. This simplicity does not compromise functionality but ensures codebases remain maintainable and comprehensible.

```
package main

import "fmt"

func main() {
    fmt.Println("Hello, World!")
}
```

The above example illustrates the minimalistic syntax for a simple Go program.

3. Performance

Go combines the ease of interpreted languages with the efficiency of compiled languages. The Go compiler produces statically linked native binaries that are fast and efficient. The language's design accommodates high-performance systems programming, making it suitable for tasks traditionally handled by C or C++.

4. Static Typing and Compiler Efficiency

Go's static typing and type inference increase reliability and performance. Static typing detects type errors at compile-time, reducing runtime errors. Type inference reduces verbosity, ensuring expressiveness without sacrificing type safety.

```
package main

import "fmt"

func add(a, b int) int {
    return a + b
}

func main() {
    sum := add(3, 4)
    fmt.Println(sum)
}
```

The Go compiler is known for its speed and efficiency, making the build process swift and seamless even for large codebases.

5. Standard Library

Go's robust standard library provides packages for a wide array of functionalities, from file handling to web servers, without the need for third-party dependencies. The comprehensive nature of the standard library accelerates development and enhances reliability.

```
package main

import (
    "fmt"
    "net/http"
)

func handler(w http.ResponseWriter, r *http.Request) {
    fmt.Fprintf(w, "Hello, World!")
}

func main() {
    http.HandleFunc("/", handler)
    http.ListenAndServe(":8080", nil)
}
```

The example demonstrates using the standard library to create a simple web server.

6. Cross-Platform Compatibility

Go supports cross-platform development, which means programs can be compiled to run on different operating systems like Linux, Windows, and macOS with minimal changes. The go build command makes it straightforward to build binaries for multiple platforms.

```
$ GOOS=linux GOARCH=amd64 go build -o hello-linux main.go
$ GOOS=windows GOARCH=amd64 go build -o hello.exe main.go
$ GOOS=darwin GOARCH=amd64 go build -o hello-darwin main.go
```

7. Garbage Collection

Go includes a robust garbage collector that manages memory efficiently. This eliminates the need for manual memory management and reduces the risk of memory leaks and segmentation faults while still offering high performance and low latency suitable for server software.

8. Tooling and Community Support

Go's ecosystem includes a suite of tools integrated into the language. These tools assist in tasks such as formatting (gofmt), testing (go test), and dependency management (go mod).

```
$ gofmt -w main.go % Automatically formats Go source code
$ go test ./... % Runs all tests in the current directory and subdirectories
$ go mod init % Initializes a new module in the working directory
```

Go's thriving community continually contributes to its ecosystem, providing a plethora of libraries and frameworks that expedite development.

9. Strong Backing and Real-World Adoption

Go is backed by Google, ensuring ongoing development and support. It has been adopted by numerous corporations and projects due to its efficiency, concurrency support, and simplicity.

Companies like Docker, Kubernetes, and many others use Go for their critical systems due to these reasons mentioned above, showcasing its real-world capabilities.

The amalgamation of these features and benefits establishes Go as a powerful, efficient, and highly productive programming language for modern software development.

1.6 Popular Use Cases and Applications

Go, also known as Golang, has been embraced by the software development community for a variety of applications due to its robust features, simplicity, and efficiency. This section delineates the various popular use cases and applications of Go, elucidating why it serves as a preferred choice in these domains.

Go's concurrency model, facilitated by goroutines and channels, makes it a strong candidate for network servers. The ability to handle thousands of concurrent connections with minimal overhead is a significant advantage. Prominent examples include:

- Net/http package is adept at building web servers.
- Implementation of microservices that can communicate seamlessly.

The following example demonstrates a simple web server using Go's standard library:

```
package main

import (
    "fmt"
    "net/http"
)

func handler(w http.ResponseWriter, r *http.Request) {
    fmt.Fprintf(w, "Hello, World!")
}

func main() {
    http.HandleFunc("/", handler)
    http.ListenAndServe(":8080", nil)
}
```

Upon accessing http://localhost:8080, the output produced is as follows:

```
Hello, World!
```

Go also excels in the domain of cloud computing and distributed systems. Many companies have adopted Go to build large-scale distributed systems due to its performance and simplicity. Kubernetes and Docker, two pivotal technologies in the containerization and orchestration space, have Go at their core. The concise syntax and efficient execution make it suitable for tasks such as writing cloud-native applications and microservices architecture.

In DevOps and automation, Go's compilation to static binaries facilitates easier deployments. The language's simplicity aids in writing maintainable scripts and tools. Terraform, an open-source tool for building, changing, and versioning infrastructure, showcases Go's prowess in this realm.

The following algorithm demonstrates a basic approach to managing infrastructure as code using Terraform:

Algorithm 1: Basic Terraform Workflow

Input: Infrastructure code (Terraform configuration files)
Output: Provisioned and managed infrastructure

1. Initialize the working directory containing Terraform configuration files;
2. terraform init;
3. Apply the configuration to create or update infrastructure;
4. terraform apply;

Data processing and manipulation are critical in various applications, from web scraping to data analysis. Go's standard library boasts packages such as encoding/csv, encoding/json, bufio, and io that make handling different data formats straightforward.

Here is a simple program to read and parse a CSV file:

```
package main

import (
    "encoding/csv"
    "fmt"
    "os"
)

func main() {
    file, err := os.Open("data.csv")
    if err != nil {
        fmt.Println("Error:", err)
        return
    }
    defer file.Close()

    reader := csv.NewReader(file)
    records, err := reader.ReadAll()
    if err != nil {
        fmt.Println("Error:", err)
        return
    }

    for _, record := range records {
```

```
        fmt.Println(record)
    }
}
```

The financial technology (fintech) sector also benefits from Go's capabilities. The need for high-performance and concurrent processing of transactions and data is critical. Go's ability to efficiently perform multiple tasks simultaneously makes it an ideal choice for building scalable financial applications.

In the world of game development, Go's performance and ease of use have led to its adoption for game server development. The language facilitates handling numerous simultaneous connections and real-time updates required for multiplayer games. Libraries such as Ebiten and Pixel are examples of frameworks built on Go for game development.

Furthermore, Go's static typing, garbage collection, and powerful standard library support software that's both high-level and close to the metal. For example, Golang.org/x/crypto captures various cryptographic operations, providing a solid base for security-focused applications.

Overall, Go's diverse applications in modern software development arise from its combination of simplicity, performance, and efficient concurrent processing capabilities, making it a versatile addition to the developer's toolkit. These attributes, coupled with a strong and evolving ecosystem, continue to drive Go's adoption in various domains.

1.7 Hello World in Go

The "Hello World" program is a foundational exercise for understanding the syntax and structure of a new programming language. In Go, this simple program introduces vital concepts such as package declaration, importing libraries, and defining functions. This section will dissect each element of a basic "Hello World" program in Go, ensuring a thorough grasp.

First, open your text editor or Integrated Development Environment (IDE) and create a new file named hello.go. In this file, we start by defining the package name:

```
// The package declaration specifies the package to which the file belongs.
package main
```

The keyword package is used to declare the package name. In Go, programs are organized into packages. The main package is a special package. When Go programs are executed, the main package is used as the entry point.

Next, we need to import the fmt package, which contains functions for formatting I/O operations. For a "Hello World" program, we'll use it to print text to the standard output.

```
// Importing the "fmt" package which provides I/O formatting methods.
import "fmt"
```

The import statement allows us to include code from other packages, providing access to external libraries and functions. The fmt package is part of Go's standard library.

We then define the entry point of the program with the main function:

```
// The main function serves as the entry point for program execution.
func main() {
    // Printing "Hello, World!" to the standard output using fmt.Println.
    fmt.Println("Hello, World!")
}
```

The main function is where execution begins. In Go, the func keyword declares a function. The main function has no parameters and does not return a value, consistent with its role in the program's entry.

The line fmt.Println("Hello, World!") utilizes the Println function from the fmt package to output text. The Println function formats its arguments and writes to standard output, appending a newline at the end.

The complete hello.go file looks as follows:

```
package main

import "fmt"

func main() {
    fmt.Println("Hello, World!")
}
```

To compile and run this program, navigate to the directory containing hello.go using the terminal or command prompt. Execute the following commands:

First, compile the program with:

```
$ go build hello.go
```

This command generates an executable file named hello (on Unix-like systems) or hello.exe (on Windows).

Next, run the executable:

```
$ ./hello    // On Unix-like systems
C:\> hello   // On Windows
```

The output should display:

```
Hello, World!
```

This simple program encapsulates the essential elements of a Go application: package declaration, importing libraries, defining the main function, and using the fmt package for output. Understanding this structure is fundamental for writing and organizing larger Go programs.

1.8 Basic Tools and Workflow

A robust understanding of Go's basic tools and workflow is essential for effective development. This section delves into the primary tools provided by the Go ecosystem, the structure of a Go workspace, and the steps involved in compiling and running Go programs. Each tool and process will be examined meticulously to ensure clarity and practical understanding.

The Go distribution includes several command-line tools that are pivotal in the workspace:

- go: The central tool for managing Go code.
- gofmt: A formatting tool to ensure code adheres to Go style guidelines.
- godoc: A documentation server for Go packages.
- go test: A framework for running unit tests.

The go Tool

The go tool orchestrates various development tasks. It provides commands to manage workspace, fetch dependencies, compile programs, run tests, and more. Below are some common commands facilitated by the go tool:

```
go env
go get
go mod
go build
go run
go test
go fmt
go doc
```

Workspace Structure

A Go workspace is a directory hierarchy with three specific directories at its root:

- src: Contains Go source files, organized by package imports.
- pkg: Contains package objects, primarily for dependency management.
- bin: Stores compiled binary executables.

A typical workspace might look like this:

```
myworkspace/
  src/
    github.com/user/
      myproject/
        main.go
  pkg/
    darwin_amd64/
  bin/
```

Compiling and Running a Program

To compile a Go program, navigate to the directory containing the source file and use the go build command:

```
cd path/to/source
go build
```

This produces an executable named after the containing directory. To run the program, simply execute the compiled binary:

```
./myproject
```

Alternatively, to compile and run a program in one step, use the go run command:

```
go run main.go
```

Dependency Management with go mod

Go Modules streamline the management of dependencies. A module is a collection of Go packages stored in a directory with a go.mod file at its root. To initialize a new module within your project:

```
go mod init github.com/user/myproject
```

This creates a go.mod file in the root directory of the project. To add a dependency, use the go get command:

```
go get package/path
```

This fetches the dependency and updates the go.mod file appropriately.

Formatting Code with gofmt

The gofmt tool reformats Go code to follow standard formatting conventions. It is highly recommended to use gofmt regularly to maintain code readability and consistency. To format a file, run:

```
gofmt -w main.go
```

The -w flag writes the formatted output directly to the file.

Testing with go test

The go test tool automates the testing of Go packages. Testing is crucial for ensuring code correctness and reliability. Tests are typically written in files ending with _test.go. To run tests in a package:

```
go test package_name
```

Ensure test functions follow the naming convention TestXxx and are defined using the testing package.

```
package mypackage

import "testing"

func TestFunction(t *testing.T) {
    result := SomeFunction()
    if result != expected {
        t.Errorf("unexpected result: got %v, want %v", result, expected)
    }
}
```

Documentation with godoc

The godoc tool serves documentation for Go packages. It runs a local web server, enabling developers to browse package documentation in a web browser. Start the documentation server with:

```
godoc -http=:6060
```

Visit localhost:6060 in a web browser to access the API documentation.

Understanding and effectively utilizing Go's tools and predefined workflows fundamentally enhances productivity and code quality. Each tool serves a distinct purpose, aiding in the seamless execution of development activities.

1.9 Community Resources and Support

One of the pivotal aspects of learning and mastering a programming language is the ability to connect with a community of fellow learners, experienced developers, and contributors. The Go programming language, often referred to as Golang, boasts an extensive and vibrant community that offers a multitude of resources and support channels. These resources can significantly augment your learning process, facilitate problem-solving, and provide insights into best practices and advanced usage.

The Go community embraces collaboration and open-source principles, ensuring that a wealth of knowledge is readily accessible. Key resources and support channels include official documentation, forums, user groups, online courses, and various repositories of code examples and libraries.

The first and foremost resource to utilize is the official Go documentation, which is meticulously maintained and frequently updated. The Go documentation can be accessed via the official website at https://golang.org/doc/. It includes comprehensive guides on language syntax, libraries, tools, and detailed examples that can help clarify concepts and demonstrate the practical use of features.

```
package main

import "fmt"

func main() {
    fmt.Println("Hello, World!")
}
```

Listing 1.3: Example from Go Documentation

In addition to the official documentation, the Go Forum (https://forum.golangbridge.org/) is a valuable platform for seeking help, discussing ideas, and sharing knowledge. The forum is organized into various categories, including "Getting Help," "Technical Discussion," and "Show Your Code," allowing users to find relevant information or post queries in the appropriate section.

Another essential resource is the *Go Slack Workspace*, which consists of numerous channels dedicated to different aspects of Go programming. These channels often encompass areas such as beginners' help, advanced usage, libraries, concurrency, and more. To join the Go Slack community, you can sign up at https://invite.slack.golangbridge.org/.

Moreover, the Go community is known for its localized user groups and meetups, which occur globally. These in-person or virtual meetings provide opportunities to network, attend talks and workshops, and collaborate on projects. Information about Go meetups can frequently be found on platforms like Meetup.com or via local tech community boards.

For real-time discussions and instant responses, the Go *Reddit* community (https://www.reddit.com/r/golang/) and the *Stack Overflow* forum (https://stackoverflow.com/questions/tagged/go) are indispensable. On Reddit, users post news, questions, tutorials, and interesting projects, fostering a community of sharing and learning. Meanwhile, Stack Overflow serves as an extensive archive of questions and solutions, enabling users to search for problems similar to their own or to ask new questions.

Dedicated online courses and tutorials offer structured and in-depth learning experiences. Platforms such as Coursera, Udacity, and Udemy provide courses ranging from introductory levels to advanced topics in Go. For a more hands-on approach, websites like Exercism (https://exercism.io/tracks/go) present programming exercises that cover various aspects of Go programming.

Numerous books written by experts in Go programming are available for those who prefer a formal, comprehensive approach to learning. These books often cover foundational concepts, practical exercises, and best practices, and provide deep dives into specific Go features. Titles include *T̈he Go Programming Languagë* by Alan A. A. Donovan and Brian W. Kernighan, and *G̈o in Action̈* by William Kennedy, Brian Ketelsen, and Erik St. Martin.

Open-source repositories such as GitHub (https://github.com/golang) or GitLab host countless projects, libraries, frameworks, and tools written in Go. These repositories offer insight into real-world applications, code quality, and various coding techniques. They also provide opportunities for contribution, enabling learners to gain experience and improve their skills by working on actual Go projects.

The Go community continuously expands its knowledge base through blogs, podcasts, and conference talks. Notable blogs like https://blog.golang.org/ and podcasts such as *Go Time* offer regular updates, interviews with experts, and discussions on recent developments and advanced topics in Go programming.

Finally, social media platforms, particularly Twitter and LinkedIn, serve as channels for following renowned Go developers, staying updated with the latest news, and participating in broader community discussions.

Through active engagement with these community resources and support channels, you can accelerate your learning, stay updated with the latest advancements, and contribute back to the Go ecosystem, enriching the community as a whole.

Chapter 2

Setting Up Go Environment

This chapter guides you through the process of downloading, installing, and configuring Go on your system. It explains setting up the Go workspace, environment variables, and command-line tools. Instructions for integrating Go with popular IDEs, creating and managing projects, handling dependencies with Go modules, understanding project structure, and using version control with Git are provided to ensure a smooth development experience.

2.1 Downloading and Installing Go

To begin working with Go, the initial step involves downloading and installing the Go programming language on your system. This process is straightforward and involves downloading the appropriate binary distribution for your operating system and following the installation instructions specific to your OS. Downloading the latest stable release from the official Go website ensures you have the most secure and feature-complete version.

Visit the official Go programming language website at https://golang.org/dl/ and select the download link suitable for your operating system.

- For Windows, download the .msi installer.

- For macOS, download the .pkg installer.
- For Linux, download the appropriate .tar.gz archive.

Windows Installation

For Windows users, execute the .msi installer and follow the on-screen instructions. The installer will guide you through the installation process, including setting up the necessary environment variables. By default, Go will be installed in C:\Go directory, and its binaries will be placed in the C:\Go\bin directory.

macOS Installation

macOS users should download the .pkg installer. After downloading, double-click the package file and follow the instructions in the installation wizard. The default installation path for Go is /usr/local/go. The installer will handle the setup of environment variables automatically.

Alternatively, macOS users can opt to use a package manager such as Homebrew. After installing Homebrew, execute the following terminal command:

```
brew install go
```

Linux Installation

Linux installation involves a few additional steps, given the diverse distribution ecosystem. To install Go on Linux, follow the instructions for downloading the .tar.gz archive, and then proceed with uncompressing and moving it to the appropriate directory.

Assuming the go1.x.x.linux-amd64.tar.gz file is downloaded, open a terminal and execute:

```
tar -C /usr/local -xzf go1.x.x.linux-amd64.tar.gz
```

Here, 1.x.x denotes the latest version number of Go at the time of download. This command extracts the archive to /usr/local, creating a directory /usr/local/go.

Next, you need to add /usr/local/go/bin to your PATH environment variable. Depending on your shell, this can be accomplished by adding the following line to your profile file:

For bash or sh, add to /.profile or /.bashrc:

```
export PATH=$PATH:/usr/local/go/bin
```

For zsh, add to /.zshrc:

```
export PATH=$PATH:/usr/local/go/bin
```

Reload the profile by running:

```
source ~/.profile
```

or for zsh:

```
source ~/.zshrc
```

Verifying Installation

After installation, confirm that Go has been correctly installed and the paths are set by running:

```
go version
```

You should see output indicating the installed version of Go, such as:

```
go version go1.x.x linux/amd64
```

If the version information is displayed correctly, the installation is successful, and Go is ready for use.

2.2 Setting Up Go Workspace

A Go workspace is a directory hierarchy for organizing Go source code and dependencies. Setting up a Go workspace correctly is crucial for developing and managing Go projects effectively. The standard layout makes it easy for developers to navigate through various parts of the code, and ensures compatibility with Go toolchain commands like go build and go test.

A Go workspace typically has three directories at its root:

- src: Contains Go source files organized by package.
- pkg: Stores compiled package objects.
- bin: Holds compiled executable binaries.

This directory structure allows the Go tooling to efficiently locate and handle source code and dependencies. Below, we will create a Go workspace, configure the GOPATH environment variable, and verify the setup.

```
$ mkdir -p $HOME/go/{bin,pkg,src}
```

This command creates the src, pkg, and bin directories under the $HOME/go directory.

Once the directories are set up, we need to configure the GOPATH environment variable. The GOPATH variable specifies the root of your workspace.

```
$ echo 'export GOPATH=$HOME/go' >> $HOME/.profile
$ echo 'export PATH=$PATH:$GOPATH/bin' >> $HOME/.profile
$ source $HOME/.profile
```

These commands add GOPATH and the GOPATH/bin directory to the PATH, allowing the Go toolchain to recognize and execute binaries within the workspace. The source command reloads the profile script to apply changes immediately.

Next, we will verify the setup by creating a simple "Hello, World!" program in the workspace.

```
$ mkdir -p $GOPATH/src/hello
$ cd $GOPATH/src/hello
$ nano hello.go
```

Within the hello.go file, add the following code:

```
package main

import "fmt"

func main() {
    fmt.Println("Hello, World!")
}
```

Save and exit the file. To compile and run the program, use the go build and go run commands from within the same directory.

```
$ go build
$ ./hello
```

The output should be:

```
Hello, World!
```

Alternatively, you can use the go run command to compile and execute the program in one step without producing a binary.

```
$ go run hello.go
```

The output will be:

```
Hello, World!
```

Each Go project resides in its own subdirectory of the src directory. For example, a project named myproject would be located at $GOPATH/src/myproject. This helps maintain a clean workspace and prevent namespace conflicts.

To leverage the full power of Go modules, initialize a new module within a project directory:

```
$ cd $GOPATH/src/myproject
$ go mod init myproject
```

This creates a go.mod file in the project root, which keeps track of the module's dependencies, enabling efficient dependency management.

Properly setting up a Go workspace not only enhances productivity but also ensures that the project structure remains standardized and maintainable. This foundational capability is integral for successful project development and collaboration within the Go ecosystem. Integrating these practices early on streamlines the development workflow and minimizes potential issues related to code organization and dependency management.

2.3 Configuring Go Environment Variables

Configuring environment variables is a crucial step in setting up a productive Go development environment. Proper configuration ensures that Go tools can locate the necessary files and directories, and that your development process is streamlined. This section elaborates on the essential environment variables you need to configure for Go.

GOROOT is an environment variable that specifies the directory where Go's installation is located. By default, this is typically set to the directory where you installed Go. For a Go installation on Unix-like systems, you can add the following to your .bashrc or .zshrc file:

```
export GOROOT=/usr/local/go
```

On Windows, you can set GOROOT using the System Properties GUI or via command line:

```
setx GOROOT ”C:\Go”
```

GOPATH is another essential environment variable that specifies the location of your workspace. This includes your source code, binaries, and packages. Typically, GOPATH should be set to a directory in your home folder. For example, to set GOPATH on a Unix-like system, append the following to your .bashrc or .zshrc:

```
export GOPATH=\$HOME/go
```

Correspondingly, on Windows, you can set GOPATH using:

```
setx GOPATH ”%USERPROFILE%\go”
```

To ensure the Go binaries are available from any location, it is necessary to add the Go binary directory to your PATH environment variable. This inclusion allows Go commands such as go build, go test, and go get to be executed directly from the command line.

For Unix-like systems, you can edit your shell configuration file (.bashrc, .zshrc) as follows:

```
export PATH=\$PATH:\$GOROOT/bin
export PATH=\$PATH:\$GOPATH/bin
```

On Windows, modify the PATH environment variable through the System Properties GUI, or use the command line:

```
setx PATH ”%PATH%;C:\Go\bin;%GOPATH%\bin”
```

These environment variables not only help manage your Go development environment but also facilitate the seamless execution of Go programs and tools. After updating your environment files, ensure you reload them by executing source .bashrc or . /.zshrc on Unix-like systems, or restart your terminal/command prompt on Windows.

Sometimes, additional Go-related environment variables might be necessary for specific use cases. For example, GO111MODULE=on enables Go modules, which manage project dependencies and versioning efficiently. You can set this environment variable either temporarily in the command line or permanently within your shell configuration file:

Temporary:

```
export GO111MODULE=on
```

Permanently in .bashrc or .zshrc:

```
export GO111MODULE=on
```

Windows equivalent for temporary setting:

```
set GO111MODULE=on
```

By correctly setting these environment variables, the Go tools can effectively locate the Go compiler, libraries, and your source code, ensuring an optimal development experience. Confirm the configurations by running the following commands:

```
go env GOROOT
go env GOPATH
```

The commands should output the paths you have set, verifying that your environment is correctly configured.

```
/usr/local/go
/home/username/go
```

Correctly configured environment variables play an instrumental role in ensuring Go development flows smoothly and efficiently. This foundational setup readies your system to handle Go programming tasks, ensuring all components interact seamlessly.

2.4 Using Go Command Line Tools

Go provides a suite of command-line tools for managing and building projects. These tools are an integral part of the Go ecosystem and are designed to enhance productivity and streamline various development tasks. In this section, we will explore essential Go command-line tools, including go build, go run, go fmt, go test, go doc, go get, and go mod commands, providing detailed explanations and examples for each.

The go build Command

The go build command compiles Go source code into executable binaries. It can be used to build individual packages or entire projects. When you execute go build in a directory containing Go source files, it generates an executable binary in the same directory.

```
$ go build main.go
```

If the build is successful, no output is displayed, but you will find an executable file named main (or main.exe on Windows) in the current directory. To build all packages within a project, simply run:

```
$ go build ./...
```

This command traverses the current directory recursively and builds all packages it finds.

The go run Command

The go run command is useful for quickly compiling and running Go programs without creating a separate executable file. It combines the actions of go build and executing the binary in a single step.

```
$ go run main.go
```

This command compiles the main.go file and directly runs the resulting binary.

The go fmt Command

Code formatting is crucial for maintaining readability and consistency across a codebase. The go fmt command automatically formats Go source code according to the language's style guidelines.

To format a single file, execute:

```
$ go fmt main.go
```

To format all files in the current directory and its subdirectories, use:

```
$ go fmt ./...
```

The go test Command

Unit testing is an essential practice in software development. Go provides a built-in testing framework and the go test command to run tests within your project. Tests are defined in files with names ending in _test.go and typically use the testing package.

To run all tests in a package, execute:

```
$ go test
```

The command finds, compiles, and executes tests, displaying the results directly in the terminal.

```
ok    package-name 0.123s
```

To run tests across all packages in a project, use:

```
$ go test ./...
```

The go doc Command

Documentation is vital for understanding code. The go doc command allows you to view package documentation directly in the terminal.

To display documentation for a specific package, such as fmt, use:

```
$ go doc fmt
```

To view documentation for a specific function within a package, include the function name:

```
$ go doc fmt.Println
```

The go get Command

Managing external dependencies is simplified with the go get command. It retrieves and installs packages from remote repositories, such as those hosted on GitHub.

To install a package, use:

```
$ go get example.com/user/package
```

This command downloads the specified package and its dependencies to the $GOPATH.

The go mod Command

Dependency management in Go is handled through Go modules. The go mod command is central to managing these modules.

To initialize a new module in your project, use:

```
$ go mod init example.com/myproject
```

This creates a go.mod file containing module path and dependency information.

To add a new dependency, use:

```
$ go get example.com/some/dependency
```

This updates the go.mod and go.sum files with the new dependency.

The go mod tidy command cleans up the go.mod file by removing unnecessary dependencies:

```
$ go mod tidy
```

These Go command-line tools are crucial for effective project management, from building and running code, ensuring code quality, handling dependencies, to managing documentation and testing. Understanding and utilizing these tools will streamline your Go development process.

2.5 Setting Up an Integrated Development Environment (IDE)

Integrated Development Environments (IDEs) are powerful tools that offer a range of functionalities beyond simple code editing. They provide integrated compilation, debugging, and testing capabilities that enhance a developer's productivity. This section explores setting up popular IDEs for Go development, including Visual Studio Code (VS Code), GoLand, and Vim.

Visual Studio Code (VS Code) VS Code is a highly popular, open-source IDE developed by Microsoft, with an extensive marketplace for extensions. Setting up VS Code for Go development involves the following steps:

Download and Install VS Code:

- Navigate to the official VS Code website: https://code.visualstudio.com/
- Download the appropriate installer for your operating system.
- Follow the installation wizard steps to complete the installation process.

Install Go Extension:

- Open VS Code.
- Navigate to the Extensions view by clicking on the Extensions icon in the Activity Bar on the side of the window.
- Search for Go in the Extensions Marketplace.
- Install the Go extension (provided by the VS Code Go team).

Configure Go Environment:

```
$ mkdir -p $HOME/go/{bin,src,pkg}
$ export GOPATH=$HOME/go
$ export PATH=$PATH:$GOPATH/bin
```

In VS Code, make sure your environment variables are correctly set in the integrated terminal by adding the following lines to your shell's configuration file (e.g., .bashrc, .zshrc):

```
$ source ~/.bashrc
```

Restart VS Code or open a new terminal to apply these changes.

GoLand GoLand is a commercial IDE by JetBrains, specifically designed for Go development. It provides advanced features such as intelligent code completion, on-the-fly error detection, and powerful debugging tools.

Download and Install GoLand:

- Navigate to the official GoLand website: https://www.jetbrains.com/go/
- Download the installer suitable for your operating system.
- Follow the setup instructions to install GoLand.

First-time Setup:

- Open GoLand.
- Upon initial startup, configure the IDE by specifying the Go SDK path. Typically, the Go SDK path will be /usr/local/go (default installation path) or as defined by your installation.
- GoLand will automatically detect and configure GOPATH if it follows the standard directory structure.

Vim Vim is a highly configurable text editor that can be augmented with plugins to support Go development. To configure Vim for Go:
Install Vim:

- On Linux:

```
$ sudo apt-get install vim
```

- On macOS (via Homebrew):

```
$ brew install vim
```

Configure Vim for Go Development:

- Install vim-go plugin using a plugin manager (e.g., Vim-Plug):

```
# Add the following line to your .vimrc
Plug 'fatih/vim-go', { 'do': ':GoUpdateBinaries' }

# Run the following commands to install vim-go
$ vim +PlugInstall +qall
```

- Configure Go installation within .vimrc:

```
let g:go_gopath = $HOME."/go"
let g:go_bin_path = $HOME."/go/bin"
```

Usage:

- Open a Go source file in Vim and execute :GoInstallBinaries to install necessary Go tools.
- Use commands such as :GoBuild, :GoTest, and :GoRun within Vim to build, test, and run your Go programs.

The process detailed for each IDE aims to provide a comprehensive setup experience. By configuring an IDE optimally for Go development, you can take advantage of powerful features like intelligent code completion, integrated debugging, and automated code formatting, which significantly enhances productivity.

2.6 Creating Your First Go Project

Creating a Go project involves initializing a new module, writing a simple Go program, and executing it. This process provides a foundational understanding of how Go projects are structured and managed. Follow these steps to create your first Go project:

Step 1: Initialize the Project

Open your terminal or command prompt. Navigate to the directory where you want to create your Go project. It is customary to keep Go projects within the $GOPATH workspace, but with Go modules, this is optional. Initiate a new Go module using the following command:

```
$ mkdir myfirstproject
$ cd myfirstproject
$ go mod init myfirstproject
```

The go mod init command initializes a new module rooted at the current directory, creating a go.mod file that tracks dependencies for your project. The go.mod file will look like this:

```
module myfirstproject

go 1.19
```

The module directive specifies the module path, and the go directive indicates the Go language version.

Step 2: Write Your Go Program

Create a new Go source file. The convention is to name the main file main.go. Open this file in your preferred text editor or integrated development environment (IDE) and write a simple Go program:

```
package main

import "fmt"

func main() {
    fmt.Println("Hello, World!")
}
```

This program prints Hello, World! to the console. The main package tells the Go compiler that this is the executable application. The main function is the entry point of the program. The fmt package is imported to use the Println function, which outputs text to the standard output.

Step 3: Build and Run Your Program

To build and run your program, use the go run command:

```
$ go run main.go
```

The output should be:

```
Hello, World!
```

The go run command compiles and runs the Go program in one step. If no errors are detected, the program's output will be displayed.

For production use, you may want to compile the program into an executable binary. This can be done using the go build command:

```
$ go build
$ ./myfirstproject
```

go build compiles the source files and produces an executable named myfirstproject (or myfirstproject.exe on Windows). Running the executable will produce the same Hello, World! output.

Step 4: Module Management

In Go projects, dependencies are managed via Go modules. When you import packages that are not part of the Go standard library, the go get command fetches them. For example, if you want to use an external package:

```
import "github.com/sirupsen/logrus"
```

Run:

```
$ go get github.com/sirupsen/logrus
```

This will download the package and add it to your go.mod file. Over time, the go.sum file, which maintains the cryptographic checksums of modules used in your project, will also be updated.

Step 5: Project Structure

A well-organized project structure is crucial for maintainability and clarity. Here is a typical Go project structure:

```
myfirstproject/
  go.mod
  go.sum
  main.go
  cmd/
    myfirstproject/
      main.go
  pkg/
    ...
  internal/
    ...
  README.md
```

In this structure:

- cmd/ contains subdirectories for each command the project can produce.
- pkg/ holds library code that's safe to be used by other projects (exportable).

- internal/ holds package code only accessible within the project.
- README.md documents the project.

The structure ensures that code is modular and accessible according to the developer's intentions.

Understanding and setting up a project correctly streamlines development and maintenance activities.

2.7 Managing Dependencies with Go Modules

Go modules provide an efficient and straightforward way to manage dependencies in Go projects. Unlike the traditional GOPATH-based dependency management system, Go modules allow you to work outside of the GOPATH directory and enable more precise version control over third-party packages. This section will cover the basics of Go modules, including initialization, adding dependencies, versioning, and best practices.

Initializing a Go Module

To start using Go modules in your project, you need to initialize a module in your project directory. This can be done using the go mod init command followed by the module path, which typically corresponds to the location where your project will be published, such as a repository URL.

```
go mod init github.com/username/projectname
```

This command creates a new file named go.mod in your project directory. The go.mod file is the primary source for defining the module and managing its dependencies. A simple go.mod file might look like this:

```
module github.com/username/projectname
go 1.17
```

Adding Dependencies

To add dependencies to your project, you use the go get command. When you run go get followed by the package path, Go fetches the latest version of the package and adds it to your project.

```
go get example.com/some/package
```

After running this command, the dependencies are listed in the go.mod file, and a go.sum file is generated or updated. The go.sum file ensures that the recorded checksum for each module is verified to avoid tampering.

go.mod might look like this after adding a dependency:

```
module github.com/username/projectname

go 1.17

require example.com/some/package v1.2.3
```

And the go.sum file will include checksums:

```
example.com/some/package v1.2.3 h1:xxxxxxxxxxxxxxxxxxxxxxxxxxxxxx=
example.com/some/package v1.2.3/go.mod h1:yyyyyyyyyyyyyyyyyyyyyyyyyyyyyy=
```

Versioning Dependencies

With Go modules, you can specify the version of the dependency you want to use. By default, go get fetches the latest version, but you can also specify a version, a specific commit, or a pre-release version with a suffix like -beta or -rc.

```
go get example.com/some/package@v1.2.3
go get example.com/some/package@latest
go get example.com/some/package@<commit-hash>
```

For fine-grained control over dependency versions, you can directly edit the go.mod file:

```
require example.com/some/package v1.2.3
```

Tidying Up Dependencies

As you add and remove dependencies, your go.mod and go.sum files may accumulate unnecessary entries. To clean up these files, use the go mod tidy command. This command removes any dependencies that are no longer required and ensures that the module files are up-to-date.

```
go mod tidy
```

Best Practices for Managing Dependencies

- Always commit the go.mod and go.sum files to version control. This ensures that everyone working on the project uses the same set of dependencies.
- Regularly run go mod tidy to clean up your module files and prevent bloated dependency lists.
- When updating dependencies, thoroughly test your project to ensure that new versions do not introduce breaking changes.
- Use the replace directive in the go.mod file to deal with incompatible or broken dependencies temporarily. However, avoid keeping replace directives in your go.mod file for extended periods.

```
replace example.com/broken/package => example.com/fixed/package v1.2.3
```

- Leverage the semantic versioning of dependencies to manage your module versions more effectively.

Understanding and effectively managing dependencies with Go modules is crucial for maintaining a stable and efficient development environment. Ensuring that the correct versions of dependencies are used and keeping your module files clean aids in smoother project builds and deployments.

2.8 Understanding Go Project Structure

In the Go programming language, the project structure plays a crucial role in both development and maintenance. Adopting a conventionally structured project enables consistent practices across teams and simplifies the management of codebases. The Go project structure typically adheres to conventions and principles that streamline the workflow, especially when dealing with package management and build processes.

At the core of a Go project is the workspace, which is organized into three directories: src, pkg, and bin. The src directory holds source code, pkg contains compiled package objects, and bin stores compiled executable binaries.

Let's examine a sample Go project structure:

```
myproject/
 bin/
 pkg/
    darwin_amd64/
    linux_amd64/
 src/
     github.com/
         user/
             myproject/
                 main.go
                 utils/
                     helper.go
                 config/
                     config.go
```

In this example, myproject is the root of the workspace. The src directory here mirrors a typical URL path, github.com/user/myproject, which aligns with Go's approach of defining packages by import paths. This structure significantly aids in dependency management and collaboration as it is aligned with source control repositories.

main.go contains the entry point of the program with the main package. In Go, the main package defines an executable program, and the main() function within it serves as the entry point.

```
package main

import (
    "fmt"
    "github.com/user/myproject/utils"
)

func main() {
    fmt.Println("Hello, Go project structure!")
    utils.HelperFunction()
}
```

The utils directory contains a subpackage that provides utility functions. The helper function defined in helper.go can be called from main.go as it has been imported.

```
package utils

import "fmt"

func HelperFunction() {
    fmt.Println("This is a utility function.")
}
```

Another directory, config, might contain configuration structs and functions. For instance, config.go could have definitions to manage application settings.

```
package config
```

```
type Config struct {
    DatabaseURL string
    Port int
}
```

When the bin directory is populated, it contains executable binaries named after their respective commands. Compiling main.go places the binary in bin, enabling execution of the project.

pkg directory, subdivided by platform (darwin_amd64, linux_amd64), stores installed packages compiled to platform-specific binaries. This reduces compilation time by reusing precompiled packages.

Each Go project should also include a go.mod file, enabling module management which is central to managing dependencies effectively. A go.mod file can be created using:

```
go mod init github.com/user/myproject
```

Here's what the go.mod file might look like:

```
module github.com/user/myproject

go 1.18

require (
    github.com/some/dependency v1.2.3
    golang.org/x/tools v0.1.5
)
```

This file establishes the module, specifies the Go version, and lists dependencies along with their versions. These dependencies are fetched and handled by Go's module system to ensure reproducibility and version consistency.

It's critical to maintain clear organization in source files. The established convention for naming directories based on functionality (e.g., utils, config) ensures code is modular and readable. Functions and types should be aptly named to encapsulate their purpose, following Go's naming conventions which prefer short and concise names for the most common entities.

Tools such as go fmt and go vet play a role in maintaining readability and correctness. go fmt auto-formats code to align with Go standards, while go vet inspects code for potential issues. It's advisable to integrate these tools in your workflow via build systems or IDEs.

The structure described here is a starting point, and it's essential to adapt it to specific project needs while adhering to Go's idioms. Prioritizing maintainability and clarity within your project structure is foundational to developing robust Go applications.

2.9 Building and Running Go Programs

In Go programming, building and running a program are fundamental tasks that transition your source code from text files into an executable binary. Understanding how to effectively use the Go tools go build and go run is crucial for efficient development and testing.

The go build command compiles the packages, resulting in an executable binary, whereas go run compiles and immediately executes the source code. Each serves specific purposes within the development cycle.

To begin, let us consider a basic Go program. This simple "Hello, World!" example will demonstrate the steps involved in building and running a program.

```
package main

import "fmt"

func main() {
    fmt.Println("Hello, World!")
}
```

To compile this program using go build, open the terminal and navigate to the directory containing the source file named main.go. Execute the following command:

```
go build main.go
```

Upon successful execution, this command produces an executable file named main (or main.exe on Windows). You can run this binary directly from the terminal:

```
./main
```

The output is straightforward:

```
Hello, World!
```

For running the program without creating an executable file, go run is more convenient. The command is as follows:

```
go run main.go
```

The output remains identical:

```
Hello, World!
```

The go run command internally compiles the source code before execution, making it suitable for quick tests and small applications. However, for deployment or performance testing, the go build command's binary production is preferred.

Next, consider the case when a program spans multiple files. Suppose your directory contains two files: main.go and helper.go.

```
\\ main.go
package main

import "fmt"

func main() {
    message := getMessage()
    fmt.Println(message)
}
```

```
\\ helper.go
package main

func getMessage() string {
    return "Hello from helper!"
}
```

To build these files into a single executable, simply use the go build command within the directory without specifying filenames:

```
go build
```

This builds and links the files together into one executable. Running this executable will yield:

```
Hello from helper!
```

Alternatively, to execute the program using go run, list all source files:

```
go run main.go helper.go
```

For larger projects following Go's project structure conventions, involving multiple packages, the commands scale similarly. Consider a directory structure as follows:

```
project/
    main.go
    helpers/
        helper.go
```

Here, the main.go file imports the helpers package:

```
\\ main.go
package main

import (
    "fmt"
    "project/helpers"
)

func main() {
    message := helpers.GetMessage()
    fmt.Println(message)
}
```

```
\\ helpers/helper.go
package helpers

func GetMessage() string {
    return "Hello from packaged helper!"
}
```

Building the project in this structure requires positioning the terminal in the project's root directory and using:

```
go build
```

Running the produced binary demonstrates the multi-package integration:

```
Hello from packaged helper!
```

Executing the program with go run also necessitates being in the project's root directory and specifying only the main package's source file:

```
go run main.go
```

Complex projects may utilize build tags, environment-specific variables, and optimized build settings via clever use of build constraints, the go build flags, and specialized files such as go.mod for module specifics. The precise control over the build process provided by these tools facilitates efficient and adaptable software development workflows tailored to diverse deployment environments. Understand the nuances of these features augments the proficiency in managing Go projects.

2.10 Setting Up Version Control with Git

Version control is an essential aspect of modern software development, enabling teams to manage changes to source code over time. In this section, we will focus on setting up Git for version control in your Go projects, discussing installation, configuration, common workflows, and best practices.

Installing Git

To begin using Git for version control in your Go projects, you need to install Git on your system. Git can be installed on various operating systems, and the installation instructions for the most common ones are listed below:

- **Windows**: Download the Git installer from https://git-scm.com/download/win. Run the installer and follow the on-screen instructions.
- **macOS**: Use Homebrew to install Git by executing `brew install git` in a terminal.
- **Linux**: Use your package manager. For example, on Debian-based systems, you can run `sudo apt-get install git`.

Configuring Git

Once Git is installed, you need to configure it with your user information. Open a terminal and set your name and email address:

```
git config --global user.name "Your Name"
git config --global user.email "your.email@example.com"
```

To verify your configuration, you can display it with:

```
git config --list
```

Initializing a Git Repository

Navigate to your Go project's directory and initialize a new Git repository with the following command:

```
git init
```

This command creates a new subdirectory named .git that contains all the necessary repository files. These files are used to track changes in the project.

Staging and Committing Changes

To start tracking changes, you need to add files to the staging area and commit them to the repository. For example, if you have created a new Go file named main.go, you can add it to the staging area:

```
git add main.go
```

Following this, you can commit the staged changes:

```
git commit -m "Initial commit"
```

The -m flag is used to provide a commit message. It is important to write meaningful commit messages to describe the changes made.

Creating and Managing Branches

Branches are used to develop features, fix bugs, or experiment independently of the main codebase. To create a new branch and switch to it, use:

```
git checkout -b feature-branch
```

To view all branches in your repository, run:

```
git branch
```

To switch back to the main branch, use:

```
git checkout main
```

When your work on the feature branch is complete, merge it back into the main branch:

```
git checkout main
git merge feature-branch
```

Pushing to a Remote Repository

To collaborate with others, you should push your local repository to a remote server such as GitHub. First, create a repository on GitHub. Then, add the remote repository to your local repository:

```
git remote add origin https://github.com/yourusername/your-repo.git
```

Push your changes to the remote repository:

```
git push -u origin main
```

The -u flag sets origin as the default remote for future pushes.

Pulling Changes from a Remote Repository

To synchronize your local repository with changes from the remote repository, use the pull command:

```
git pull origin main
```

Best Practices for Using Git

Following best practices ensures a smooth and efficient workflow:

- Write clear, concise commit messages.
- Commit often with small, manageable chunks of code.
- Use branches for feature development and bug fixes.
- Regularly pull changes from the remote repository to stay updated.
- Resolve merge conflicts promptly and cautiously.

Integrating Git into your Go development process will streamline collaboration, track code changes systematically, and enhance project management. Configure Git correctly, adhere to best practices, and ensure a seamless version control experience.

[illegible]

Pulling Changes from a Remote Repository

[illegible]

Best Practices for Using Git

[illegible]

- [illegible]
- [illegible]
- [illegible]
- [illegible]
- [illegible]

[illegible]

Chapter 3

Basic Syntax and Data Types

This chapter introduces the basic syntax of the Go programming language, covering program structure, keywords, and identifiers. It discusses variables, constants, and the fundamental data types available in Go, along with type conversion and inference. The chapter also explores strings, character encoding, pointers, memory management, operators, expressions, and basic input/output operations, providing a solid foundation for understanding and writing Go code.

3.1 Basic Program Structure

A Go program's structure typically begins with the package declaration, followed by import statements, and then the main function or other functions. The main function serves as the entry point for the program. Below is a detailed breakdown of each component and their roles within the structure of a Go program.

```
package main

import "fmt"

func main() {
    fmt.Println("Hello, World!")
}
```

Listing 3.1: Basic Go Program Structure

Package Declaration

Every Go source file starts with a package declaration. This is crucial as it defines the package to which the file belongs. In the simplest form, a standalone executable program will have main as its package name, designating it as an entry point for execution.

```
package main
```

Listing 3.2: Package Declaration

For reusable packages, the package name can be any valid identifier, and it is conventionally named the same as the directory in which the source files reside.

Import Statements

Following the package declaration, the program can import other packages. The import keyword allows you to import remote and standard libraries, giving access to a plethora of pre-built functions and data structures. Multiple packages can be imported with either individual import statements or grouped together in parentheses.

```
import "fmt"
```

Listing 3.3: Single Import Statement

```
import (
    "fmt"
    "math"
    "strings"
)
```

Listing 3.4: Grouped Import Statements

fmt is a standard library package used for formatted I/O operations, math provides basic constants and mathematical functions, and strings contains functions for manipulating UTF-8 encoded strings.

Function Declarations

Functions in Go begin with the func keyword followed by the function name, its parameters, return type, and the function body enclosed in curly braces. The main function forms the entry point of the program.

```
func main() {
```

```
    fmt.Println("Hello, World!")
}
```

Listing 3.5: Main Function

fmt.Println() is a function call that outputs a string to the standard output, adding a newline at the end.

Organizing Programs with Packages

To enhance modularity and maintainability, Go encourages the use of packages. A package in Go is a collection of source files in the same directory that are compiled together. Each Go source file in a directory must have the same package name.

Suppose we have a source file mathutils.go intended for mathematical utilities:

```
package mathutils

func Add(a int, b int) int {
    return a + b
}
```

Listing 3.6: mathutils.go

We can then create another Go file in the same directory:

```
package main

import (
    "fmt"
    "path/to/mathutils"
)

func main() {
    sum := mathutils.Add(3, 4)
    fmt.Println("Sum:", sum)
}
```

Listing 3.7: main.go

Here, mathutils.Add is a function call to the Add function defined in the mathutils package. The import path "path/to/mathutils" must be the correct path relative to the GOPATH or go.mod file, depending on the project setup.

Comments and Documentation

To maintain code readability, Go supports single-line comments using // and multi-line comments with /* ... */. Comments are crucial for explaining the purpose of code blocks, parameters, and overall program logic.

```
// Single-line comment

/*
Multi-line comment
spanning multiple lines
*/
```

Listing 3.8: Comments in Go

Go also includes a special convention for writing documentation comments. Documentation comments begin with the element being described (e.g., package, function), and are processed by the godoc tool to generate HTML documentation.

```
// Add adds two integers and returns the sum.
func Add(a int, b int) int {
    return a + b
}
```

Listing 3.9: Documenting a Function

The logical flow of a Go program from the package declaration to imports, function definitions, and potential documentation, exhibits a clear and efficient structure. This organized approach ensures readability and maintainability, essential for both small scripts and large-scale software projects.

3.2 Go Keywords and Identifiers

Go keywords are reserved words in the language that have special meaning and cannot be used for naming variables, functions, or any other user-defined entities. These keywords form the basic building blocks of the language syntax, ensuring consistency and readability in Go code.

Here is a list of all 25 Go keywords:

- break
- case
- chan

- const
- continue
- default
- defer
- else
- fallthrough
- for
- func
- go
- goto
- if
- import
- interface
- map
- package
- range
- return
- select
- struct
- switch
- type
- var

These keywords cannot be redeclared or used as identifiers.

Identifiers in Go are names used to identify variables, constants, functions, types, package names, etc. The naming conventions for identifiers in Go are:

- An identifier must start with a letter (A-Z or a-z) or an underscore (_).
- Following the first letter, it may contain letters, digits (0-9), or underscores.

Identifiers are case-sensitive, meaning myVar and myvar would be considered different identifiers. Identifiers can be short names (e.g., x and y) or more descriptive names (e.g., housePrice, clientName). Descriptive names are preferred for better readability.

The following example demonstrates valid and invalid identifiers:

```
package main

import "fmt"

func main() {
    // Valid identifiers
    var amount int = 100
    var housePrice float64 = 500000.50
    var client_name string = "John Doe"

    fmt.Println(amount, housePrice, client_name)

    // Invalid identifiers (uncomment to see errors)
    // var 123name string // Invalid: starts with a digit
    // var client-name string // Invalid: contains a hyphen
    // var var int // Invalid: uses a keyword
}
```

Listing 3.10: Valid and Invalid Identifiers

Output:

```
100 500000.5 John Doe
```

The Go compiler provides errors for any invalid identifiers, helping enforce these rules effectively.

To further understand the scope and visibility of identifiers, we can look at how Go handles exporting identifiers. In Go, an identifier's first letter determines its visibility:

- If the identifier starts with a capital letter, it is exported, meaning it will be accessible from other packages.
- If it starts with a lowercase letter, it will be unexported and private to the package it is declared in.

Consider the following example demonstrating exporting and non-exporting identifiers:

```
package main

import (
    "fmt"
    "example/mypackage"
)

func main() {
    // Accessing exported identifier
    fmt.Println(mypackage.ExportedVar) // Accessible

    // Accessing unexported identifier
    // fmt.Println(mypackage.unexportedVar) // Error: unexportedVar not
        exported by package mypackage
}
```

Listing 3.11: Exporting and Non-exporting Identifiers

Here, the mypackage package might contain the following code:

```
package mypackage

// Exported variable
var ExportedVar string = "I am visible from other packages"

// Unexported variable
var unexportedVar string = "I am only visible within this package"
```

Listing 3.12: Defining Exported and Non-exported Identifiers in a Package

When writing Go code, adhering to proper naming conventions and understanding the reserved nature of keywords is essential for readability and maintainability. This ensures that the code remains consistent and free of syntax-related issues.

3.3 Variables and Constants

Variables and constants are central to programming in Go, serving as the building blocks for data storage and manipulation. A variable is a named location in memory that stores a value, which can change during the execution of a program. In contrast, a constant is a named value that cannot be altered once assigned.

Variables are defined using the var keyword and can be initialized when declared or assigned a value later. Go supports both explicit declaration and type inference for variables.

```
package main

import "fmt"

func main() {
    var a int // Explicit declaration without initialization
    var b int = 10 // Explicit declaration with initialization

    // Type inference
    var c = 20 // Type of c is inferred as int
    d := 30 // Short variable declaration (Type inferred as int)

    fmt.Println(a) // Output: 0 (default zero value for int)
    fmt.Println(b) // Output: 10
    fmt.Println(c) // Output: 20
    fmt.Println(d) // Output: 30
}
```

Listing 3.13: Variable Declaration and Initialization

The default zero value depends on the type of the variable:

- int and float64 have a zero value of 0.
- bool has a zero value of false.
- string has a zero value of an empty string "".
- Pointers have a zero value of nil.

Variables can also be grouped together for convenience in declaration:

```
package main

import "fmt"

func main() {
    var (
        x int = 5
        y float64 = 7.8
        z string = "Go"
    )
    fmt.Println(x, y, z) // Output: 5 7.8 Go
}
```

Listing 3.14: Grouped Variable Declaration

Constants are declared using the `const` keyword. Unlike variables, constants cannot be declared using the short declaration syntax and must have their type or value specified explicitly.

```
package main

import "fmt"

const Pi float64 = 3.14159
const Greeting = "Hello, World" // Type inferred as string

func main() {
    const x = 123 // Unnamed constant; type is inferred as int
    fmt.Println(Pi)
    fmt.Println(Greeting)
    fmt.Println(x)
}
```

Listing 3.15: Constant Declaration

Constants may also be grouped together similarly to variables:

```
package main

import "fmt"

const (
    A = 1
    B = "Constant"
    C = 3.14
)

func main() {
    fmt.Println(A, B, C)
}
```

Listing 3.16: Grouped Constant Declaration

Go supports the iota identifier which simplifies the creation of incrementing sequences of constants. Iota starts at 0 and increments by 1 within a constant block.

```
package main

import "fmt"

const (
    Sunday = iota // 0
    Monday // 1
    Tuesday // 2
    Wednesday // 3
    Thursday // 4
```

```
    Friday // 5
    Saturday // 6
)

func main() {
    fmt.Println(Sunday, Monday, Tuesday, Wednesday, Thursday, Friday,
        Saturday)
    // Output: 0 1 2 3 4 5 6
}
```

Listing 3.17: Using iota for Sequential Constants

Variables and constants can have different scopes defined by where and how they are declared:

- Local variables: Defined inside a function and accessible only within that function.
- Global variables: Defined outside any function and accessible throughout the package.
- Block scope: Variables defined within a block (such as if, for, or switch statements) are accessible only within that block.

Understanding the scope helps manage the lifetime and visibility of variables, preventing unintended side effects and enhancing code maintainability.

The concept of variable shadowing occurs when a variable declared within a narrower scope (e.g., inside a function or block) has the same name as one in an outer scope. The inner variable overrides the outer one within its scope.

```
package main

import "fmt"

var x = 10 // Global variable

func main() {
    x := 20 // Local variable shadows the global variable
    {
        var x = 30 // Inner block variable shadowing the outer block variable
        fmt.Println(x) // Output: 30
    }
    fmt.Println(x) // Output: 20 (outer block variable)
}
```

Listing 3.18: Variable Shadowing

Proper use of variables and constants enhances the efficiency and readability of Go programs, providing a foundation upon which more complex constructs can be built.

3.4 Basic Data Types

In Go, basic data types form the foundation upon which more complex data structures are built. These types are intrinsically supported by the language, providing developers with the essential tools necessary for a myriad of programming tasks. Understanding these types is crucial for effective and efficient Go programming.

Go's basic data types are categorized as follows:

- Boolean types
- Numeric types
- String types

Boolean Types: Go supports a single boolean type, represented by the keyword bool. A bool type can hold one of two values: true or false. Booleans are commonly used in conditional statements and control flow structures to make decisions.

```
// Example of boolean declaration and usage
var isAvailable bool = true
if isAvailable {
  fmt.Println("The resource is available.")
} else {
  fmt.Println("The resource is not available.")
}
```

```
Output:
The resource is available.
```

Numeric Types: Numeric types in Go are divided into three main categories: integers, floating-point numbers, and complex numbers.

Integer Types: Integers represent whole numbers and are divided into signed and unsigned types. Signed integers can hold both positive and negative values, whereas unsigned integers can only hold non-negative values.

The signed integer types are:

- int8
- int16
- int32
- int64
- int (Platform-dependent size)

The unsigned integer types are:

- uint8 (also known as byte)
- uint16
- uint32
- uint64
- uint (Platform-dependent size)

```
// Examples of integer declarations
var smallInt int8 = 127
var largeUInt uint64 = 18446744073709551615

fmt.Printf("Signed int8 value: %d\n", smallInt)
fmt.Printf("Unsigned uint64 value: %d\n", largeUInt)
```

```
Output:
Signed int8 value: 127
Unsigned uint64 value: 18446744073709551615
```

Floating-Point Types: The floating-point types represent numbers with fractional components. Go supports IEEE-754 standard 32-bit and 64-bit floating-point numbers.

- float32
- float64

```
// Examples of floating-point declarations
var pi float32 = 3.14159
var e float64 = 2.718281828459045

fmt.Printf("Value of pi: %f\n", pi)
fmt.Printf("Value of e: %f\n", e)
```

```
Output:
Value of pi: 3.141590
Value of e: 2.718282
```

Complex Types: Complex numbers consist of a real and an imaginary part. In Go, complex numbers have two types:

- complex64 (comprising float32 real and imaginary parts)
- complex128 (comprising float64 real and imaginary parts)

```
// Examples of complex number declarations
var c1 complex64 = 1 + 2i
var c2 complex128 = complex(5.5, 7.2)

fmt.Printf("Complex64 number: %v\n", c1)
fmt.Printf("Complex128 number: %v\n", c2)
```

```
Output:
Complex64 number: (1+2i)
Complex128 number: (5.5+7.2i)
```

String Types: Strings in Go are sequences of bytes used to represent text. They are immutable, meaning once a string is created, its contents cannot be altered.

```
// Example of string declaration and usage
var greeting string = "Hello, World!"
fmt.Println(greeting)
```

```
Output:
Hello, World!
```

Strings can be concatenated using the + operator.

```
// Concatenation of strings
var part1 string = "Hello"
var part2 string = "World"
var message string = part1 + ", " + part2 + "!"
fmt.Println(message)
```

```
Output:
Hello, World!
```

To extract individual characters from a string, use indexing. Note that Go treats strings as read-only slices of bytes.

```
// Accessing characters in a string
var str string = "Sample"
firstChar := str[0]
fmt.Printf("First character: %c\n", firstChar)
```

```
Output:
First character: S
```

Strings in Go support a variety of operations, including slicing and string formatting, which will be explored in further sections.

Understanding and utilizing Go's basic data types correctly enhances program correctness and efficiency. These fundamental building blocks are essential for all Go programmers to master.

3.5 Type Conversion and Type Inference

In Go, type conversion and type inference are crucial concepts for managing and manipulating data effectively. This section delves into the mechanisms provided by Go to convert and infer types, ensuring seamless operations and efficient memory usage.

Go is a statically typed language, meaning the variable type is known at compile time. Each variable in Go must be explicitly declared with a specific type, which ensures type safety. However, Go provides flexibility through type conversion and type inference, which simplifies coding by reducing redundancy.

Type conversion in Go requires explicit syntax. Implicit type conversion, often referred to as "type coercion" in other languages, is not supported in Go, preventing unexpected behaviors and promoting code clarity. To convert between different types, the syntax is $\mathrm{T(v)}$, where T is the target type, and v is the value to be converted. Consider the following exemplary scenario:

```
var i int = 42
var f float64 = float64(i)
var u uint = uint(f)
```

In this example:

- The integer i is explicitly converted to a float64 type.
- The resulting float64 value f is further converted to an uint.

This explicit type conversion ensures that the programmer is always aware of the types involved in operations, thereby reducing the chance of bugs and unexpected results. However, it is crucial to note that converting between types can lead to data loss or overflow, especially when dealing with floating-point numbers and integers. To illustrate, consider converting a float64 value to an int:

```
var f float64 = 3.14
var i int = int(f)
```

Here, the floating-point number 3.14 is truncated to the integer 3. This operation results in the loss of the decimal portion. Thus, it is vital to be aware of the possible consequences of type conversion on data.

Conversely, type inference in Go simplifies variable declarations by allowing the Go compiler to deduce the type of a variable from the context of its initial assignment, using the := syntax. Type inference enhances code readability and reduces verbosity. For example:

```
var i = 42 // Explicit type declaration
f := 3.14 // Type inferred as float64
text := "Hello, Go!" // Type inferred as string
```

In this example, the types of f and text are inferred by the Go compiler, eliminating the need for explicit type definitions. The compiler automatically determines:

- f to be of type float64,
- text to be of type string.

This can be particularly useful when working with composite types or functions that return multiple values. Consider the following example of inferring types from function return values:

```
func getValues() (int, float64, string) {
    return 1, 2.5, "Go"
}

func main() {
    i, f, s := getValues()
}
```

Here, the function getValues returns multiple values of different types. The variables i, f, and s in the main function will have their types inferred correctly based on the function's return values. This convenience simplifies the code and makes it more maintainable.

Go also allows mixing explicit type declarations and type inference for variables within the same scope, which can be helpful in complex programs where certain variables must be explicitly typed for clarity or performance reasons.

```
var i int // Explicit type declaration
j := i + 42 // Type inferred from context
```

In this snippet, i is explicitly declared as an integer, and j is inferred to be an integer based on the context of its initialization expression.

To summarize, type conversion in Go mandates explicit syntax to prevent ambiguity and maintain predictable behavior, while type inference provides a compact syntax that retains type safety and enhances code legibility. Understanding and effectively utilizing these features allows developers to write more robust and maintainable Go programs.

3.6 Strings and Character Encoding

In Go, the concept of strings and character encoding is pivotal for dealing with textual data. A string in Go is an immutable sequence of bytes, typically but not exclusively representing text encoded in UTF-8. This immutability means that once a string is created, it cannot be altered. Any manipulation of a string results in the creation of a new string. This immutable nature is a key characteristic that ensures the integrity and reliability of string data in concurrent programming scenarios.

Strings are declared using double quotes ("") for literal strings and backticks (‘) for raw string literals. Raw string literals can span multiple lines and do not interpret any escape sequences. Here is how to declare and initialize strings in Go:

```
package main

import "fmt"

func main() {
    var strLiteral string = "Hello, World!"
    var rawStrLiteral string = `This is a raw
    string literal spanning multiple lines.`

    fmt.Println(strLiteral)
    fmt.Println(rawStrLiteral)
}
```

Listing 3.19: String Declaration and Initialization

Output:

```
Hello, World!
This is a raw
string literal spanning multiple lines.
```

Go's strings are encoded in UTF-8 by default, making it compatible with the vast majority of text data used globally. UTF-8 is a variable-length character encoding capable of encoding all valid character code points in Unicode using one to four one-byte (8-bit) code units. This encoding design positions Go well for processing international text.

For accessing individual bytes or characters within a string, the indexing operation can be utilized. Since a string is an immutable array of bytes, the indexing operation returns the byte at the specified position. To handle multi-byte characters correctly, it is necessary to decode the string into runes. A rune in Go is an alias for int32, and it signifies a Unicode code point.

Example of traversing a string byte-wise and rune-wise:

```
package main

import "fmt"

func main() {
    str := "Golang"
    fmt.Println("Byte-wise traversal:")
    for i := 0; i < len(str); i++ {
        fmt.Printf("%c ", str[i])
    }
    fmt.Println("\nRune-wise traversal:")
    for _, r := range str {
        fmt.Printf("%c ", r)
    }
}
```

Listing 3.20: Byte-wise and Rune-wise Traversal

Output:

```
Byte-wise traversal:
G o l a n g
Rune-wise traversal:
G o l a n g
```

For extended Unicode strings, the above approach ensures correct handling of characters irrespective of their byte length. Note however that indexing directly into a string may not yield the full character if it is multi-byte; instead, specific bytes of the character are accessed.

To convert a string to a slice of runes and vice versa, Go provides built-in functions:

```
package main

import "fmt"

func main() {
    str := "Hello, Go!"
    runes := []rune(str)
    fmt.Println("Runes:", runes)

    newStr := string(runes)
    fmt.Println("String from runes:", newStr)
}
```

Listing 3.21: String to Rune Slice Conversion

Output:

```
Runes: [72 101 108 108 111 44 32 71 111 33]
String from runes: Hello, Go!
```

String manipulation functions are typically provided in the strings package. Common operations include obtaining the length of a string, finding substrings, and splitting strings. Note that the length function returns the number of bytes, not characters, which is significant in the context of UTF-8 encoded strings:

```
package main

import (
    "fmt"
    "strings"
)

func main() {
    str := "Hello,   !"
    fmt.Println("Length in bytes:", len(str))
    fmt.Println("Length in runes:", len([]rune(str)))

    substr := "  "
    fmt.Println("Contains substring:", strings.Contains(str, substr))
    fmt.Println("Index of substring:", strings.Index(str, substr))
    fmt.Println("Splitting string:", strings.Split(str, ","))
}
```

Listing 3.22: String Manipulation Functions

Output:

```
Length in bytes: 13
```

```
Length in runes: 9
Contains substring: true
Index of substring: 7
Splitting string: [Hello    !]
```

Special attention is required when concatenating strings, as excessive concatenation can result in inefficient memory usage due to their immutability. For extensive string manipulation tasks, it is prudent to utilize a strings.Builder:

```
package main

import (
    "fmt"
    "strings"
)

func main() {
    var builder strings.Builder
    builder.WriteString("Hello")
    builder.WriteString(", ")
    builder.WriteString("Go!")

    result := builder.String()
    fmt.Println(result)
}
```

Listing 3.23: Efficient String Concatenation with strings.Builder

Output:

```
Hello, Go!
```

By understanding string immutability, UTF-8 encoding, and efficient manipulation techniques, developers can handle textual data in Go with confidence and efficiency.

3.7 Pointers and Memory Management

Pointers in Go provide a way to directly manage memory, allowing for more efficient and flexible manipulation of variables. Understanding pointers is crucial for optimizing performance and reducing memory usage in Go programs.

A pointer is a variable that holds the memory address of another variable. This allows the programmer to manipulate the variable's value indirectly through its memory address.

To declare a pointer in Go, use the * operator in front of the type to which the pointer will point. Here is an example of how to declare a pointer to an int:

```
var p *int
```

Once declared, a pointer must be assigned the address of a variable before it can be used. The address-of operator & is used to retrieve the address of a variable. Consider the following example:

```
var a int = 58
p = &a
```

In this example, the address of the variable a is assigned to the pointer p. Now, p holds the address of a, and we can manipulate a's value through p using the dereferencing operator *.

Dereferencing a pointer means accessing the value stored at the memory address. Here is how it is done:

```
fmt.Println(*p) // Prints the value of 'a', which is 58
*p = 100 // Changes the value of 'a' to 100
```

Pointers are particularly useful in functions. When passing variables to functions, Go uses pass-by-value by default, meaning it copies the value of the variable. However, using pointers, we can pass the address of a variable and thus avoid copying and allow the function to modify the original variable:

```
func updateValue(val *int) {
    *val = 200
}

func main() {
    var num int = 50
    updateValue(&num)
    fmt.Println(num) // Prints 200
}
```

In this example, updateValue takes a pointer to an int and modifies the value at the given address.

Memory management in Go is handled primarily through the use of garbage collection, which automatically reclaims memory allocated by your program when it detects that the memory is no longer in use. This reduces the complexity of memory management compared to languages like C or C++ but doesn't eliminate the programmer's responsibility to write efficient code.

To allocate memory dynamically in Go, use the new and make functions.

The new function allocates memory for a variable of a specified type and returns a pointer to it. For instance:

```
p := new(int)
*p = 500
fmt.Println(*p) // Prints 500
```

In contrast, the make function is used for the creation and initialization of slices, maps, and channels, which are specific built-in data types in Go. For example, to create a slice of integers, you can use:

```
s := make([]int, 5) // Creates a slice of 5 integers
```

Understanding memory allocation and efficient memory usage is vital. While Go simplifies memory management through garbage collection, relying too heavily on dynamic allocation without careful consideration can lead to performance problems.

One important practice is to minimize the scope of variables to reduce the lifespan of objects and allow the garbage collector to reclaim memory sooner. Avoid unnecessary global variables and long-lived heap allocations.

Moreover, be cautious when using slices and maps as they can quickly consume large amounts of memory. Slices, in particular, can lead to memory leaks if the underlying array remains in memory because a small portion of it is still referenced by a long-lived slice. Here's an example to illustrate this:

```
data := make([]int, largeSize) // Allocates a large array
slice := data[:smallSize] // Creates a slice of smaller size

// Even though 'slice' is small, 'data' is not garbage collected
// if 'slice' references it.
```

To prevent such leaks, it is sometimes useful to explicitly copy the needed elements into a new slice:

```
sliceCopy := append([]int(nil), data[:smallSize]...)
```

For long-lived programs, tracking and optimizing memory allocation patterns can significantly improve performance. Go's runtime package provides tools like runtime.GC() to manually trigger garbage collection and runtime.MemStats to inspect memory usage, enabling better control and understanding of memory behavior in your applications.

Example of using runtime.MemStats:

```
var memStats runtime.MemStats
runtime.ReadMemStats(&memStats)
```

```
fmt.Printf("Alloc: %v MB\n", memStats.Alloc / 1024 / 1024)
```

With these strategies and concepts in mind, effective memory management ensures robust and efficient Go applications.

3.8 Operators and Expressions

Operators are fundamental components of many basic and complex expressions in the Go programming language. Operators are used to perform operations on variables and values. Go supports various categories of operators including arithmetic, relational, logical, bitwise, assignment, and miscellaneous operators, such as increment and decrement. Understanding these operators and how to build expressions is crucial for mastering Go programming.

Arithmetic operators in Go perform basic mathematical operations like addition, subtraction, multiplication, division, and modulo. Consider the following example that demonstrates the usage of arithmetic operators:

```
package main

import "fmt"

func main() {
    a := 10
    b := 3

    sum := a + b
    diff := a - b
    prod := a * b
    quot := a / b
    rem := a % b

    fmt.Printf("Sum: %d\n", sum)
    fmt.Printf("Difference: %d\n", diff)
    fmt.Printf("Product: %d\n", prod)
    fmt.Printf("Quotient: %d\n", quot)
    fmt.Printf("Remainder: %d\n", rem)
}
```

The output of the above program will be:

```
Sum: 13
Difference: 7
Product: 30
Quotient: 3
Remainder: 1
```

In addition to standard arithmetic operators, Go also includes unary arithmetic operators, such as the unary plus (+) and minus (-), which can be used to indicate the positive or negative value of an operand.

Relational operators, sometimes called comparison operators, are used to compare two values. The relational operators in Go are: ==, !=, <, >, <=, and >=. These operators return a boolean value, true or false. For instance:

```
package main

import "fmt"

func main() {
    x := 5
    y := 10

    fmt.Println(x == y) // false
    fmt.Println(x != y) // true
    fmt.Println(x < y) // true
    fmt.Println(x > y) // false
    fmt.Println(x <= y) // true
    fmt.Println(x >= y) // false
}
```

Logical operators are used to combine multiple boolean expressions or values and provide logical conjunctions and disjunctions. Go includes three logical operators: && (logical AND), || (logical OR), and ! (logical NOT). Here is an example:

```
package main

import "fmt"

func main() {
    a := true
    b := false

    fmt.Println(a && b) // false
    fmt.Println(a || b) // true
    fmt.Println(!a) // false
    fmt.Println(!b) // true
}
```

Bitwise operators work at the bit-level and are used for manipulating data at the binary level. Go provides several bitwise operators including AND (&), OR (|), XOR ^(), AND NOT (&), left shift («), and right shift (»). An example demonstrating bitwise operators is shown below:

```
package main
```

```
import "fmt"

func main() {
    x := 6 // 110 in binary
    y := 3 // 011 in binary

    fmt.Printf("x & y: %d\n", x & y) // AND
    fmt.Printf("x | y: %d\n", x | y) // OR
    fmt.Printf("x ^ y: %d\n", x ^ y) // XOR
    fmt.Printf("x &^ y: %d\n", x &^ y) // AND NOT
    fmt.Printf("x << 1: %d\n", x << 1) // left shift
    fmt.Printf("x >> 1: %d\n", x >> 1) // right shift
}
```

The output of the above program will be:

```
x & y: 2
x | y: 7
x ^ y: 5
x &^ y: 4
x << 1: 12
x >> 1: 3
```

Assignment operators are used to assign values to variables. The basic assignment operator is =. Go also supports compound assignment operators, which combine an arithmetic or bitwise operation with assignment. These include +=, -=, *=, /=, %=, &=, |=, ^=, «=, and »=. Here's an example:

```
package main

import "fmt"

func main() {
    var a int = 5
    var b int = 10

    a += 1 // equivalent to a = a + 1
    b -= 2 // equivalent to b = b - 2

    fmt.Println("a:", a)
    fmt.Println("b:", b)
}
```

The output of the above program will be:

```
a: 6
b: 8
```

Finally, Go contains miscellaneous operators like the increment (++)

and decrement (–) operators. These operators increase or decrease the value of a variable by one. They can only be used as a suffix (var++ or var–) and not as a prefix (++var or –var).

Expressions in Go are combinations of values, variables, operators, and function calls that evaluate to a value. Expressions can be simple, such as the literal value 5, or complex, involving multiple operators and operands. The correct application of operators within expressions follows the standard precedence and associativity rules. For instance, multiplication and division have higher precedence than addition and subtraction, which means they are evaluated first in the absence of parentheses. Here's an example of a complex expression evaluated according to precedence rules:

```
package main

import "fmt"

func main() {
    result := 10 + 5*2 - 3/1
    fmt.Println("Result:", result) // Result: 17
}
```

Wrapping up, operators and expressions are crucial for performing calculations, comparisons, and logical operations that are essential in programming. Mastery of operators and their proper application within expressions is a fundamental skill in Go programming, aiding in the creation of efficient and maintainable code.

3.9 Basic Input and Output

Input and output operations are fundamental aspects of most programs, enabling interaction with users and manipulation of data. Go provides a rich set of libraries and types to handle I/O operations efficiently. The most commonly used package for standard I/O is the fmt package. This section delves into the basic mechanisms of performing input and output operations in Go.

To begin, let us examine how to print text to the standard output, typically the console. The fmt package offers various functions for formatted output, such as fmt.Print, fmt.Println, and fmt.Printf. The simplest function, fmt.Print, prints its arguments to the standard output:

```
package main
```

```
import "fmt"

func main() {
    fmt.Print("Hello, World!")
}
```

The above program outputs the text "Hello, World!" without a trailing newline. To include a newline at the end of the output, use fmt.Println:

```
package main

import "fmt"

func main() {
    fmt.Println("Hello, World!")
}
```

```
Hello, World!
```

For formatted output, fmt.Printf comes into play, allowing complex formatting using format specifiers. Format specifiers begin with a percent sign (%), and they define the type of formatting to be applied. Here are common format specifiers:

- %d - decimal integer
- %f - floating-point number
- %s - string
- %t - boolean

Consider the following program, which demonstrates various format specifiers:

```
package main

import "fmt"

func main() {
    var i int = 42
    var f float64 = 3.14159
    var s string = "Go Language"
    var b bool = true

    fmt.Printf("Integer: %d\n", i)
    fmt.Printf("Float: %f\n", f)
```

```
    fmt.Printf("String: %s\n", s)
    fmt.Printf("Boolean: %t\n", b)
}
```

```
Integer: 42
Float: 3.141590
String: Go Language
Boolean: true
```

Input operations in Go can be performed using fmt.Scan, fmt.Scanln, and fmt.Scanf. These functions read from the standard input, typically the keyboard. The fmt.Scan function reads space-separated values, fmt.Scanln reads values separated by a newline, and fmt.Scanf reads input according to a specified format.

Here is a simple example using fmt.Scan:

```
package main

import "fmt"

func main() {
    var name string
    var age int
    fmt.Print("Enter your name: ")
    fmt.Scan(&name)
    fmt.Print("Enter your age: ")
    fmt.Scan(&age)
    fmt.Printf("Hello, %s! You are %d years old.\n", name, age)
}
```

```
Enter your name: Alice
Enter your age: 30
Hello, Alice! You are 30 years old.
```

In this example, the fmt.Scan function takes pointers to variables where the input values will be stored. The & operator is used to pass the address of the variables name and age.

When handling more complex input formats, fmt.Scanf can be utilized. fmt.Scanf reads input according to the specified format, similar to fmt.Printf. Consider the following example:

```
package main

import "fmt"

func main() {
    var name string
```

```
    var age int
    fmt.Print("Enter your name and age: ")
    fmt.Scanf("%s %d", &name, &age)
    fmt.Printf("Hello, %s! You are %d years old.\n", name, age)
}
```

```
Enter your name and age: Bob 25
Hello, Bob! You are 25 years old.
```

For scenarios requiring multiline input, bufio can be used. The bufio.NewReader function creates a new reader instance that can read from standard input line by line. Here's an example:

```
package main

import (
    "bufio"
    "fmt"
    "os"
)

func main() {
    reader := bufio.NewReader(os.Stdin)
    fmt.Print("Enter a line of text: ")
    text, _ := reader.ReadString('\n')
    fmt.Printf("You entered: %s", text)
}
```

In this program, bufio.NewReader reads an entire line up to the newline character.

Understanding these basic input and output operations is vital for developing interactive programs in Go. From simple console applications to more sophisticated I/O-dependent programs, mastering these fundamental techniques lays the groundwork for more complex implementations.

3.10 Comments and Documentation

Documentation is a crucial aspect of programming, as it ensures that your code is understandable not only to others but also to your future self. In Go, comments serve as the primary means of documentation. There are two types of comments in Go: single-line comments and multi-line comments.

Single-line comments start with // and extend to the end of the line. They are generally used for short explanations or notes within the code.

```
// This is a single-line comment
package main

import "fmt"

func main() {
    // Print a message to the console
    fmt.Println("Hello, World!")
}
```

Multi-line comments start with /* and end with */. They can span multiple lines and are often used for more extensive explanations or documentation. Multi-line comments can also be nested within each other.

```
package main

import "fmt"

/*
This is a multi-line comment.
It can span multiple lines.
*/

/* Multi-line comments can be nested.
/* This is a nested comment. */
This is the outer comment. */

func main() {
    fmt.Println("Hello, World!")
}
```

Go also supports a form of documentation comments, which are comments that directly precede a package, type, function, or variable declaration. These comments are extracted by the godoc tool to generate documentation for your code.

```
package main

import "fmt"

// main is the entry point for the program.
func main() {
    fmt.Println("Hello, World!")
}

// add returns the sum of two integers.
func add(x int, y int) int {
    return x + y
}
```

The godoc tool processes these comments and produces detailed documentation. To generate HTML documentation for a Go package, you may use the command:

```
godoc -http=:6060
```

Navigate to http://localhost:6060/ in your web browser to view the documentation. This documentation will include not only comments but also detailed information about the structure and usage of the code.

When writing comments and documentation in Go, it is essential to follow conventions and best practices to ensure clarity and maintainability. Here are some best practices:

- Write comments in complete sentences.
- Use proper grammar and punctuation.
- Be concise but informative.
- Avoid stating the obvious or repeating what the code already makes clear.
- Place comments on the same level of indentation as the code they refer to.
- For documentation comments, begin with the name of the element being documented (e.g., add returns the sum of two integers).

Using comments judiciously and adhering to these practices will make your code easier to understand and maintain. Well-documented code not only helps others understand your work but also aids in debugging and future development.

It is also important to note that excessive commenting can be detrimental. Section off your code logically and document blocks of code where necessary, rather than adding redundant comments for every single line.

Employing comments and documentation effectively strikes a balance between maintainability and readability, thereby enhancing the overall quality of your Go programs.

Chapter 4

Control Structures

This chapter explores control structures in Go, including conditional statements like if-else and switch, and looping constructs such as for loops. It covers loop control mechanisms like break and continue, nested loops, and labels. Additionally, the chapter discusses deferred function calls, the panic and recover mechanism, and advanced features like type switch and type assertions, providing a comprehensive understanding of flow control in Go programs.

4.1 Introduction to Control Structures

Control structures are fundamental constructs in programming languages that enable the direction of the flow of execution based on certain conditions or repetitive tasks. They form the backbone of logical decision-making and iterative processes, making it possible to write dynamic and functional programs. In Go, control structures are designed with simplicity and clarity in mind while offering robust functionality.

Control structures in Go encompass:

- Conditional statements: if-else and switch.
- Looping constructs: for loops, including their various forms.
- Loop control mechanisms: break and continue.

- Special constructs: deferred function calls, panic, and recover mechanisms.
- Advanced features: type switch and type assertions.

```
if condition {
    // block of code to be executed if the condition is true
} else {
    // block of code to be executed if the condition is false
}
```

Listing 4.1: Basic structure of an if-else statement in Go

The if-else statement is essential for decision-making in Go programs. When the condition evaluates to true, the code within the first block is executed; otherwise, the code within the else block runs. Conditions in if statements can include relational and logical operations, contributing to robust decision-making capabilities.

```
switch expression {
case value1:
    // code to be executed if expression equals value1
case value2:
    // code to be executed if expression equals value2
default:
    // code to be executed if expression does not equal any case
}
```

Listing 4.2: Basic structure of a switch statement in Go

The switch statement serves as a convenient alternative to multiple if-else branches. It evaluates an expression once and compares it to the values specified in each case. If a match is found, the corresponding code block executes. If no match is found and a default case is provided, the default block executes. This structure is highly readable and reduces code clutter.

```
for i := 0; i < 10; i++ {
    fmt.Println(i)
}
```

Listing 4.3: Example of a for loop in Go

Looping constructs enable repeated execution of a block of code. The for loop is the only looping construct in Go, versatile enough to handle typical loop scenarios: initialization, condition-checking, and post-iteration steps. This loop will print numbers from 0 to 9. The simplicity and power of the for loop are evident, making it suitable for a wide variety of tasks.

Loop control mechanisms such as break and continue provide further control within loops. break terminates the loop immediately, whereas continue skips the current iteration and proceeds to the next iteration.

```
for i := 0; i < 10; i++ {
    if i == 5 {
        break
    }
    if i%2 == 0 {
        continue
    }
    fmt.Println(i)
}
```

Listing 4.4: Usage of break and continue in a for loop

In this code, when i equals 5, the break statement terminates the loop. The continue statement causes the loop to skip the print statement when i is even, only printing odd numbers less than 5.

Deferred function calls, the panic, and recover mechanisms introduce more advanced control flows, ensuring resource cleanup and error handling. Deferred function calls use the defer keyword:

```
func main() {
    defer fmt.Println("This statement is deferred")
    fmt.Println("This statement is executed first")
}
```

Listing 4.5: Example of deferred function call in Go

In this example, the deferred statement executes after the surrounding function completes. The panic and recover mechanisms handle runtime errors gracefully, maintaining program stability whenever possible.

```
func main() {
    defer func() {
        if r := recover(); r != nil {
            fmt.Println("Recovered from panic:", r)
        }
    }()
    panic("an unexpected error occurred")
}
```

Listing 4.6: Example of panic and recover in Go

Upon invoking panic, the program flow jumps to the deferred function.

If there is a call to recover and the error is non-nil, the error is handled, and the program can continue execution from a safe state.

Incorporating type switch constructs and type assertions further enhances control flow capabilities, allowing developers to handle interface types dynamically based on their underlying concrete types.

```
func doSomething(x interface{}) {
    switch x.(type) {
    case int:
        fmt.Println("x is int")
    case string:
        fmt.Println("x is string")
    default:
        fmt.Println("x is another type")
    }
}
```

Listing 4.7: Example of type switch in Go

In a type switch, the .(type) syntax is used to assert the dynamic type of the interface. Each case block handles a specific type, ensuring type-specific logic can be executed based on the runtime type of the variable.

This integral understanding of control structures lays the groundwork for constructing well-architected and responsive Go applications. As we delve deeper into each of these constructs, the mechanism of writing concise, efficient, and manageable code in Go becomes progressively clear.

4.2 Conditional Statements: if-else

Conditional statements are fundamental in Go programming for enabling decision-making within a program. These statements allow the execution of code segments based on the evaluation of boolean expressions. The if-else construct in Go is straightforward and powerful, providing a clear way to control the flow of execution.

The basic structure of an if statement in Go is as follows:

```
if condition {
    // code to execute if condition is true
}
```

Here, condition must be an expression that evaluates to a boolean value. If condition is true, the code block inside the curly braces is executed.

For example:

```
package main

import "fmt"

func main() {
    num := 10
    if num > 5 {
        fmt.Println("num is greater than 5")
    }
}
```

The above code snippet will print "num is greater than 5" because the condition num > 5 is true.

An if statement may also include an else clause to specify an alternative set of statements to execute if the condition evaluates to false:

```
if condition {
    // code to execute if condition is true
} else {
    // code to execute if condition is false
}
```

For instance:

```
package main

import "fmt"

func main() {
    num := 3
    if num > 5 {
        fmt.Println("num is greater than 5")
    } else {
        fmt.Println("num is not greater than 5")
    }
}
```

This code will output "num is not greater than 5" because the condition num > 5 is false.

Additionally, Go supports the else if construct for multiple conditions. This allows for the chaining of conditions in a clean and readable manner:

```
if condition1 {
    // code to execute if condition1 is true
```

```
} else if condition2 {
    // code to execute if condition2 is true
} else {
    // code to execute if all conditions are false
}
```

Consider the following example demonstrating else if:

```
package main

import "fmt"

func main() {
    num := 7
    if num > 10 {
        fmt.Println("num is greater than 10")
    } else if num > 5 {
        fmt.Println("num is greater than 5 but less than or equal to 10")
    } else {
        fmt.Println("num is 5 or less")
    }
}
```

Here, the output will be "num is greater than 5 but less than or equal to 10" as the condition num > 5 is true while num > 10 is false.

In Go, an if statement can also include a short statement to execute before the condition itself is evaluated. This can be useful for scoping variables only within the context of the if statement:

```
if err := someFunction(); err != nil {
    // handle the error
}
```

In this example, the variable err is declared and assigned within the if statement. This variable is accessible in the if block and all associated else and else if clauses.

Consider a case where the short statement is utilized:

```
package main
import (
    "fmt"
    "strconv"
)

func main() {
    if num, err := strconv.Atoi("42a"); err != nil {
        fmt.Println("Conversion error:", err)
    } else {
```

```
        fmt.Println("Converted number:", num)
    }
}
```

Running this example would produce the output:

```
Conversion error: strconv.Atoi: parsing "42a": invalid syntax
```

Here, strconv.Atoi("42a") attempts to convert the string "42a" to an integer. Since "42a" is not a valid integer, the conversion fails, setting err to a non-nil value and executing the first code block of the if statement.

An understanding of if-else constructs is foundational for more complex control structures. Although the syntax and semantics are relatively simple, mastery of these constructs is essential for effective conditional logic implementation in Go programs.

4.3 Switch Statements

switch statements in Go provide a powerful way to handle multiple conditional branches with clean and concise syntax. They represent a more elegant alternative to chained if-else statements, and are versatile enough to be used for both value-based and type-based comparisons.

Basic Syntax and Usage

The basic structure of a switch statement in Go is as follows:

```
switch variable {
case value1:
    // statements
case value2:
    // statements
default:
    // statements
}
```

The expression following the switch keyword is evaluated once, and the result is compared against the expression in each case clause. When a match is found, the associated block of code is executed. If no match is found, the default block is executed, if it is provided.

```
package main

import (
    "fmt"
```

```
)

func main() {
    day := 3
    switch day {
    case 1:
        fmt.Println("Monday")
    case 2:
        fmt.Println("Tuesday")
    case 3:
        fmt.Println("Wednesday")
    case 4:
        fmt.Println("Thursday")
    case 5:
        fmt.Println("Friday")
    default:
        fmt.Println("Weekend")
    }
}
```

```
Wednesday
```

Switching without an Expression

Go allows the usage of a switch statement without a specific expression. This defaults to true for each case condition, effectively acting as a cleaner form of a series of if-else statements.

```
package main

import (
    "fmt"
)

func main() {
    score := 85
    switch {
    case score >= 90:
        fmt.Println("Grade A")
    case score >= 80:
        fmt.Println("Grade B")
    case score >= 70:
        fmt.Println("Grade C")
    case score >= 60:
        fmt.Println("Grade D")
    default:
        fmt.Println("Grade F")
    }
}
```

```
Grade B
```

Multiple Expressions in Case Statements

Each case in a switch statement can contain multiple comma-separated expressions. The case block executes if any of the expressions match the switch expression.

```
package main

import (
    "fmt"
)

func main() {
    letter := "B"
    switch letter {
    case "A", "E", "I", "O", "U":
        fmt.Println("Vowel")
    default:
        fmt.Println("Consonant")
    }
}
```

```
Consonant
```

Fallthrough Behavior

By default, Go switch statements do not fall through to subsequent case blocks as in some other languages. To explicitly allow fallthrough, the fallthrough keyword must be used.

```
package main

import (
    "fmt"
)

func main() {
    num := 2
    switch num {
    case 1:
        fmt.Println("One")
        fallthrough
    case 2:
        fmt.Println("Two")
        fallthrough
    case 3:
        fmt.Println("Three")
    default:
        fmt.Println("Number not between 1 and 3")
    }
}
```

```
Two
Three
Number not between 1 and 3
```

Type Switches

Type switches are a special form of the switch statement to determine the type of an interface. This functionality is particularly useful for handling cases when an interface can hold values of different types.

```
package main

import (
    "fmt"
)

func typeSwitchExample(x interface{}) {
    switch v := x.(type) {
    case int:
        fmt.Printf("Integer: %d\n", v)
    case string:
        fmt.Printf("String: %s\n", v)
    case bool:
        fmt.Printf("Boolean: %t\n", v)
    default:
        fmt.Printf("Unknown type\n")
    }
}

func main() {
    typeSwitchExample(42)
    typeSwitchExample("Hello")
    typeSwitchExample(true)
}
```

```
Integer: 42
String: Hello
Boolean: true
```

Switch statements in Go, with their various features such as multiple expressions per case, implicit and explicit fallthrough, and type switches, provide a robust mechanism for control flow in a straightforward and readable format.

4.4 Loops: for

The for loop is the only looping construct in Go, providing exceptional flexibility and expressiveness. In Go, the for loop can be used in several variations: the standard for-loop, the for-range loop, the while-like loop, and the infinite loop. This section details each of these variations with examples.

The syntax for the standard for loop in Go is as follows:

```
for initialization; condition; post {
    // body of the loop
}
```

Here, initialization is executed once at the beginning of the loop, the condition is evaluated before each iteration, and post is executed after each iteration. If the condition evaluates to false, the loop terminates. Below is an example of a simple for loop that prints numbers from 1 to 5:

```
for i := 1; i <= 5; i++ {
    fmt.Println(i)
}
```

The output of this code will be:

```
1
2
3
4
5
```

The for loop can also be used in a manner similar to a while loop. When initialization and post statements are omitted, the loop continues until the condition evaluates to false:

```
i := 1
for i <= 5 {
    fmt.Println(i)
    i++
}
```

This loop has the same effect as the previous example. The output is identical:

```
1
2
3
4
5
```

The infinite loop is a variation of the for loop with no condition, initialization, or post statements. This loop will continue indefinitely unless interrupted by a break statement or other control flow mechanism:

```
for {
    // infinite loop
    fmt.Println("Infinite Loop")
}
```

To prevent an infinite loop from running indefinitely and potentially crashing the program, the break statement is commonly used to terminate the loop under specific conditions. Consider the following example:

```
i := 1
for {
    if i > 5 {
        break
    }
    fmt.Println(i)
    i++
}
```

The loop will terminate when i exceeds 5. The output from this code will be:

```
1
2
3
4
5
```

Another powerful variation of the for loop is the for-range loop, which iterates over elements in a collection, such as an array, slice, string, map, or channel. The syntax for a for-range loop when iterating over a slice is:

```
numbers := []int{1, 2, 3, 4, 5}
for index, value := range numbers {
    fmt.Printf("Index: %d, Value: %d\n", index, value)
}
```

The output will be:

```
Index: 0, Value: 1
Index: 1, Value: 2
Index: 2, Value: 3
Index: 3, Value: 4
Index: 4, Value: 5
```

In cases where the index is not needed, it can be omitted by using an underscore (_):

```
numbers := []int{1, 2, 3, 4, 5}
for _, value := range numbers {
    fmt.Printf("Value: %d\n", value)
}
```

The output of the above code will be:

```
Value: 1
Value: 2
Value: 3
Value: 4
Value: 5
```

For strings, the for-range loop iterates over Unicode code points. This is particularly useful when dealing with multi-byte characters:

```
str := "hello"
for index, runeValue := range str {
    fmt.Printf("Index: %d, Rune: %c\n", index, runeValue)
}
```

For maps, the for-range loop iterates over keys and values:

```
m := map[string]int{"Alice": 30, "Bob": 25, "Charlie": 35}
for key, value := range m {
    fmt.Printf("Key: %s, Value: %d\n", key, value)
}
```

The output will be:

```
Key: Alice, Value: 30
Key: Bob, Value: 25
Key: Charlie, Value: 35
```

The for loop is versatile enough to handle different kinds of iteration requirements in Go. Its ability to iterate over slices, arrays, maps, and strings, as well as providing a mechanism for infinite loops, makes it a fundamental construct for coding in Go.

4.5 Loop Control: break and continue

In Go programming, control structures within loops play a critical role in managing the flow of execution. Two essential loop control statements are break and continue. Understanding these constructs is vital for efficient loop management, allowing the programmer to exit loops early or skip iterations based on specific conditions.

break is used to terminate the execution of the nearest enclosing loop, effectively ending the loop when certain conditions are met. On the other hand, continue is used to skip the remaining code inside the loop for the current iteration and proceed directly to the beginning of the next iteration.

```
package main

import "fmt"

func main() {
    // Example using 'break'
    fmt.Println("Example of 'break' in a loop")
    for i := 0; i < 10; i++ {
        if i == 5 {
            break // Exit the loop when i equals 5
        }
        fmt.Println(i)
    }

    // Example of using 'continue'
    fmt.Println("Example of 'continue' in a loop")
    for j := 0; j < 10; j++ {
        if j % 2 == 0 {
            continue // Skip the rest of the loop when j is even
        }
        fmt.Println(j)
    }
}
```

Listing 4.8: Using break and continue in loops

Executing this program yields the following output:

```
Example of 'break' in a loop
0
1
2
3
4
Example of 'continue' in a loop
1
3
5
7
9
```

In the first loop controlled by break, the output displays numbers from 0 to 4, demonstrating that the loop terminates as soon as i equals 5. The second loop, using continue, outputs only odd numbers from 0 to 9, skipping the even numbers.

Using break and continue can increase the efficiency and readability of your code. However, it's crucial to use these statements judiciously to avoid creating complex and hard-to-follow control flows.

Let's consider another example where both break and continue are utilized within nested loops. In nested loops, break and continue affect the control flow of the innermost enclosing loop.

```
package main

import "fmt"

func main() {
    fmt.Println("Nested loops with `break` and `continue`")
    for m := 1; m <= 3; m++ {
        for n := 1; n <= 3; n++ {
            if m * n == 4 {
                break // Break the inner loop when m * n equals 4
            }
            if n % 2 == 0 {
                continue // Skip the even values of n
            }
            fmt.Printf("m: %d, n: %d\n", m, n)
        }
    }
}
```

Listing 4.9: Control flow in nested loops with break and continue

The output of this program is as follows:

```
Nested loops with `break` and `continue`
m: 1, n: 1
m: 2, n: 1
m: 3, n: 1
```

In this example, the nested loop structure includes conditional logic such that when m * n == 4, the break statement halts the inner loop, proceeding with the next iteration of the outer loop. Additionally, the continue statement skips the remaining code in the inner loop for the current iteration if n is even, thus avoiding the print statement for those cases.

Regarding practical applications, break is commonly utilized to exit a loop when a certain condition is met, often used in search algorithms or situations where an early termination criterion is defined. For example, to find the first occurrence of a value within a slice:

```
package main
```

```
import "fmt"

func main() {
    values := []int{10, 20, 30, 40, 50}
    target := 30
    found := false
    for _, value := range values {
        if value == target {
            found = true
            break // Exit the loop immediately once the target is found
        }
    }

    if found {
        fmt.Println("Target value found in slice.")
    } else {
        fmt.Println("Target value not found in slice.")
    }
}
```

Listing 4.10: Applying break to find an element in a slice

The use of continue is advantageous in scenarios requiring the skipping of specific iterations, often employed in filter operations or conditions where the iteration should bypass certain entries. Consider filtering non-positive numbers:

```
package main

import "fmt"

func main() {
    numbers := []int{-2, -1, 0, 1, 2}
    for _, number := range numbers {
        if number <= 0 {
            continue // Skip non-positive numbers
        }
        fmt.Println(number)
    }
}
```

Listing 4.11: Using continue to filter a slice

The output for the above code is:

```
1
2
```

In this context, continue allows the loop to proceed by bypassing non-positive numbers and ensuring that only positive numbers are printed.

In conclusion, mastering break and continue is essential for controlling the flow within Go loops effectively. Proper use of these constructs streamlines loop operation, enhances readability, and addresses specific conditions crucial for various algorithm implementations.

4.6 Nested Loops and Labels

Nested loops are an indispensable aspect of many computational algorithms, allowing the execution of looped statements within other loops. In the Go programming language, a nested loop is simply a loop inside another loop. Each iteration of the outer loop triggers a complete iteration through the inner loop(s). This structure enables the traversal of multidimensional arrays, the generation of combinations, and the implementation of complex algorithms.

Consider the following example where we use nested loops to iterate over a two-dimensional slice:

```
package main

import "fmt"

func main() {
    matrix := [][]int{
        {1, 2, 3},
        {4, 5, 6},
        {7, 8, 9},
    }

    for i := 0; i < len(matrix); i++ {
        for j := 0; j < len(matrix[i]); j++ {
            fmt.Printf("%d ", matrix[i][j])
        }
        fmt.Println()
    }
}
```

In this example, the outer loop iterates over the rows of the matrix, while the inner loop iterates over the elements within each row. The program prints each element in a row and proceeds to the next row upon the completion of the inner loop. The output is:

```
1 2 3
4 5 6
7 8 9
```

Next, consider scenarios where we need to control the execution flow within nested loops more precisely. Go provides the break, continue, and goto statements, which can be enhanced by labels to manage looping control.

A common requirement in nested looping is breaking out of an inner loop and halting the execution of an outer loop. In Go, this is achieved elegantly using labeled break statements.

Here is an example of using labeled breaks to exit out of nested loops:

```
package main

import "fmt"

func main() {
    matrix := [][]int{
        {1, 2, 3},
        {4, 5, 0},
        {7, 8, 9},
    }

outerLoop:
    for i := 0; i < len(matrix); i++ {
        for j := 0; j < len(matrix[i]); j++ {
            if matrix[i][j] == 0 {
                fmt.Println("Found 0, breaking out of loops")
                break outerLoop
            }
            fmt.Printf("%d ", matrix[i][j])
        }
        fmt.Println()
    }
    fmt.Println("Completed the loops.")
}
```

In this program, a label, outerLoop, is defined before the outer loop. When a zero is found in the matrix, the break outerLoop statement halts the execution of both the inner and outer loops. The program prints:

```
1 2 3
4 5
Found 0, breaking out of loops
Completed the loops.
```

Labels in Go can also be used with the goto statement to provide finer control, though its use is relatively discouraged due to potential complexity and readability concerns. However, it's essential to understand its functionality and proper usage.

Consider the following example where the goto statement is used:

```
package main

import "fmt"

func main() {
    for i := 0; i < 5; i++ {
        for j := 0; j < 5; j++ {
            if i == 2 && j == 2 {
                fmt.Println("Skipping position (2,2)")
                goto skip
            }
            fmt.Printf("(%d,%d) ", i, j)
        }
        fmt.Println()
    }
    return

skip:
    fmt.Println("Exited the nested loop at position (2,2)")
}
```

In this snippet, the goto statement jumps to the labeled skip when the condition i == 2 && j == 2 is met. This terminates the execution of the nested loops prematurely and skips to the code following the skip label. The output is:

```
(0,0) (0,1) (0,2) (0,3) (0,4)
(1,0) (1,1) (1,2) (1,3) (1,4)
Skipping position (2,2)
Exited the nested loop at position (2,2)
```

Proper utilization of nested loops and labels facilitates the development of efficient and readable code for complex logical operations. Recognizing both the power and potential pitfalls of these constructs is crucial for mastering control structures in Go. Labelling should be used judiciously, as overuse or misuse may lead to complicated and hard-to-maintain source code.

4.7 Deferred Function Calls

Deferred function calls in Go provide a mechanism to ensure that a function is executed after the surrounding function completes. The defer statement is used to schedule a function call to be run after the function in which the defer statement is executed returns. This is particularly useful for resource management, such as closing files, releasing locks, or cleaning up resources, regardless of whether the function exits normally or due to a panic.

A defer statement immediately evaluates the parameters of the deferred function call and pushes the call onto a stack. The deferred calls are executed in the reverse order of their addition when the surrounding function returns.

The syntax for the defer statement is as follows:

```
defer functionName(parameters)
```

Consider the following example demonstrating the use of defer:

```
package main

import (
    "fmt"
)

func main() {
    fmt.Println("Start of main function")
    defer fmt.Println("This will be executed last")
    fmt.Println("End of main function")
}
```

The output of the above program will be:

```
Start of main function
End of main function
This will be executed last
```

In this example, the defer statement defers the execution of the fmt.Println("This will be executed last") call until the surrounding function main() exits. As a result, it gets executed after fmt.Println("End of main function"), despite the order in which the statements appear in the source code.

Multiple Deferred Calls

When multiple defer calls are present within a function, they are executed in last-in, first-out (LIFO) order. This behavior can be illustrated with the following example:

```
package main

import (
    "fmt"
)

func main() {
    defer fmt.Println("First deferred call")
    defer fmt.Println("Second deferred call")
    defer fmt.Println("Third deferred call")
```

```
    fmt.Println("End of main function")
}
```

Running this program will produce the following output:

```
End of main function
Third deferred call
Second deferred call
First deferred call
```

Here, the third deferred call is executed first, followed by the second, and finally the first.

Practical Applications of defer

One of the common use cases of defer is to ensure that a resource allocation operation (such as file opening or lock acquisition) is paired with a corresponding deallocation (such as file closing or lock release), even in the presence of errors or early returns within the function.

For example, consider a function that opens a file and reads its content. Using defer can ensure that the file is properly closed regardless of how the function exits:

```
package main

import (
    "fmt"
    "os"
)

func readFile(filepath string) error {
    file, err := os.Open(filepath)
    if err != nil {
        return err
    }
    defer file.Close() // Ensures the file is closed when the function returns

    // Read the file content here
    // ...

    fmt.Println("File reading completed")
    return nil
}

func main() {
    err := readFile("example.txt")
    if err != nil {
        fmt.Println("Error:", err)
    }
}
```

In this example, the file.Close() call is deferred, ensuring that the file is closed after the readFile function completes, regardless of whether it exits due to an error.

Deferred Function Calls with Anonymous Functions

Deferred function calls can also utilize anonymous functions for more complex cleanup tasks:

```
package main

import "fmt"

func main() {
    defer func() {
        fmt.Println("Deferred anonymous function call")
    }()
    fmt.Println("Main function body")
}
```

Output:

```
Main function body
Deferred anonymous function call
```

In this scenario, an anonymous function is deferred and executed after the main function body completes. This pattern is useful when the cleanup logic requires access to function-scoped variables.

Limitations and Considerations

While defer provides an elegant way to handle cleanup, it is worth noting some limitations and considerations:

- defer statements add a slight overhead due to the management of the deferred call stack.
- The number of deferred calls should be kept reasonable to avoid excessive memory usage, especially in long-running functions or loops.
- The execution of deferred calls occurs before the function returns, potentially affecting performance if the deferred calls are time-consuming.

Deferred function calls are a powerful feature in Go, offering a reliable way to manage resources and ensure clean-up operations are performed as required.

4.8 Panic and Recover Mechanism

In Go, the panic and recover mechanism provides a way to handle runtime errors and manage exceptional conditions gracefully. This mechanism is particularly useful for handling unexpected situations and ensuring that program state can be recovered or cleaned up before the application terminates.

A panic is a built-in function that stops the ordinary flow of control and begins panicking. When the function panic is called, it immediately stops execution of the function and starts to unwind the stack, running any deferred functions along the way. If the panic reaches the top of the goroutine's stack, the program crashes. This is illustrated in the following simple panic example:

```
package main

import "fmt"

func main() {
    fmt.Println("Starting the program...")
    panic("A severe error occurred!")
    fmt.Println("This line will not be executed.")
}
```

Executing this code results in the following output:

```
Starting the program...
panic: A severe error occurred!

goroutine 1 [running]:
main.main()
        /path/to/your/code.go:6 +0x39
exit status 2
```

In the code above, the line containing fmt.Println("This line will not be executed.") does not execute because the panic function call causes the program to terminate prematurely.

To manage panics and allow the program to continue execution, Go provides the recover function. The recover function can only be called within deferred functions. This function stops the unwinding process initiated by panic and returns the value passed to the call of panic. If recover is called outside the deferred function, it will return nil.

An example of using recover is provided below:

```
package main
```

```
import "fmt"

func main() {
    defer func() {
        if r := recover(); r != nil {
            fmt.Println("Recovered from:", r)
        }
    }()

    fmt.Println("Starting the program...")
    panic("A severe error occurred!")
    fmt.Println("This line will not be executed.")
}
```

When this program is executed, the output will be:

```
Starting the program...
Recovered from: A severe error occurred!
```

In this instance, the deferred anonymous function utilizes recover to capture the panic and prevent the program from terminating. The line containing fmt.Println("This line will not be executed.") does not execute because the control flow is still interrupted by panic, but the program does not crash, allowing subsequent code to run normally.

To understand the practical use of panic and recover, consider a function that divides two numbers and uses panic to handle a division by zero scenario:

```
package main

import "fmt"

func divide(a, b int) int {
    if b == 0 {
        panic("division by zero")
    }
    return a / b
}

func main() {
    defer func() {
        if r := recover(); r != nil {
            fmt.Println("Recovered in main from:", r)
        }
    }()

    result := divide(10, 2)
    fmt.Println("Result:", result)
```

```
    result = divide(10, 0)
    fmt.Println("This will not be printed:", result)
}
```

Output when executed:

```
Result: 5
Recovered in main from: division by zero
```

In this example, if divide is called with a non-zero denominator, it executes normally and returns the result. However, if a division by zero is attempted, panic is invoked. The deferred function in main captures this panic using recover, preventing the program from crashing and allowing for a controlled exit or further processing.

A sophisticated use case involves the interaction between multiple function calls. Consider the following code:

```
package main

import "fmt"

func handleArithmetic() {
    defer func() {
        if r := recover(); r != nil {
            fmt.Println("Recovered in handleArithmetic from:", r)
        }
    }()

    fmt.Println("Performing division...")
    divide(10, 0)
    fmt.Println("This will not be printed.")
}

func divide(a, b int) int {
    if b == 0 {
        panic("division by zero")
    }
    return a / b
}

func main() {
    handleArithmetic()
    fmt.Println("Continuing execution in main...")
}
```

Output when executed:

```
Performing division...
Recovered in handleArithmetic from: division by zero
Continuing execution in main...
```

Here, handleArithmetic is responsible for invoking divide. When panic occurs during the division by zero, the deferred function in handleArithmetic recovers from it, ensuring that the program can continue executing in main without interruption.

In scenarios involving goroutines, recover must be employed judiciously within the goroutine itself, as each goroutine has its own stack. This ensures that panics within one goroutine do not affect others:

```
package main

import (
    "fmt"
    "time"
)

func safeGoroutine() {
    defer func() {
        if r := recover(); r != nil {
            fmt.Println("Recovered in goroutine from:", r)
        }
    }()

    fmt.Println("Goroutine is panicking...")
    panic("panic in goroutine")
}

func main() {
    go safeGoroutine()
    time.Sleep(1 * time.Second) // wait for goroutine to finish
    fmt.Println("Continuing execution in main...")
}
```

Output when executed:

```
Goroutine is panicking...
Recovered in goroutine from: panic in goroutine
Continuing execution in main...
```

In this example, the panic occurring in safeGoroutine is contained and recovered within the goroutine itself. This isolation prevents the main execution flow from being disrupted.

The panic and recover mechanism in Go is a powerful tool for managing error states and ensuring that applications maintain stability, even when encountering severe errors. By strategically placing recover calls in deferred functions, developers can design robust systems that gracefully handle exceptions and maintain consistent operation.

4.9 Type Switch and Type Assertions

Type switches and type assertions are valuable features in the Go programming language, enhancing flexibility when working with interfaces and type-safe operations.

Type Switches:

A type switch is a construct that allows a program to dispatch execution based on the type of an interface. This capability can be particularly useful when handling values of an interface type and needing to perform type-specific operations. The syntax for a type switch is similar to that of a regular switch statement.

Consider this example which determines the type of a variable v and performs an action accordingly:

```
package main

import "fmt"

func main() {
    var i interface{} = "hello"

    switch v := i.(type) {
    case int:
        fmt.Printf("v is an integer: %d\n", v)
    case string:
        fmt.Printf("v is a string: %s\n", v)
    default:
        fmt.Printf("v is of a different type\n")
    }
}
```

In this example, i is an empty interface, which means it can hold any type. The type switch uses the syntax i.(type), and within each case clause, v is of the specified type. Here fmt.Printf is called with format specifiers suitable for the type of v.

Type Assertions:

Type assertions provide access to the dynamic type of an interface. A type assertion takes the following form: i.(T), where i is an interface type and T is asserted to be a specific type. The result of a type assertion is the value stored inside the interface if it is of type T. If i does not hold a T, a run-time panic occurs.

Here's a basic example demonstrating a type assertion:

```
package main

import "fmt"

func main() {
    var i interface{} = 42

    v, ok := i.(int)
    if ok {
        fmt.Printf("Integer value: %d\n", v)
    } else {
        fmt.Printf("i is not an integer\n")
    }
}
```

In this program, i is an empty interface holding an integer value. The type assertion i.(int) attempts to convert i to an integer. The ok value indicates whether the assertion succeeded. If ok is true, the program safely prints the integer value; otherwise, it reports that i is not an integer.

Type assertions can also be directly used without the 'ok' pattern, though this is more risky as it may cause a runtime panic:

```
package main

import "fmt"

func main() {
    var i interface{} = 42

    // Unsafe type assertion, may panic if i is not int.
    v := i.(int)
    fmt.Printf("Integer value: %d\n", v)
}
```

Use this pattern with caution, ensuring that the type being asserted is likely held by the interface value.

Practices for Type Safety:

It is crucial to validate the interface type before performing operations to avoid panics. Using type switches for handling multiple types can lead to cleaner code and reduced risk when compared to sequences of type assertions.

For example, handling different types within a single code block can become cumbersome with multiple type assertions:

```
package main
```

```
import "fmt"

func handle(i interface{}) {
    if v, ok := i.(int); ok {
        fmt.Printf("Integer value: %d\n", v)
    } else if v, ok := i.(string); ok {
        fmt.Printf("String value: %s\n", v)
    } else {
        fmt.Printf("Unknown type\n")
    }
}

func main() {
    handle(42)
    handle("hello")
}
```

Contrast this with a type switch which succinctly handles various type cases:

```
package main

import "fmt"

func handle(i interface{}) {
    switch v := i.(type) {
    case int:
        fmt.Printf("Integer value: %d\n", v)
    case string:
        fmt.Printf("String value: %s\n", v)
    default:
        fmt.Printf("Unknown type\n")
    }
}

func main() {
    handle(42)
    handle("hello")
}
```

By adopting type switches, the code becomes more readable and maintainable. This is especially significant in complex programs where interfaces may hold values of various types.

Understanding and effectively utilizing type switches and type assertions enable Go programmers to write more flexible and robust code, aligning with the language's type safety principles while exploiting its dynamic features.

Chapter 5

Functions in Go

This chapter delves into the concept of functions in Go, explaining how to define and call them. It covers parameters, return values, named return values, and variadic functions. The chapter also introduces anonymous functions and closures, discusses recursion, and explains higher-order functions. Additionally, it introduces the defer statement, its usage, and how to handle errors within functions, providing a thorough understanding of functional programming in Go.

5.1 Introduction to Functions

In Go, functions are first-class citizens, which means they can be assigned to variables, passed as arguments to other functions, and returned from other functions. Understanding functions in Go is essential for writing clean, efficient, and reusable code.

A function in Go is a group of statements that together perform a task. Every Go program has at least one function, namely the main function, which is automatically called when the program is executed. Functions allow for modularity in code, facilitating the division of a complex problem into smaller, manageable tasks.

```
package main

import "fmt"
```

```
// Declare a function named greet
func greet() {
    fmt.Println("Hello, world!")
}

// Main function
func main() {
    // Call the greet function
    greet()
}
```

Listing 5.1: Basic Function Syntax in Go

In this example, we define a simple function named greet that prints "Hello, world!" to the console. The main function calls the greet function, demonstrating how functions can be invoked.

Functions are defined using the keyword func, followed by the function name, a list of zero or more parameters enclosed in parentheses, and the function body enclosed in braces. The general syntax for a function definition is as follows:

```
func functionName(parameterList) returnType {
    // function body
}
```

Listing 5.2: General Syntax for Defining a Function in Go

parameterList is a comma-separated list of parameters, where each parameter has a name and a type. The returnType specifies the type of value the function returns. If a function does not return any value, the returnType is omitted.

```
package main

import "fmt"

// Function that takes two integers and returns their sum
func add(a int, b int) int {
    return a + b
}

// Main function
func main() {
    result := add(3, 4)
    fmt.Println("Sum:", result)
}
```

Listing 5.3: Function with Parameters and Return Value

In this example, the add function takes two int parameters and returns their sum. The main function calls add with the arguments 3 and 4, and prints the result.

Go supports multiple return values, allowing functions to return more than one value. This feature is particularly useful for functions that can return a result along with an error indication.

```
package main

import (
    "errors"
    "fmt"
)

// Function that divides two integers and returns the result and an error
func divide(a int, b int) (int, error) {
    if b == 0 {
        return 0, errors.New("division by zero")
    }
    return a / b, nil
}

// Main function
func main() {
    numerator := 10
    denominator := 2
    result, err := divide(numerator, denominator)
    if err != nil {
        fmt.Println("Error:", err)
    } else {
        fmt.Println("Result:", result)
    }
}
```

Listing 5.4: Function with Multiple Return Values

In this example, the divide function performs integer division and returns two values: the result of the division and an error value. If the denominator is zero, the function returns an error; otherwise, it returns the division result and a nil error.

Additionally, functions in Go can be assigned to variables and passed as arguments to other functions, demonstrating their first-class status. This capability enables powerful programming paradigms such as higher-order functions and function literals.

```
package main

import "fmt"

// Function that prints a message
```

```
func printMessage(message string) {
    fmt.Println(message)
}

// Function that takes another function as an argument
func executeFunction(f func(string), message string) {
    f(message)
}

// Main function
func main() {
    // Assign the printMessage function to a variable
    var messagePrinter func(string) = printMessage

    // Call the function using the variable
    messagePrinter("Hello from a function variable")

    // Pass the function as an argument to another function
    executeFunction(printMessage, "Hello from a higher-order function")
}
```

Listing 5.5: Assigning Functions to Variables and Passing Them as Arguments

In this example, printMessage is assigned to the variable messagePrinter, and the function is then called using this variable. The executeFunction function demonstrates how to pass a function as an argument. It takes a function and a string, calling the function with the string argument.

These foundational concepts establish a basis for more advanced features and practices involving Go functions.

5.2 Defining and Calling Functions

In Go, functions serve as the fundamental building blocks of code organization and reuse. A function is a group of statements that together perform a task. Every Go program has at least one function, which is the main function. You can divide your code into separate functions, which can make the code easier to manage and understand. To define a function in Go, you use the func keyword, followed by the function name, a list of parameters within parentheses, and a block of code that represents the function body. The general syntax for defining a function is as follows:

```
func functionName(parameter1 type, parameter2 type) returnType {
    // function body
```

```
}
```

The returnType is optional. If the function does not return any value, you can omit it.

Let's start with a simple example of defining and calling a function that adds two integers and returns the result.

```
package main

import "fmt"

func add(a int, b int) int {
    return a + b
}

func main() {
    result := add(3, 4)
    fmt.Println("Result:", result)
}
```

In the above example, we define a function named add that takes two parameters, a and b, both of type int. The function returns an int value which is the sum of a and b. The main function calls the add function with the arguments 3 and 4, stores the result in the variable result, and prints it.

Functions can have multiple parameters, and the parameters must be specified with their types. When you call a function, the arguments must be passed in the same order as the parameters are defined.

Go also supports multiple return values. You can return more than one value from a function by specifying the return types within parentheses. Here's an example of a function that returns multiple values:

```
package main

import "fmt"

func swap(a, b int) (int, int) {
    return b, a
}

func main() {
    x, y := swap(1, 2)
    fmt.Println("Swapped values:", x, y)
}
```

In this example, the swap function takes two integer parameters and returns two integers. The function swaps the values of a and b and returns them. The main function calls swap with the arguments 1 and 2, and captures the returned values x and y, then prints the swapped values.

Parameters in Go functions can also be named the same way we name any variable. However, when naming parameters, it is a good practice to choose meaningful names. Parameters with the same type can be grouped together to reduce redundancy. For example:

```
func multiply(a, b int) int {
    return a * b
}
```

Here, a and b are grouped together because they share the same type, int.

Go functions are first-class citizens. This means that functions can be assigned to variables, passed as arguments to other functions, and returned as values from other functions.

Consider the following example:

```
package main

import "fmt"

func foo() {
    fmt.Println("foo was called")
}

func bar(f func()) {
    f() // calling the passed function
}

func main() {
    bar(foo) // passing foo as an argument to bar
}
```

In this example, the bar function takes a function f as a parameter and calls f within its body. The main function passes the foo function to bar, which then calls foo. This demonstrates how functions can be used as arguments, enabling higher-order functions.

An important aspect of function calling in Go is the way arguments are passed. By default, Go uses pass-by-value, meaning that a copy of the argument's value is passed to the function. Modifying this copy within the function doesn't affect the original value. However, if a function needs to modify the original value, you can pass a pointer to the argument.

Here's an example of passing a pointer to a function:

```
package main

import "fmt"
```

```
func increment(val *int) {
    *val++
}

func main() {
    num := 5
    increment(&num)
    fmt.Println("Incremented value:", num) // Output: Incremented value: 6
}
```

In the example above, the increment function takes a pointer to an integer parameter, val. Inside the function, the value at the address pointed to by the pointer is incremented. The main function calls increment and passes the address of num using the & operator. This allows increment to modify the original num variable.

It's also worth noting that named return values can be used to simplify function declarations. When you use named return values, you can return without explicitly specifying the values, making the code more concise.

Here's an example using named return values:

```
package main

import "fmt"

func divide(a, b int) (quotient int, remainder int) {
    quotient = a / b
    remainder = a % b
    return
}

func main() {
    q, r := divide(10, 3)
    fmt.Println("Quotient:", q, "Remainder:", r) // Output: Quotient: 3 Remainder: 1
}
```

In this example, the divide function calculates the quotient and remainder of the division operation and uses named return values. The main function captures these values and prints them.

5.3 Parameters and Return Values

Understanding parameters and return values in Go is fundamental to effectively harnessing the power of functions. Go's design emphasizes simplicity and clarity, which is reflected in its function parameter and return value syntax.

Function parameters in Go are defined within the parentheses following the function name. Each parameter must have a name and a type, and multiple parameters are separated by commas. Additionally, Go supports type inference for multiple parameters of the same type, allowing for a more concise syntax.

```
func add(a int, b int) int {
    return a + b
}
```

In the add function above, a and b are parameters of type int. The function returns an int, as specified after the closing parenthesis of the parameter list. This basic syntax is consistent across all functions in Go.

For functions with multiple return values, Go allows you to specify the types of each return value within parentheses.

```
func divide(a float64, b float64) (float64, error) {
    if b == 0.0 {
        return 0.0, errors.New("division by zero")
    }
    return a / b, nil
}
```

The divide function returns a float64 and an error. It checks for division by zero and returns an appropriate error if necessary. Multiple return values enhance the function's utility, allowing it to return both a result and an error status.

The order of parameters and return values should be considered to enhance the readability and maintainability of your code. Leveraging Go's support for named return values can further improve code clarity. Named return values are declared by name in the function signature and behave as variables within the function scope.

```
func calculate(a int, b int) (sum int, product int) {
    sum = a + b
    product = a * b
    return
}
```

In the calculate function, the return values sum and product are named, and therefore automatically initialized to the zero value of their type (in this case, int). The return statement can be used without explicitly specifying the values to return, as the named return values are used by default.

Variadic functions are another powerful feature in Go, enabling a function to accept a variable number of arguments of the same type. To define a variadic function, use an ellipsis (...) before the type of the final parameter.

```
func sum(nums ...int) int {
    total := 0
    for _, num := range nums {
        total += num
    }
    return total
}
```

In the sum function, the nums parameter is variadic, allowing it to accept any number of int values. Within the function, nums behaves like a slice. Variadic parameters can simplify the function call syntax and enhance flexibility.

When a function requires a specific number of initial parameters followed by a variable number, the variadic parameter must be the last in the parameter list.

```
func printStrings(prefix string, texts ...string) {
    for _, text := range texts {
        fmt.Println(prefix, text)
    }
}
```

The printStrings function takes a prefix string and any number of texts strings. The function prints each text with the given prefix. This demonstrates the utility of combining fixed and variadic parameters to create more versatile functions.

Go also provides a mechanism for converting between slices and variadic parameters. A slice can be passed to a variadic function by appending an ellipsis after the slice variable.

```
nums := []int{1, 2, 3, 4, 5}
result := sum(nums...)
fmt.Println(result)
```

In this example, the slice nums is passed to the sum function using the variadic parameter syntax. This feature is crucial for building flexible functions that interoperate seamlessly with slices.

Error handling in functions often involves using multiple return values to signal errors without exceptions. Functions can return a result value along with an error value to indicate success or failure.

```
func readFile(fileName string) ([]byte, error) {
    data, err := os.ReadFile(fileName)
    if err != nil {
        return nil, err
    }
    return data, nil
}
```

The readFile function exemplifies this practice by returning the content of a file and an error. When an error occurs, it returns nil for the data and the error itself.

Conciseness and readability in function signatures are essential. Grouping parameters of the same type and using named return values are effective strategies. Variadic functions offer flexibility, and leveraging multiple return values for error handling is a powerful idiom in Go. Understanding these concepts is crucial for writing effective and idiomatic Go code.

5.4 Named Return Values

In Go, functions can return multiple values, which is a unique feature of the language allowing more flexibility and simplifying error handling. Named return values extend this feature further by enabling you to return values with pre-declared names. This capability can make your code clearer and more readable by documenting the purpose of each return value directly in the function signature.

When you declare named return values, Go automatically initializes these variables to their zero values upon function entry. At the end of the function, the values of these named variables are returned with a simple return statement without any arguments. This mechanism simplifies the code and reduces the potential for mistakes, especially when dealing with multiple return values.

Here is the syntax for defining a function with named return values:

```
func functionName(param1 type1, param2 type2) (result1 type1, result2 type2) {
    // function body
    // variables result1 and result2 can be used directly
    return
}
```

The result1 and result2 are named return values that are automatically initialized to their zero values when the function begins execution.

Consider the following example where named return values are implemented in a function that performs a simple arithmetic operation:

```
func divideAndRemainder(a, b int) (quotient int, remainder int) {
    if b == 0 {
        fmt.Println("Division by zero is not allowed.")
        return
    }
    quotient = a / b
    remainder = a % b
    return // implicitly returns quotient, remainder
}
```

In this example, the function divideAndRemainder performs integer division, calculating both the quotient and the remainder. The named return values, quotient and remainder, are declared in the function signature. Inside the function body, these variables are assigned values, and when the return statement is reached, Go returns the current values of quotient and remainder.

Using named return values can also aid in making the function's purpose and the role of each return value more explicit, which is particularly useful in functions with more complex logic. For instance:

```
func calculateStatistics(numbers []int) (sum int, mean float64, stddev float64) {
    count := len(numbers)
    if count == 0 {
        return
    }
    // Calculate sum
    for _, num := range numbers {
        sum += num
    }
    // Calculate mean
    mean = float64(sum) / float64(count)
    // Calculate standard deviation
    var variance float64
    for _, num := range numbers {
        variance += (float64(num) - mean) * (float64(num) - mean)
    }
    stddev = math.Sqrt(variance / float64(count))
    return
}
```

Here, the function calculateStatistics takes a slice of integers and returns three named values: sum, mean, and stddev. This clear declaration of the return values makes it easier to understand the purpose and output of the function. The named return values help avoid potential mistakes by allowing you to directly manipulate the variables that are ultimately returned.

Although named return values enhance code readability and maintainability, they should be used judiciously. In cases where the function logic is simple or only a single value is returned, unnamed return values might be more appropriate. The choice between using named versus unnamed return values should be guided by the complexity of the function and the need for clarity.

For complex functions, named return values can also facilitate the handling of multiple exit points by ensuring that all return variables are declared in one place, thus reducing the chances of inconsistent return value handling. Nevertheless, it is crucial to balance readability and simplicity—the primary goal is to write clear, understandable, and maintainable code.

Consider another example that demonstrates the advantages of named return values in error handling situations:

```
func parseConfig(configData []byte) (config Config, err error) {
    err = json.Unmarshal(configData, &config)
    if err != nil {
        return
    }
    // Additional validation logic if necessary
    return
}
```

In this function, parseConfig, the named return values are config and err. If an error occurs during the JSON unmarshalling process, the function immediately returns with the error. The named return values improve the function's readability and show at a glance what will be returned in case of an error.

Proper usage of named return values is a powerful tool in the Go programmer's arsenal. By leveraging them appropriately, one can write more cohesive, self-explanatory functions that convey their purpose and behavior directly through their signatures.

5.5 Variadic Functions

Variadic functions in Go allow for a flexible interface where a function can accept an indefinite number of arguments. This is useful when the number of parameters isn't known beforehand, offering greater versatility in how functions are utilized. Variadic functions consume slice values of a specific type and collect them into a single variable.

A variadic parameter is denoted by ellipsis (...) followed by the type. For instance, a variadic function that accepts any number of integers would have a signature like func myFunc(nums ...int).

```
package main

import (
    "fmt"
)

func sum(values ...int) int {
    total := 0
    for _, value := range values {
        total += value
    }
    return total
}

func main() {
    fmt.Println(sum(1, 2, 3)) // Output: 6
    fmt.Println(sum(10, 20, 30, 40)) // Output: 100
    fmt.Println(sum()) // Output: 0
}
```

In this example, the sum function uses a variadic parameter values ...int to facilitate the addition of an arbitrary number of integers. Within the function body, the variadic parameter values behaves like a slice of integers, []int, which allows iteration over its elements using a for loop.

The function can be invoked with any number of integer arguments, including none. When no arguments are supplied, the slice is empty, and the function operates accordingly.

A critical observation about variadic functions is their versatility with existing slices. Passing a slice to a variadic function is straightforward using the spread operator (...):

```
package main

import (
    "fmt"
)

func printAll(strings ...string) {
    for _, str := range strings {
        fmt.Println(str)
    }
}
```

```
func main() {
    messages := []string{"Hello", "World", "from", "Go"}

    printAll(messages...) // Spread operator
}
```

In this script, the slice messages is passed to the variadic function printAll using the spread operator, which acts as syntactic sugar to expand the slice into individual arguments. Otherwise, passing the slice directly would result in a compilation error because the function expects a variable number of arguments, not a slice.

Combining Variadic Parameters with Regular Parameters

A variadic function may also have regular parameters. The regular parameters must precede the variadic parameter:

```
package main

import (
    "fmt"
)

func greet(message string, names ...string) {
    for _, name := range names {
        fmt.Printf("%s, %s!\n", message, name)
    }
}
func main() {
    greet("Hello", "Alice", "Bob", "Charlie")
}
```

In this example, the greet function features a regular string parameter message and a variadic string parameter names. When invoking the function, the first argument always corresponds to the message, and the remaining arguments are collected into the names slice.

```
Hello, Alice!
Hello, Bob!
Hello, Charlie!
```

Functions with regular and variadic parameters provide greater control by combining fixed and flexible interface parts.

Using Variadic Functions in Recursion

Variadic functions can also be employed recursively. Consider an example of a function that finds the maximum value from a list of integers, using recursion:

```
package main

import (
    "fmt"
)

func max(numbers ...int) int {
    if len(numbers) == 0 {
        return 0
    }
    if len(numbers) == 1 {
        return numbers[0]
    }
    restMax := max(numbers[1:]...)
    if numbers[0] > restMax {
        return numbers[0]
    }
    return restMax
}

func main() {
    fmt.Println(max(1, 3, 5, 2, 8, 4)) // Output: 8
}
```

In this example, the max function employs recursion to determine the highest integer from a variable set of arguments. The base cases handle slices with zero or one element. Recursive calls are made on progressively smaller slices until the base cases are achieved.

```
8
```

When designing variadic functions, it is crucial to consider performance implications and possible impacts on readability. Unnecessary use of variadic parameters can lead to complex and less maintainable codebases. Employ this feature judiciously to maintain code quality and efficiency.

5.6 Anonymous Functions and Closures

Anonymous functions, also known as function literals, are functions that are defined without a name. They are a central feature of Go and are used frequently in Go programming to encapsulate functionality and handle concurrency. An anonymous function can be declared and invoked at the same time, allowing the creation of one-off functions with a scope limited to the place of their use. They are particularly useful for short-lived operations or cases where the function's logic needs to access local variables defined outside its own scope.

To define an anonymous function in Go, use the func keyword followed directly by the function's parameters and body. Consider the following example that demonstrates the definition and invocation of an anonymous function:

```
package main

import "fmt"

func main() {
    message := "Hello, Go!"
    func(msg string) {
        fmt.Println(msg)
    }(message)
}
```

In this example, the anonymous function is immediately invoked with the argument message. The function takes a single parameter, msg, and prints it. Because message falls within the scope of the main function, the anonymous function can access it.

Closures extend the concept of anonymous functions by allowing them to capture and access variables from the environment in which they are defined. A closure is formed when an anonymous function accesses variables defined outside its immediate scope. This feature leverages lexical scoping to provide a powerful means of maintaining state across function calls without resorting to global variables.

Consider the following example, which demonstrates closures by incrementing an internal counter:

```
package main

import "fmt"

func main() {
    counter := func() func() int {
        count := 0
        return func() int {
            count++
            return count
        }
    }()

    fmt.Println(counter()) // Output: 1
    fmt.Println(counter()) // Output: 2
```

```
    fmt.Println(counter()) // Output: 3
}
```

In this example, the counter variable is assigned an anonymous function that returns another anonymous function. The inner function increments count and returns the new value each time it is called. The count variable is captured by the closure formed by the returned anonymous function, allowing count to persist and accumulate values across multiple calls to counter().

The use of closures in Go often arises in the context of concurrent programming with goroutines. Goroutines can utilize closures to maintain state within their associated anonymous functions. This can be particularly beneficial for managing shared resources or encapsulating operations that need to run independently. Consider the following example which leverages closures in the context of goroutines:

```
package main

import (
    "fmt"
    "time"
)

func main() {
    for i := 0; i < 5; i++ {
        go func(n int) {
            fmt.Printf("Goroutine %d\n", n)
        }(i)
    }
    time.Sleep(time.Second)
}
```

The anonymous function passed to the go statement captures the loop variable i via its parameter n. Each goroutine independently prints its respective value of n.

It is essential to be cautious when using closures inside loops. The loop variable should be passed as an argument to the anonymous function to avoid capturing its pointer, which would lead to unexpected behavior. If the loop variable is not correctly managed, all goroutines might end up printing the same value, typically the last value of the loop variable. Here is an example demonstrating incorrect use and its correction:

Incorrect closure usage in a loop:

```
for i := 0; i < 5; i++ {
    go func() {
```

```
        fmt.Println(i)
    }()
}
```

In the above example, all goroutines print the same value because they capture the pointer to i, which is incremented after each iteration.

Corrected closure usage in a loop:

```
for i := 0; i < 5; i++ {
    go func(n int) {
        fmt.Println(n)
    }(i)
}
```

By passing i as an argument to the anonymous function, each goroutine prints its respective value of i correctly.

Anonymous functions and closures enhance the flexibility and expressiveness of Go. They allow temporary functions to be written in places where named functions would be cumbersome, enabling more compact and readable code. The ability of closures to capture and manipulate variables from their defining scope makes them a powerful tool for managing state, particularly in concurrent programming scenarios.

5.7 Recursion in Go

Recursion is a powerful programming technique in which a function calls itself to solve a problem. Recursive functions are particularly useful in algorithmic situations where the problem can be divided into smaller subproblems of the same nature. In Go, recursion is implemented by defining a function that makes a call to itself. However, it's essential to ensure that the recursive case progresses towards a base case to avoid infinite recursion and stack overflow errors.

A typical recursive function consists of two parts:

- **Base Case:** This condition terminates the recursive calls. When the function reaches this condition, it returns a value without performing any further recursive calls.
- **Recursive Case:** This part of the function reduces the problem into smaller subproblems and recursively calls the function to solve them.

To understand recursion in Go, let's examine a classic example: computing the factorial of a number. The factorial of a number n (denoted as $n!$) is the product of all positive integers less than or equal to n. Mathematically, it is defined as:

$$n! = \begin{cases} 1 & \text{if } n = 0 \\ n \times (n-1)! & \text{if } n > 0 \end{cases}$$

In Go, the recursive implementation of the factorial function can be defined as follows:

```
func factorial(n int) int {
    // Base case: if n is 0 or 1, return 1
    if n == 0 || n == 1 {
        return 1
    }
    // Recursive case: n * factorial(n-1)
    return n * factorial(n-1)
}

func main() {
    fmt.Println(factorial(5)) // Output: 120
}
```

Listing 5.6: Recursive Factorial Function in Go

In this code snippet, the factorial function calls itself with the parameter n-1, and the recursion continues until n reaches 0 or 1. When n is 0 or 1, the base case is met, and the function returns 1.

Another common example of recursion is computing the Fibonacci sequence. The Fibonacci sequence is a series of numbers in which each number (after the first two) is the sum of the two preceding ones. It is defined as:

$$F(n) = \begin{cases} 0 & \text{if } n = 0 \\ 1 & \text{if } n = 1 \\ F(n-1) + F(n-2) & \text{if } n > 1 \end{cases}$$

The Go implementation of the Fibonacci sequence using recursion is illustrated below:

```
func fibonacci(n int) int {
    // Base case: if n is 0, return 0; if n is 1, return 1
    if n == 0 {
        return 0
    } else if n == 1 {
```

```
        return 1
    }
    // Recursive case: fibonacci(n-1) + fibonacci(n-2)
    return fibonacci(n-1) + fibonacci(n-2)
}

func main() {
    fmt.Println(fibonacci(5)) // Output: 5
}
```

Listing 5.7: Recursive Fibonacci Function in Go

In the fibonacci function, the base cases handle when n is 0 or 1, directly returning 0 and 1, respectively. For values of n greater than 1, the function makes recursive calls to fibonacci(n-1) and fibonacci(n-2), and returns their sum.

While recursion provides a concise and elegant solution to certain problems, it is not always the most efficient approach. For example, the recursive Fibonacci function unnecessarily recalculates values multiple times, leading to exponential time complexity. An alternative, more efficient solution would use memoization or iterative techniques. Here's an example of the Fibonacci function with memoization:

```
var memo = map[int]int{}

func fibonacciMemo(n int) int {
    // Check if result is already computed
    if result, exists := memo[n]; exists {
        return result
    }
    // Base case
    if n == 0 {
        return 0
    } else if n == 1 {
        return 1
    }
    // Recursive case with memoization
    memo[n] = fibonacciMemo(n-1) + fibonacciMemo(n-2)
    return memo[n]
}

func main() {
    fmt.Println(fibonacciMemo(5)) // Output: 5
}
```

Listing 5.8: Fibonacci Function with Memoization in Go

In the fibonacciMemo function, a map is used to store previously computed results, avoiding redundant calculations and significantly improving performance.

When using recursion, it's also important to be aware of the limitations imposed by the call stack. Each recursive call consumes stack space, and deep recursion may lead to a stack overflow error. Therefore, always consider the depth of recursion and whether an iterative approach might be more appropriate for the problem at hand.

Recursion is a fundamental concept that, when used judiciously, can simplify the implementation of complex algorithms and problems. Understanding its mechanics and recognizing its limitations are crucial for writing efficient and effective Go programs.

5.8 Higher-Order Functions

Higher-order functions are functions that take other functions as arguments, return a function as a result, or both. In Go, higher-order functions enhance code flexibility and reusability. This concept aligns well with Go's focus on simplicity and efficiency.

A function in Go is a first-class citizen, meaning it can be treated like any other variable. We can pass a function to another function, return it from a function, or store it in a variable. Consider a simple example that demonstrates how to pass a function as an argument:

```
package main

import "fmt"

// Define a function type
type Operation func(int, int) int

// Functions that conform to the Operation type
func add(a int, b int) int {
    return a + b
}

func multiply(a int, b int) int {
    return a * b
}

// A higher-order function that takes another function as an argument
func compute(op Operation, a int, b int) int {
    return op(a, b)
}

func main() {
```

```
    x, y := 5, 10

    // Using the higher-order function with different operations
    fmt.Printf("Add: %d\n", compute(add, x, y))
    fmt.Printf("Multiply: %d\n", compute(multiply, x, y))
}
```

Listing 5.9: Defining and Using Higher-Order Functions

In this example, we define an Operation type, which is a function that takes two int parameters and returns an int. We then create two functions, add and multiply, that match this type signature. The compute function is a higher-order function that accepts an Operation and two integers. Depending on the function passed to compute, it performs addition or multiplication.

Higher-order functions can also return other functions. This is useful for creating function generators or for implementing patterns such as currying. Here is an example that demonstrates a higher-order function producing another function:

```
package main

import "fmt"

// A higher-order function that returns a function
func incrementer(step int) func(int) int {
    return func(x int) int {
        return x + step
    }
}

func main() {
    incByOne := incrementer(1)
    incByTwo := incrementer(2)

    // Using the returned functions
    fmt.Printf("Increment by 1: %d\n", incByOne(5))
    fmt.Printf("Increment by 2: %d\n", incByTwo(5))
}
```

Listing 5.10: Returning Functions from Higher-Order Functions

Here, incrementer is a higher-order function that takes an integer step and returns a new function. This returned function itself takes an integer x and increments it by step. In the main function, we create two incrementing functions, incByOne and incByTwo, and use them to increment the number 5 by 1 and 2, respectively.

The ability to pass and return functions adds a layer of abstraction, enabling developers to create more modular and reusable code. This is particularly powerful in scenarios involving common patterns like filtering and mapping, which are commonplace in many programming paradigms.

Consider the following example, which demonstrates a higher-order function for filtering slices of integers:

```
package main

import "fmt"

// A function type for predicates
type Predicate func(int) bool

// A higher-order function for filtering slices
func filter(data []int, pred Predicate) []int {
    var result []int
    for _, v := range data {
        if pred(v) {
            result = append(result, v)
        }
    }
    return result
}

// Predicates
func isEven(n int) bool {
    return n%2 == 0
}

func isPositive(n int) bool {
    return n > 0
}

func main() {
    data := []int{1, 2, -3, 4, -5, 6}

    evenNumbers := filter(data, isEven)
    positiveNumbers := filter(data, isPositive)

    fmt.Printf("Even numbers: %v\n", evenNumbers)
    fmt.Printf("Positive numbers: %v\n", positiveNumbers)
}
```

Listing 5.11: Filtering with Higher-Order Functions

In this code, we define a Predicate type, a function that takes an integer and returns a boolean. The filter function is a higher-order function that accepts a slice of integers data and a Predicate pred. It iterates over the slice and includes the elements for which the predicate returns true in the result.

We then define two predicates, isEven and isPositive, which we use to filter even and positive numbers, respectively. Here, higher-order functions allow for concise and clear implementations of common filtering operations.

Higher-order functions are powerful constructs that, when effectively utilized, can lead to more concise, maintainable, and scalable code. Understanding and mastering them leads to expressing complex operations succinctly, improving both code readability and reusability.

5.9 Defer Statement and Its Usage

The defer statement in Go is a powerful tool used for executing a function call at a later point in time, specifically when the surrounding function returns. This mechanism is often used to ensure that certain cleanup tasks are performed, such as closing files, releasing resources, or unlocking a mutex.

The syntax of the defer statement is straightforward. It consists of the defer keyword followed by a function call. This function call can be either a named function or an anonymous function. The deferred function will execute its stated operations after all other statements in the surrounding function have been completed but before the surrounding function itself returns.

```
package main

import (
    "fmt"
)

func main() {
    fmt.Println("Start")

    defer fmt.Println("Deferred execution")

    fmt.Println("End")
}
```

When the above code is run, the output is as follows:

```
Start
End
Deferred execution
```

The defer statement in this example demonstrates its fundamental behavior. Upon entering the main function, "Start" is printed. The defer fmt.Println("Deferred execution") statement registers the deferred function call, but does not execute it immediately. "End" is then printed, followed by the execution of the deferred function, printing "Deferred execution".

Common Use Cases for defer

Defer statements are particularly useful in the following scenarios:

- **Resource Management:** Ensuring that resources such as files or network connections are properly closed.
- **Mutex Locking:** Guaranteeing that a locked mutex is always unlocked.
- **Error Handling:** Streamlining and centralizing cleanup operations in the event of an error.

Resource Management

Consider a scenario in which a file is opened for reading, and we need to ensure that the file is closed when it is no longer needed. Without defer, this would typically involve placing the file.Close() call at every possible return point, making the function cumbersome and error-prone. Here is an example of using defer to manage file closing:

```
package main

import (
    "fmt"
    "os"
)

func readFile(filename string) error {
    file, err := os.Open(filename)
    if err != nil {
        return err
    }
    defer file.Close() // Ensures file is closed when function returns

    // Read file logic here
    // ...
    return nil
```

```
}

func main() {
    err := readFile("example.txt")
    if err != nil {
        fmt.Println("Error:", err)
    }
}
```

In the readFile function, the defer file.Close() statement ensures that the file is closed when the function readFile returns, regardless of whether the return occurs due to an error or after reading the file's contents.

Mutex Locking

The defer statement is also pivotal in synchronizing access to shared resources using mutexes. For example:

```
package main

import (
    "fmt"
    "sync"
)

var (
    mu sync.Mutex
    data = make(map[string]string)
)

func writeData(key, value string) {
    mu.Lock()
    defer mu.Unlock() // Ensures mutex is unlocked on function exit

    data[key] = value
    fmt.Println("Data written:", key, value)
}

func main() {
    writeData("name", "Go Programming")
}
```

In this example, the defer mu.Unlock() statement ensures that the mutex is unlocked after the function writeData returns, preventing potential deadlocks.

Multiple Defer Statements

Go supports multiple defer statements in a single function. These deferred function calls are stacked in the order they appear and executed in the reverse order (last-in, first-out) upon function completion.

```
package main

import (
    "fmt"
)

func multipleDefer() {
    defer fmt.Println("First defer")
    defer fmt.Println("Second defer")
    defer fmt.Println("Third defer")
}

func main() {
    multipleDefer()
}
```

The output illustrates the last-in, first-out behavior of defer statements:

```
Third defer
Second defer
First defer
```

Arguments Evaluation in Deferred Calls

One critical detail to note about the defer statement in Go is that the arguments to a deferred function call are evaluated immediately when the defer statement is executed, not when the function call itself executes. Consider the following example:

```
package main

import (
    "fmt"
)

func printValue(val int) {
    fmt.Println("Value:", val)
}

func main() {
    val := 10
    defer printValue(val)
```

```
    val = 20
    fmt.Println("Main Value:", val)
}
```

The output of the program is:

```
Main Value: 20
Value: 10
```

When defer printValue(val) is executed, val holds the value 10. This value is captured at the point of the defer statement and used when printValue is eventually called.

Using Anonymous Functions with Defer

Anonymous functions are often used with defer to capture the current state of variables more flexibly. Adjusting the previous example:

```
package main

import (
    "fmt"
)

func main() {
    val := 10
    defer func(v int) {
        fmt.Println("Value:", v)
    }(val)

    val = 20
    fmt.Println("Main Value:", val)
}
```

The output remains the same, but the use of an anonymous function passed the immediate evaluation constraint by explicitly capturing the current state of val.

This thorough exploration of the defer statement reveals its critical role in managing resource lifecycle, synchronizing access, handling errors, and ensuring that essential cleanup operations are not overlooked. The precise and deterministic nature of deferred calls makes them an indispensable part of robust Go programming.

5.10 Error Handling in Functions

Error handling is a critical aspect of programming, enabling developers to build robust, maintainable software that can gracefully handle and recover from unexpected conditions. In Go, error handling is implemented using the built-in error type. This section explores the mechanisms of error handling within functions, providing thorough insights on best practices, idiomatic approaches, and practical examples.

Returning Errors from Functions

In Go, it is common practice to return an error as the last return value from a function. The error type is an interface that has a single method, Error(), which returns a string message. Here is an example of a function that returns an error:

```
package main

import (
    "errors"
    "fmt"
)

// divide performs division and returns an error in case of division by zero.
func divide(a, b float64) (float64, error) {
    if b == 0 {
        return 0, errors.New("division by zero")
    }
    return a / b, nil
}

func main() {
    result, err := divide(4, 0)
    if err != nil {
        fmt.Println("Error:", err)
    } else {
        fmt.Println("Result:", result)
    }
}
```

The divide function performs division and returns an error if the divisor is zero. In the main function, the error is checked, and appropriate action is taken based on whether an error occurred.

Using the fmt.Errorf for Formatted Error Messages

Go provides the fmt.Errorf function to create formatted error messages. This function works similarly to fmt.Sprintf but returns an error. Here is an example:

```
package main

import (
```

```
    "fmt"
)

// divide performs division and returns an error in case of division by zero, using fmt.
    Errorf for formatted error messages.
func divide(a, b float64) (float64, error) {
    if b == 0 {
        return 0, fmt.Errorf("cannot divide %f by zero", a)
    }
    return a / b, nil
}

func main() {
    result, err := divide(4, 0)
    if err != nil {
        fmt.Println("Error:", err)
    } else {
        fmt.Println("Result:", result)
    }
}
```

Custom Error Types

For more complex scenarios, custom error types can be created by implementing the error interface. This approach allows for more granular control over error information and handling.

```
package main

import (
    "fmt"
)

// DivideError represents a custom error type for division errors.
type DivideError struct {
    Dividend float64
    Divisor float64
    Message string
}

func (e *DivideError) Error() string {
    return fmt.Sprintf("cannot divide %f by %f: %s", e.Dividend, e.Divisor, e.Message)
}

// divide performs division and returns a custom error in case of division by zero.
func divide(a, b float64) (float64, error) {
    if b == 0 {
        return 0, &DivideError{
            Dividend: a,
            Divisor: b,
            Message: "division by zero is not allowed",
        }
    }
    return a / b, nil
}

func main() {
    result, err := divide(4, 0)
    if err != nil {
        fmt.Println("Error:", err)
```

```
    } else {
        fmt.Println("Result:", result)
    }
}
```

In this example, DivideError is a custom error type that includes additional context about the error. This information can be invaluable for debugging and logging purposes.

Panic and Recover

Go also provides the panic and recover mechanisms for handling severe errors that are not expected to occur under normal operation. A panic stops the normal execution of a program and begins panicking, unwinding the stack. The recover function can be used to regain control of the program from a panic. Here is an example:

```
package main

import (
    "fmt"
)

// divide performs division and panics in case of division by zero.
func divide(a, b float64) float64 {
    if b == 0 {
        panic("division by zero")
    }
    return a / b
}

// safeDivide calls divide and recovers from any panic that occurs.
func safeDivide(a, b float64) (result float64, err error) {
    defer func() {
        if r := recover(); r != nil {
            err = fmt.Errorf("panic occurred: %v", r)
        }
    }()
    return divide(a, b), nil
}

func main() {
    result, err := safeDivide(4, 0)
    if err != nil {
        fmt.Println("Error:", err)
    } else {
        fmt.Println("Result:", result)
    }
}
```

In this example, safeDivide uses defer and recover to catch a panic caused by a division by zero and convert it into an error that can be handled gracefully.

Best Practices

- Always return errors as the last return value from functions. - Use descriptive and informative error messages. - Prefer using existing error mechanisms such as errors.New and fmt.Errorf for simple errors. - Create custom error types for more complex error scenarios to include additional context. - Use panic and recover sparingly, only for unexpected situations where the program cannot continue normal execution.

Adhering to these best practices ensures that error handling in Go functions is consistent, maintainable, and effective, allowing programs to handle and recover from erroneous states gracefully.

Chapter 6

Working with Arrays, Slices, and Maps

This chapter covers the use of composite data types in Go, focusing on arrays, slices, and maps. It explains how to define, create, and manipulate arrays and slices, including multi-dimensional slices and their operations. The chapter also introduces maps, demonstrating how to create, use, and iterate over them. Key concepts such as slice capacity, reslicing, and common use cases are discussed to provide a comprehensive understanding of these essential data structures.

6.1 Introduction to Composite Data Types

Composite data types in Go provide a structured way to organize and manage collections of data. These data types allow developers to group related data together, making it easier to handle and manipulate complex data structures. The primary composite data types in Go are arrays, slices, and maps. Understanding these concepts forms the backbone of efficient and effective programming in Go, enabling the creation of more complex and powerful applications.

Arrays in Go are fixed-length sequences of elements of the same type. The length of an array is part of its type, meaning that the size of an array cannot be altered after it is declared. Arrays are useful when you need to store a collection of elements where the number of elements is known and fixed at compile-time.

Slices are more flexible and powerful than arrays. Unlike arrays, the length of a slice is not part of its type, allowing slices to be resized dynamically. Slices are built on top of arrays and provide a more convenient and versatile way to work with sequences of elements. They support operations like append, which can dynamically grow the underlying array as needed.

Maps are hash tables that store key-value pairs, allowing for fast retrieval, insertion, and deletion of data based on keys. They provide an efficient way to associate values with unique keys, which can be of any comparable type. Maps are particularly useful for tasks where efficient data retrieval is required, such as in databases and caches.

```
package main

import "fmt"

func main() {
    // Defining an array
    var arr [5]int
    arr[0] = 10
    arr[1] = 20
    arr[2] = 30
    arr[3] = 40
    arr[4] = 50

    fmt.Println("Array:", arr)

    // Creating and using a slice
    slc := []int{10, 20, 30, 40, 50}
    slc = append(slc, 60)

    fmt.Println("Slice:", slc)

    // Creating and using a map
    m := make(map[string]int)
    m["one"] = 1
    m["two"] = 2

    fmt.Println("Map:", m)
}
```

Listing 6.1: Example of defining and using arrays, slices, and maps

```
Output:
Array: [10 20 30 40 50]
Slice: [10 20 30 40 50 60]
Map: map[one:1 two:2]
```

Arrays, slices, and maps in Go are strongly typed, which means that the type of their elements is explicitly defined and enforced by the compiler. This reduces the likelihood of runtime errors due to type mismatches and enhances code readability and maintainability.

To define an array in Go, you specify the number of elements and the type of each element. This can be done using the syntax var arrayName [length]elementType. Arrays are indexed starting from zero, and each element can be accessed using its index.

Unlike arrays, slices do not require the length to be specified at the time of their creation. Instead, you can create a slice with a known set of elements directly using a slice literal, or by using the make function. The make function allows you to create a slice with a specified length and capacity, where the capacity is the number of elements the slice can grow to before it needs to allocate more memory.

Maps are created using the make function or by specifying a map literal. The type of the keys and values in the map must be defined. You can add elements to the map by assigning values to specific keys and retrieve elements by referencing the corresponding key. If you try to access a key that does not exist in the map, Go will return the zero value of the map's value type.

The introduction of composite data types in Go allows for more dynamic and efficient data structures, providing significant functionality for various programming needs.

6.2 Arrays: Definition and Usage

Arrays in Go are a fundamental composite data type that provides a way to store sequentially indexed data elements of the same type. An array has a fixed size determined at the time of its creation. This section explicates both the syntax and semantics of array definition and its utilization in Go.

An array is declared by specifying its length and the type of its elements. The general syntax for array declaration is:

```
var arrayName [length]elementType
```

For example, to declare an array of 10 integers:

```
var integers [10]int
```

Arrays in Go can also be initialized at the time of declaration by providing values in a comma-separated list enclosed in braces:

```
var numbers = [5]int{1, 2, 3, 4, 5}
```

If the initialization values are known, the length of the array can be inferred by the compiler:

```
var autoNumbers = [...]int{10, 20, 30, 40, 50}
```

Here, the length of the array autoNumbers is determined by the number of elements provided.

Accessing and modifying elements within an array is straightforward using an index, with indexing starting at 0:

```
var a [3]int // Declare an array of 3 integers
a[0] = 42 // Assign 42 to the first element
a[1] = 27 // Assign 27 to the second element
fmt.Println(a[0]) // Outputs: 42
fmt.Println(a[1]) // Outputs: 27
```

Attempting to access an index outside of the array bounds will result in a run-time panic. Carefully monitor array bounds to ensure the program's stability.

It is important to recognize that arrays in Go are value types. When an array is assigned to another array, a copy of the original array is created:

```
a := [3]int{1, 2, 3}
b := a
b[0] = 9
fmt.Println(a) // Outputs: [1 2 3]
fmt.Println(b) // Outputs: [9 2 3]
```

In this example, b becomes a copy of a. Changes to b do not affect a, showcasing the independent nature of the copied array.

Arrays can be iterated using the for loop. The range keyword provides a convenient way to iterate over arrays, returning both the index and the value of each element:

```
for index, value := range numbers {
    fmt.Printf("Index: %d, Value: %d\n", index, value)
}
```

The output of the above iteration:

```
Index: 0, Value: 1
Index: 1, Value: 2
Index: 2, Value: 3
```

```
Index: 3, Value: 4
Index: 4, Value: 5
```

Arrays can also be multidimensional. For example, to declare a two-dimensional array, use the following syntax:

```
var matrix [3][4]int
```

This creates a 2D array with 3 rows and 4 columns. Elements can be accessed using compound indices:

```
matrix[0][1] = 7 // Assign 7 to the element at row 0, column 1
```

Similarly, initializing a multi-dimensional array can be done in-line:

```
var matrix2 = [2][3]int{
    {1, 2, 3},
    {4, 5, 6},
}
```

Arrays in Go offer the foundational building block for managing sequences of data. Their fixed size and value type semantics ensure predictable behavior, but for dynamic-sized collections, slices are often preferred. The following sections will dive deeper into slices, providing a flexible alternative for working with collections of data.

Arrays set the baseline, slices extend the utility. This understanding sets the stage for deeper explorations into collections in Go.

6.3 Array Operations

Arrays in Go are fixed-length sequences of elements, all of the same type. Once an array is defined, its size and type cannot be altered. Understanding how to efficiently operate on arrays is crucial for effective programming in Go as it provides a foundation for working with more complex data structures.

The following operations are fundamental when working with arrays.

Initialization and Assignment

To initialize an array in Go, you can either specify the length and individual elements or use the ... operator to let Go determine the length from the initial values. Here's an example:

```
var days = [7]string{"Sunday", "Monday", "Tuesday", "Wednesday", "Thursday", "
    Friday", "Saturday"}
```

This line of code initializes an array named days with a length of 7, containing the names of the days of the week. Alternatively, Go can infer the array length:

```
days := [...]string{"Sunday", "Monday", "Tuesday", "Wednesday", "Thursday", "Friday
    ", "Saturday"}
```

Individual elements can be accessed or altered using their index, starting from 0:

```
days[0] = "Sun"
fmt.Println(days[0]) // Output: Sun
```

Iteration

To process each element of an array, the for loop or the range keyword can be utilized. The for loop is a common approach:

```
for i := 0; i < len(days); i++ {
    fmt.Println(days[i])
}
```

Alternatively, the range keyword iterates over each element, providing both the index and the value:

```
for index, value := range days {
    fmt.Printf("Index: %d, Value: %s\n", index, value)
}
```

The output will look like this:

```
Index: 0, Value: Sunday
Index: 1, Value: Monday
Index: 2, Value: Tuesday
Index: 3, Value: Wednesday
Index: 4, Value: Thursday
Index: 5, Value: Friday
Index: 6, Value: Saturday
```

Copying

Copying an array is straightforward; you can simply assign one array to another of the same type and length:

```
var weekDays [7]string
```

```
weekDays = days
```

This creates a new array weekDays which is an exact copy of days. Changing elements in weekDays will not affect days.

Array Equality

Arrays in Go can be compared using the equality operator (==). Two arrays are considered equal if and only if they have the same length and corresponding elements are equal:

```
a := [3]int{1, 2, 3}
b := [3]int{1, 2, 3}
c := [3]int{3, 2, 1}

fmt.Println(a == b) // Output: true
fmt.Println(a == c) // Output: false
```

Multidimensional Arrays

Arrays can have more than one dimension, and these are often referred to as multidimensional arrays. They are declared by specifying additional pairs of square brackets:

```
var matrix [3][3]int
```

This code declares a 3x3 matrix of integers. Multidimensional arrays can be initialized with nested array literals:

```
matrix := [3][3]int{
    {1, 2, 3},
    {4, 5, 6},
    {7, 8, 9},
}
```

Individual elements can be accessed and modified using two indices:

```
matrix[1][2] = 10
fmt.Println(matrix[1][2]) // Output: 10
```

Bound Checking

Go includes automatic boundary checking for arrays. Accessing an index outside the range of the array will cause a runtime panic:

```
fmt.Println(days[7]) // This will trigger a runtime panic since the index is out of range.
```

Because of this built-in safety feature, developers can avoid many common errors associated with array usage in other programming languages.

These fundamental array operations are essential for manipulating data efficiently and form the basis for more complex data structures and algorithms. Proficiency in these operations is vital for mastering Go programming.

6.4 Introduction to Slices

A slice is a flexible and powerful data structure in Go, offering a more convenient and versatile alternative to arrays. Unlike arrays, slices are dynamically sized, enabling efficient manipulation of sequences of data without the need for frequent resizing operations. Slices in Go are essentially references to a segment of an array, providing a view into the underlying array data. This section delves into the conceptual framework and practical applications of slices, emphasizing their critical role in Go programming.

Slices are defined using the []T notation, where T represents the slice's element type. A slice is characterized by its length, which specifies the number of elements it contains, and its capacity, which defines the number of elements the slice can hold before it needs to be resized. Below is an example of slice declaration and initialization:

```
var numbers []int // Declaring a slice of integers
numbers = []int{1, 2, 3, 4, 5} // Initializing the slice with values
```

Here, the slice numbers is declared without explicitly specifying its length, embodying the dynamic nature of slices. The slice numbers is later assigned an array of integers directly.

Slices can be derived from arrays or other slices using slicing syntax. The slicing operation returns a new slice referencing the segment specified by the half-open range [low:high], where low is the starting index (inclusive) and high is the ending index (exclusive). Consider the following example:

```
arr := [5]int{1, 2, 3, 4, 5} // Array declaration
s := arr[1:4] // Slice creation from array
```

In this case, s references the elements [2, 3, 4] from the array arr. Notably, modifying s will reflect changes in the underlying array arr, demonstrating the reference semantics of slices:

```
s[0] = 10
fmt.Println(arr) // Output: [1 10 3 4 5]
```

Slices are integral to the Go language due to their flexibility and efficiency. The zero value of a slice is nil, and it has a length and capacity of zero. Slices can be dynamically expanded using the built-in append function, which adds new elements to the end of a slice and returns a new slice if the underlying array no longer has sufficient capacity:

```
numbers = append(numbers, 6, 7)
fmt.Println(numbers) // Output: [1 2 3 4 5 6 7]
```

When append is called, it may allocate a new underlying array, thus returning a new slice potentially referencing a different array. This ensures that slices can grow as elements are appended without manual reallocation.

An important aspect of slices is their interaction with the make function. The make function can be used to create slices with a specified length and capacity, providing explicit control over these properties:

```
sl := make([]int, 3, 5) // Slice with length 3 and capacity 5
fmt.Println(sl) // Output: [0 0 0]
```

In the example above, the slice sl is pre-allocated with a length of 3 and a capacity of 5. The initial values are zeroed according to the type of the slice (integers in this case).

Manipulating slices involves operations like copying, appending, and slicing. The copy function is used to copy elements from one slice to another, preserving their values but not their capacities:

```
source := []int{1, 2, 3}
destination := make([]int, len(source))
copy(destination, source)
fmt.Println(destination) // Output: [1 2 3]
```

The above example demonstrates copying elements from source to destination, ensuring the two slices contain the same values without sharing the same underlying array.

As a more advanced feature, slices can be effectively used in conjunction with variadic functions, which accept a variable number of arguments. By using the ellipsis syntax (...), slices can be passed as arguments to such functions seamlessly:

```
func sum(nums ...int) int {
    total := 0
    for _, num := range nums {
        total += num
    }
    return total
}

result := sum(1, 2, 3, 4, 5)
fmt.Println(result) // Output: 15
```

By employing slices, Go enables developers to handle collections of data with ease and efficiency. The dynamic and flexible nature of slices affords a robust mechanism for managing dynamic arrays, iterating over data, and interfacing with functions. These properties make slices a fundamental construct in the Go programming language.

6.5 Creating and Using Slices

Slices in Go provide a dynamic and flexible way to work with sequences of elements. Unlike arrays, slices are of variable length and provide more powerful and convenient operations. Slices are built on top of arrays, providing a more intuitive and efficient interface for various operations.

To create a slice, we can use the built-in make function or directly slice an existing array. Here are several ways to create and use slices in Go.

Creating a Slice with make

The make function is the most common method to create a slice in Go. It is used as follows:

```
// Syntax: make([]Type, length, capacity)
slice := make([]int, 5, 10)
```

In this example, a slice of integers is created with an initial length of 5 and a capacity of 10. Length refers to the number of elements the slice currently contains, while capacity refers to the number of elements the underlying array can hold.

You can also create a slice with only the length, in which case the capacity will be equal to the length:

```
slice := make([]int, 5)
```

Creating a Slice from an Array

Another way to create a slice is by slicing an array:

```
// Creating an array
arr := [5]int{1, 2, 3, 4, 5}

// Creating a slice from the array
slice := arr[1:4]
```

In this example, slice contains the elements arr[1], arr[2], and arr[3], corresponding to the values 2, 3, 4 respectively. The range specified by arr[1:4] follows the pattern of including the start index and excluding the end index.

Appending to a Slice

The append function is used to add elements to a slice. The function dynamically increases the slice's capacity if needed:

```
slice := []int{1, 2, 3}
slice = append(slice, 4, 5, 6)
```

The append function here adds elements 4, 5, 6 to the existing slice. Note that since slices do not support adding elements directly, we must reassign the returned result to the slice variable.

Copying Slices

Go provides the copy function to copy elements from one slice to another. Note that this function copies the minimum number of elements from the source slice to the destination slice based on their lengths:

```
src := []int{1, 2, 3}
dest := make([]int, 2)
copy(dest, src)
```

In this case, only the first two elements of src (1, 2) are copied to dest. The length of dest determines the number of elements copied.

Iterating Over Slices

Slices can be iterated over using the for loop, with the range keyword being particularly useful for this purpose:

```
slice := []int{1, 2, 3, 4, 5}
for index, value := range slice {
    fmt.Printf("Index: %d, Value: %d\n", index, value)
}
```

Outputs:

```
Index: 0, Value: 1
```

```
Index: 1, Value: 2
Index: 2, Value: 3
Index: 3, Value: 4
Index: 4, Value: 5
```

The range keyword provides both the index and value of each element in the slice.

Understanding Nil Slices

A slice declared without initialization is called a nil slice. Nil slices have a length and capacity of zero and are different from empty slices:

```
var nilSlice []int
fmt.Printf("Nil slice: len=%d cap=%d nil=%v\n", len(nilSlice), cap(nilSlice), nilSlice
    == nil)
```

Outputs:

```
Nil slice: len=0 cap=0 nil=true
```

While both nil and empty slices can act similarly, they are not the same internally.

Passing Slices to Functions

Slices are passed to functions by reference, allowing the functions to modify the original slice elements. Here is an example of passing a slice to a function:

```
func modifySlice(s []int) {
    s[0] = 10
}

slice := []int{1, 2, 3}
modifySlice(slice)
fmt.Println(slice)
```

Outputs:

```
[10 2 3]
```

In this example, the function modifySlice changes the first element of the slice to 10, and this change is reflected in slice after the function call.

Slices form a crucial aspect of Go programming, providing a powerful and flexible way to handle collections of data. Understanding their creation and usage is fundamental to proficient Go programming, offering enhanced capabilities over arrays.

6.6 Slice Operations

Slices provide a flexible and powerful way to work with sequences of data in Go. They are more versatile than arrays due to their dynamic nature. This section delves into various operations that can be performed on slices, illustrating each with examples. Understanding these operations is crucial for effective Go programming.

Appending to a Slice
One of the fundamental operations on a slice is appending elements. The built-in append function allows you to add elements to the end of a slice. The basic syntax is:

```
slice = append(slice, element1, element2, ...)
```

Here is an example demonstrating how to append elements to a slice:

```
package main

import "fmt"

func main() {
    var numbers []int
    numbers = append(numbers, 1, 2, 3)
    fmt.Println(numbers)

    moreNumbers := []int{4, 5, 6}
    numbers = append(numbers, moreNumbers...)
    fmt.Println(numbers)
}
```

The output will be:

```
[1 2 3]
[1 2 3 4 5 6]
```

When appending another slice, the ellipsis (...) is necessary to indicate that all elements of the slice should be appended.

Copying a Slice
Another common operation is copying elements from one slice to another. The copy function is used for this purpose. It copies elements from one slice to another and returns the number of elements copied. The syntax is as follows:

```
copiedElements := copy(destinationSlice, sourceSlice)
```

An example of copying slices is given below:

```
package main

import "fmt"

func main() {
    source := []int{1, 2, 3, 4}
    destination := make([]int, len(source))
    copiedElements := copy(destination, source)
    fmt.Println(destination)
    fmt.Println("Number of elements copied:", copiedElements)
}
```

The output will be:

```
[1 2 3 4]
Number of elements copied: 4
```

Only the minimum number of elements from either the source or destination slice will be copied if their lengths differ.

Slicing a Slice

Slicing a slice means creating a new slice that points to a specified range of elements from an existing slice. The syntax for slicing is slice[low:high]. Both low and high are indices, where low is inclusive, and high is exclusive:

```
slice := []int{0, 1, 2, 3, 4, 5}
newSlice := slice[2:5]
```

The above example shows how to create a new slice from an existing slice:

```
package main

import "fmt"

func main() {
    original := []int{0, 1, 2, 3, 4, 5}
    sliced := original[2:5]
    fmt.Println(sliced)
}
```

The output will be:

```
[2 3 4]
```

Indices can be omitted to use defaults: from the start for low and to the end for high. For example, slice[:3] slices from the start to index 2, and slice[3:] slices from index 3 to the end.

Deleting an Element

Since Go does not provide a built-in function to delete an element from a slice, you must manage this by utilizing 'append' and slicing operations. To remove an element at index i, you can do the following:

```
slice = append(slice[:i], slice[i+1:]...)
```

Here is an example:

```
package main

import "fmt"

func main() {
    numbers := []int{1, 2, 3, 4, 5}
    indexToRemove := 2
    numbers = append(numbers[:indexToRemove], numbers[indexToRemove
        +1:]...)
    fmt.Println(numbers)
}
```

The output will be:

```
[1 2 4 5]
```

Iterating Over a Slice

Iterating over a slice typically involves using the for loop along with the range keyword. The range keyword returns both the index and the value of each element, allowing for iteration over both indices and elements:

```
for index, value := range slice {
    // Use index and value
}
```

A practical example is shown below:

```
package main

import "fmt"

func main() {
    fruits := []string{"apple", "banana", "cherry"}
    for index, fruit := range fruits {
        fmt.Printf("Index: %d, Fruit: %s\n", index, fruit)
    }
}
```

The output will be:

```
Index: 0, Fruit: apple
```

```
Index: 1, Fruit: banana
Index: 2, Fruit: cherry
```

Slices provide a robust way to handle data sequences. Enhanced by operations like appending, copying, and slicing, they enable efficient and dynamic manipulation of data in Go programs.

6.7 Multi-Dimensional Slices

Multi-dimensional slices in Go provide a mechanism to represent and manipulate matrices or multi-dimensional arrays. They extend the concept of slices, allowing the programmer to work with grids or tables efficiently. This section explores the creation, initialization, and manipulation of multi-dimensional slices.

Definition and Creation: In Go, a slice of a slice can be used to create a multi-dimensional slice. Conceptually, a two-dimensional slice can be visualized as a slice where each element is another slice.

To define a two-dimensional slice:

```
var multiDimSlice [][]int
```

In this example, multiDimSlice is a slice where each element is a slice of int. Initially, multiDimSlice is nil.

Initialization: There are multiple ways to initialize a multi-dimensional slice. One can use nested loops or append function to create and populate the slice.

Example of initializing a 3x3 multi-dimensional slice using nested loops:

```
rows, cols := 3, 3
multiDimSlice := make([][]int, rows)
for i := range multiDimSlice {
    multiDimSlice[i] = make([]int, cols)
}
```

In this code snippet, make function creates a slice of size 3, and each element of this slice is initialized to another slice of size 3.

Populating Multi-Dimensional Slices:

After creation, multi-dimensional slices can be populated just like normal slices. It is essential to use nested loops for indexing into the appropriate dimensions.

```
for i := 0; i < rows; i++ {
```

```
    for j := 0; j < cols; j++ {
        multiDimSlice[i][j] = i * cols + j
    }
}
```

This code will populate the multiDimSlice with values from 0 to 8 in a row-wise manner.

Accessing Elements:

Accessing elements in multi-dimensional slices is similar to single-dimensional slices, but with an extra level of indexing.

```
value := multiDimSlice[1][2]
fmt.Println(value)
```

This will print the value located at row 1, column 2.

Iterating Over Multi-Dimensional Slices:

Iterating over the elements of a multi-dimensional slice involves nested loops:

```
for i := 0; i < rows; i++ {
    for j := 0; j < cols; j++ {
        fmt.Print(multiDimSlice[i][j], " ")
    }
    fmt.Println()
}
```

This loop structure will print all elements of the multi-dimensional slice in a matrix format.

Reslicing Multi-Dimensional Slices:

Just as with single-dimensional slices, multi-dimensional slices can be resliced. However, care must be taken as only the outer slice will be resliced, not the inner slices or their elements.

```
newSlice := multiDimSlice[1:]
```

This operation creates a new slice starting from the second row of multiDimSlice. The inner slices remain unchanged.

Using Multi-Dimensional Slices for Matrices:

Multi-dimensional slices are particularly useful for operations requiring matrix-like structures. For example, one can represent a game board or perform mathematical matrix operations.

Example of a simple matrix multiplication algorithm using multi-dimensional slices:

Algorithm 2: Matrix Multiplication

Data: Two matrices A and B, both of size $n \times m$

Result: Matrix C which is the result of $A \times B$

Initialize an $n \times m$ matrix C with zeros;

for $i = 0$ **to** $n - 1$ **do**

  for $j = 0$ **to** $m - 1$ **do**

    for $k = 0$ **to** $m - 1$ **do**

      $C[i][j] = C[i][j] + A[i][k] * B[k][j]$;

Here, A and B are input matrices, and C is the resultant matrix. The triple nested loops perform the dot product of rows and columns to compute the elements of C.

Appending to Multi-Dimensional Slices:

Appending to a multi-dimensional slice works similarly to single-dimensional slices. However, when appending new rows, every new row should itself be a slice.

```
newRow := []int{9, 10, 11}
multiDimSlice = append(multiDimSlice, newRow)
```

This appends newRow as a new row to multiDimSlice.

Example: Representing a Tic-Tac-Toe Board:

A practical application of multi-dimensional slices is representing a Tic-Tac-Toe board. Here is an example of initializing and displaying a Tic-Tac-Toe board:

```
board := [][]string{
    {"X", "O", "X"},
    {"O", "X", "O"},
    {"X", "O", "X"},
}

for i := 0; i < len(board); i++ {
    fmt.Println(board[i])
}
```

This code creates a 3x3 Tic-Tac-Toe board and prints each row.

Understanding and utilizing multi-dimensional slices can greatly enhance a programmer's ability to manage complex data structures in Go.

6.8 Understanding Capacity and Reslicing

In this section, we delve into the concepts of capacity and reslicing in Go, key aspects for effectively managing and optimizing slices. Comprehending these concepts is instrumental in writing resource-efficient Go programs.

The capacity of a slice, represented by cap(slice), indicates the maximum size up to which the slice can grow when elements are appended. It is crucial to note that the capacity of a slice is not necessarily equal to its length, although the length is always less than or equal to the capacity.

To understand the distinction between length and capacity, consider the example below:

```
package main

import "fmt"

func main() {
    s := make([]int, 5, 10)

    fmt.Println("Length of the slice:", len(s)) // Outputs: 5
    fmt.Println("Capacity of the slice:", cap(s)) // Outputs: 10
}
```

This program initializes a slice s with a length of 5 and a capacity of 10. While the length represents the number of elements the slice currently holds, the capacity defines how many elements it can hold before needing to allocate more memory. This distinction is vital for optimized memory allocation and performance tuning.

Reslicing refers to creating a new slice that references the array underlying an existing slice. This operation is highly efficient as it does not involve copying data but simply reallocates the pointers within the underlying array. Reslicing modifies the view over the existing array elements while preserving the initial data.

Consider the following example demonstrating reslicing:

```
package main

import "fmt"

func main() {
    original := []int{0, 1, 2, 3, 4, 5, 6, 7, 8, 9}
    fmt.Println("Original slice:", original) // Outputs: [0 1 2 3 4 5 6 7 8 9]
```

```
    resliced := original[2:5]
    fmt.Println("Resliced slice:", resliced) // Outputs: [2 3 4]

    // Modifying the resliced array
    resliced[0] = 99
    fmt.Println("Modified resliced slice:", resliced) // Outputs: [99 3 4]
    fmt.Println("Original slice after modification:", original) // Outputs: [0 1 99 3
        4 5 6 7 8 9]
}
```

In this case, original is resliced into resliced which contains elements from indices 2 to 4 (inclusive) from the original slice. Note that any mutation in resliced influences the underlying array, which is also referenced by original.

Moreover, capacity plays an essential role in reslicing. The capacity of the resliced slice is determined by the length of the segment from the start index of the reslice operation up to the capacity of the original slice. To illustrate:

```
package main

import "fmt"

func main() {
    original := make([]int, 5, 10)
    resliced := original[2:4]

    fmt.Println("Length of the resliced slice:", len(resliced)) // Outputs: 2
    fmt.Println("Capacity of the resliced slice:", cap(resliced)) // Outputs: 8
}
```

In this example, resliced starts at index 2 of original and ends at index 3 (4 - 1). The capacity of resliced is 8, which spans from index 2 to the capacity of original, which is 10.

The underlying implementation of slices ensures optimal memory reuse and performance efficiency by leveraging operations like reslicing. However, developers must remain cautious when dealing with resliced slices, as improper handling may lead to unintended data modifications and bugs.

Furthermore, the append function appends elements to a slice, creating a new slice if its capacity is exceeded. When the capacity is insufficient, Go allocates a larger array from which a new slice with increased capacity is derived. This guarantees optimized memory usage while providing flexibility in slice management.

To exemplify append's influence:

```
package main

import "fmt"

func main() {
    original := make([]int, 3, 5)
    fmt.Println("Original slice:", original, " Length:", len(original), " Capacity:",
        cap(original)) // Outputs: [0 0 0] Length: 3 Capacity: 5

    extended := append(original, 1, 2)
    fmt.Println("Extended slice:", extended, " Length:", len(extended), " Capacity:
        ", cap(extended)) // Outputs: [0 0 0 1 2] Length: 5 Capacity: 5

    extended = append(extended, 3)
    fmt.Println("Extended further:", extended, " Length:", len(extended), "
        Capacity:", cap(extended)) // Outputs: [0 0 0 1 2 3] Length: 6 Capacity:
        10
}
```

This code snippet demonstrates that append initially works within the existing capacity. When additional elements exceed the capacity, Go allocates a more extensive array and copies the existing elements. The slice length and capacity hence dynamically adjust.

Mastering the capacity and reslicing mechanisms is imperative for efficient Go programming. These operations optimize memory use, ensuring high performance and responsiveness in applications. Appropriate handling minimizes redundancies and enhances the manageability of slice data.

6.9 Introduction to Maps

Maps in Go are fundamental data structures that associate keys with values, enabling efficient key-based lookups. Similar to hash tables in other programming languages, maps are highly optimized for read and write operations. Defining and using maps correctly is crucial for effective Go programming, and this section elucidates their intricacies to offer a robust understanding.

A map type in Go is defined as map[K]V, where K represents the type of keys and V denotes the type of values. Both K and V can be any type, as long as the key type K is comparable. This comparability constraint ensures that keys in a map can be uniquely identified during lookup operations.

To declare a map in Go, use the following syntax:

```
var myMap map[string]int
```

Here, myMap is a variable that can hold a map with string keys and integer values. Initially, myMap is set to nil, indicating that it is not initialized. Attempting to use this map without initialization will lead to a runtime panic. Therefore, it is essential to initialize the map, which is typically done using the make function:

```
myMap = make(map[string]int)
```

Alternatively, you can declare and initialize a map in one step. For instance:

```
myMap := make(map[string]int)
```

Adding and retrieving values in a map relies on straightforward syntax. To insert a key-value pair, the following syntax is used:

```
myMap["one"] = 1
\myMap["two"] = 2
myMap["three"] = 3
```

In this example, the keys "one", "two", and "three" are associated with the integer values 1, 2, and 3, respectively. To retrieve a value associated with a key, use:

```
value := myMap["two"]
fmt.Println(value)
```

The output will be:

```
2
```

If a referenced key does not exist in the map, the result will be the zero value for the map's value type. For instance, querying a non-existent key in myMap will yield 0, as 0 is the zero value for the int type.

A critical feature of maps is the ability to check for the presence of a key and retrieve its associated value safely. This is achieved using the two-value assignment form:

```
value, exists := myMap["four"]
if exists {
    fmt.Println("Key found:", value)
} else {
    fmt.Println("Key not found")
```

```
}
```

In this code, the exists boolean variable is true if the key “four” is present in myMap, and false otherwise. This mechanism prevents inadvertent usage of zero-value data types when keys are absent.

Maps can also be initialized with predefined key-value pairs using composite literals:

```
predefinedMap := map[string]int{
    "apple": 5,
    "banana": 8,
    "cherry": 12,
}
```

In this declaration, predefinedMap instantly holds the specified key-value pairs.

Deleting key-value pairs from a map utilizes the built-in delete function:

```
delete(myMap, "one")
```

The delete function removes the key “one” and its associated value from myMap. If the key doesn’t exist, delete performs no operation, ensuring safe execution.

Maps support range loops for iteration over key-value pairs:

```
for key, value := range myMap {
    fmt.Println(key, value)
}
```

This loop iterates through all key-value pairs in myMap, printing each key followed by its corresponding value. The iteration order is not specified and can vary from one execution to another. This behavior is intrinsic to the underlying implementation of maps in Go.

Maps, a crucial part of Go’s toolbox for associative data storage, provide flexibility and efficiency needed in various applications. They facilitate tasks such as counting occurrences of elements, data grouping, and rapid lookups, enhancing the robustness of Go programs.

6.10 Creating and Using Maps

Maps in Go are powerful built-in data structures that associate keys with values. Unlike arrays and slices, which use integer indices, maps allow the use of any comparable type as keys, enabling more complex data modeling. This section explores the creation and manipulation of maps in Go. We will examine their initialization, insertion, retrieval, and deletion of elements, along with iteration over map elements.

```
package main

import "fmt"

func main() {
    // Declare a map with string keys and int values
    var myMap map[string]int
    fmt.Println(myMap) // Output: map[]
}
```

Listing 6.2: Basic map declaration and initialization

The above code declares a variable myMap of type map[string]int but does not initialize it. Accessing such an uninitialized map without assigning it will result in a runtime panic. To properly initialize a map, use the make function or a map literal.

```
package main

import "fmt"

func main() {
    // Initialize a map using the make function
    myMap := make(map[string]int)
    fmt.Println(myMap) // Output: map[]

    // Insert elements into the map
    myMap["apple"] = 5
    myMap["banana"] = 3
    fmt.Println(myMap) // Output: map[apple:5 banana:3]

    // Retrieve elements from the map
    fmt.Println(myMap["apple"]) // Output: 5
}
```

Listing 6.3: Initializing a map using make

Using make, we initialize myMap, avoiding the risk of runtime panics. Elements are inserted into the map by specifying a key and assigning it a value. Accessing elements is straightforward using the key within brackets.

A map can also be initialized using a literal, providing an immediate declaration and assignment of key-value pairs.

```
package main
```

```
import "fmt"

func main() {
    // Initialize a map using a literal
    myMap := map[string]int{
        "apple": 5,
        "banana": 3,
    }
    fmt.Println(myMap) // Output: map[apple:5 banana:3]
}
```

Listing 6.4: Initializing a map using literals

Maps in Go accommodate a variety of operations, including checking for the existence of a key, deleting a key-value pair, and iterating over the map.

```
package main

import "fmt"

func main() {
    myMap := map[string]int{
        "apple": 5,
        "banana": 3,
    }

    // Check for the existence of a key
    if value, ok := myMap["apple"]; ok {
        fmt.Println("The key 'apple' exists with value", value)
    } else {
        fmt.Println("The key 'apple' does not exist")
    }

    // Delete a key-value pair
    delete(myMap, "banana")
    fmt.Println(myMap) // Output: map[apple:5]
}
```

Listing 6.5: Map operations: existence check and deletion

The existence of a key can be checked using two-value assignment. The second return value is a boolean indicating whether the key exists. To remove a key-value pair from the map, use the delete function.

Iterating over maps employs the range keyword, allowing you to access both keys and values.

```
package main

import "fmt"
```

```
func main() {
    myMap := map[string]int{
        "apple": 5,
        "banana": 3,
    }

    // Iterate over the map using range
    for key, value := range myMap {
        fmt.Printf("Key: %s, Value: %d\n", key, value)
    }
}
```

Listing 6.6: Iterating over a map

In this example, the range construct iterates over the map, providing access to key-value pairs. The order of iteration over map entries is not specified in Go, meaning it can vary with each iteration.

Maps in Go support dynamic behavior. Adding a key sets its value, and retrieving a non-existent key returns the zero value of the map's value type. For example, a map of integers returns 0 for non-existent keys.

```
package main

import "fmt"

func main() {
    myMap := map[string]int{
        "apple": 5,
    }

    // Accessing a non-existent key
    fmt.Println(myMap["banana"]) // Output: 0 (zero value for int)
}
```

Listing 6.7: Retrieving a non-existent key

This behavior simplifies map usage but necessitates careful key existence checks where specific value differentiations are vital. For sophisticated applications, implementing error states or sentinel values might be required to handle such scenarios accurately.

Maps offer a robust mechanism for handling associations in Go, enhancing the language's capacity to deal with varying data relationship problems efficiently.

6.11 Map Operations and Iteration

Go provides comprehensive support for maps, which are hash tables implemented as key-value pairs. This section delves into common map operations including insertion, deletion, and retrieval of elements, as well as iteration over maps. Understanding these operations is essential for using maps effectively in Go programming.

To begin with, consider a simple map of string keys to int values:

```
scores := make(map[string]int)
```

Inserting elements into the map is straightforward. Use the key within brackets, assign it a value:

```
scores["Alice"] = 85
scores["Bob"] = 95
```

Retrieving a value from the map involves using the corresponding key:

```
var scoreAlice int = scores["Alice"]
```

To handle situations where the key might not be present in the map, use the two-value assignment form:

```
value, present := scores["Charlie"]
if present {
  fmt.Println("Charlie's score:", value)
} else {
  fmt.Println("Charlie is not present in the scores map.")
}
```

In this example, value holds the value of scores["Charlie"], and present is a boolean flag indicating the presence of the key. If present is false, this means that "Charlie" is not a key in scores.

Deletion of a key-value pair from a map is performed using the delete function:

```
delete(scores, "Alice")
```

After this operation, attempting to find the value for the key "Alice" would reveal it no longer exists in the map.

Iterating over a map in Go utilizes the range keyword. This allows you to access each key-value pair in the map efficiently:

```
for key, value := range scores {
```

```
  fmt.Printf("%s: %d\n", key, value)
}
```

Here, key and value represent the key-value pairs from the scores map. The order of iteration is not specified and should not be relied upon.

If only keys or only values are required during iteration, you can modify the range statement accordingly:

To iterate only over keys:

```
for key := range scores {
  fmt.Println("Key:", key)
}
```

To iterate only over values:

```
for _, value := range scores {
  fmt.Println("Value:", value)
}
```

The underscore (_) is used to ignore the key when only values are needed.

It is also possible to check for the existence of a map element during iteration. For instance, to calculate the average score of all students present in the scores map, you could use:

```
var total, count int
for _, value := range scores {
  total += value
  count++
}
average := float64(total) / float64(count)
fmt.Printf("Average score: %.2f\n", average)
```

This snippet first initializes total and count to zero, then iterates over each value in the scores map, incrementing both the total score and the count of scores. The average score is calculated using a type conversion to float64 to avoid integer division.

String keys and integer values are typically demonstrated, but maps in Go can contain keys and values of any types, including user-defined types. This versatility makes maps a powerful tool for a wide range of applications.

The chapter emphasized that, like slices, maps are also reference types in Go. When a map is assigned to another map, they both refer to the same underlying data. For example:

```
scores1 := map[string]int{"Alice": 87, "Bob": 92}
scores2 := scores1
scores2["Alice"] = 90
fmt.Println(scores1) // Output: map[Alice:90 Bob:92]
```

Modifying scores2["Alice"] also modifies scores1["Alice"] since scores1 and scores2 refer to the same map data. Understanding this behavior is crucial for avoiding unintended side effects.

These map operations and iterations form the basis of many algorithms and data handling processes in Go, enhancing both efficiency and code clarity.

6.12 Common Use Cases for Arrays, Slices, and Maps

Arrays, slices, and maps are foundational structures in Go that enable efficient data storage and manipulation. The versatility of these composite data types makes them essential in a wide variety of applications. This section delves into several common use cases, illustrating how arrays, slices, and maps can be utilized effectively.

1. Handling Fixed-Size Data with Arrays

Arrays are ideal for scenarios where the size of the data set is fixed and known at compile time. They offer predictable memory usage and constant-time access to elements. A common application is storing configuration constants or pre-calculated lookup tables. For instance, consider the example of storing a list of days in a week:

```
package main

import "fmt"

func main() {
    var daysOfWeek [7]string = [7]string{"Sunday", "Monday", "Tuesday", "
        Wednesday", "Thursday", "Friday", "Saturday"}
    fmt.Println(daysOfWeek)
}
```

```
[Sunday Monday Tuesday Wednesday Thursday Friday Saturday]
```

2. Dynamic Data Handling with Slices

Slices provide flexibility and ease of use when dealing with dynamic or unknown sizes of data sets. They allow for growth and the efficient addition, deletion, and manipulation of elements. A common use case involves reading and processing user inputs or data from an external source. Below is an example of storing and processing a dynamic list of integers:

```
package main

import (
    "fmt"
)

func main() {
    numbers := []int{1, 2, 3, 4, 5}
    numbers = append(numbers, 6, 7, 8)
    fmt.Println(numbers)
}
```

```
[1 2 3 4 5 6 7 8]
```

3. Multi-Dimensional Data with 2D Slices

Multi-dimensional slices are powerful for representing grid-based data. An example use case is simulating a matrix or a game board such as Sudoku. Here is an illustration of initializing and printing a 2D slice:

```
package main

import "fmt"

func main() {
    matrix := make([][]int, 3)
    for i := range matrix {
        matrix[i] = make([]int, 3)
    }
    matrix[1][1] = 5
    for _, row := range matrix {
        fmt.Println(row)
    }
}
```

```
[0 0 0]
[0 5 0]
[0 0 0]
```

4. Associative Arrays with Maps

Maps are optimal for scenarios requiring key-value pairs with efficient lookups. A pervasive application is in implementing dictionaries, caches, or managing user properties. For instance, here is how to create a simple phone book application:

```
package main

import "fmt"

func main() {
    phoneBook := map[string]string{
        "Alice": "123-4567",
        "Bob": "987-6543",
    }
    phoneBook["Charlie"] = "555-4321"
    fmt.Println(phoneBook)
}
```

```
map[Alice:123-4567 Bob:987-6543 Charlie:555-4321]
```

5. Efficient Key Lookups and Iteration

Maps are highly advantageous for quick lookups, especially in datasets with unique identifiers. They are also useful in counting occurrences or grouping data. Consider this example of counting the frequency of elements in a slice:

```
package main

import "fmt"

func main() {
    data := []string{"apple", "banana", "apple", "orange", "banana", "apple"}
    frequency := make(map[string]int)
    for _, item := range data {
        frequency[item]++
    }
    fmt.Println(frequency)
}
```

```
map[apple:3 banana:2 orange:1]
```

6. Combining Arrays, Slices, and Maps

In complex applications, it is common to combine arrays, slices, and maps to leverage their unique features. For instance, creating an inventory management system might involve arrays for fixed product categories, slices for dynamic inventory items, and maps for tracking stock count by product ID.

Consider the following hypothetical example that ties these concepts together:

```
package main

import "fmt"

func main() {
    categories := [3]string{"Electronics", "Clothing", "Groceries"}
    inventory := make([]map[string]int, len(categories))
    for i := range inventory {
        inventory[i] = make(map[string]int)
    }

    inventory[0]["Laptop"] = 15
    inventory[1]["Jeans"] = 30
    inventory[2]["Apples"] = 50

    fmt.Println("Inventory by categories:")
    for i, category := range categories {
        fmt.Printf("%s: %v\n", category, inventory[i])
    }
}
```

```
Inventory by categories:
Electronics: map[Laptop:15]
Clothing: map[Jeans:30]
Groceries: map[Apples:50]
```

The examples exhibit the flexibility and capability of arrays, slices, and maps in solving various programming tasks. Understanding these use cases enables developers to choose the appropriate data structure based on the requirements of the problem, ensuring both performance and simplicity.

Chapter 7

Structs and Methods

This chapter introduces structs in Go, detailing how to define, create, and manipulate them, including struct fields and tags. It covers embedded structs and composition, providing insights into organizing and structuring data. The chapter also explores methods, explaining how to define and use them, and differentiating between pointer receivers and value receivers. Additionally, it introduces interfaces and their role in achieving polymorphism, concluding with best practices for using structs and methods effectively.

7.1 Introduction to Structs

In Go, a `struct` is a composite data type that allows you to group together variables under a single name for easier handling and organization of data. Structs are analogous to records or classes in other programming languages and are essential in crafting complex data structures that encapsulate properties and behaviors. This section introduces the concept of structs, their syntax, and scenarios where their usage is beneficial.

A `struct` in Go is defined by the `struct` keyword followed by a set of fields. Each field has a name and a type, and they can be of any data type, including other structs. Here is a simple example of a struct definition in Go:

```
type Person struct {
```

```
    FirstName string
    LastName string
    Age int
}
```

In this example, Person is a struct type with three fields: FirstName, LastName, and Age. Each field is declared with a specified type; FirstName and LastName are string types, while Age is an int type.

Structs provide various benefits and functionalities:

- **Organization**: Grouping related data under a single name enhances code readability and maintainability.
- **Encapsulation**: Structs help in encapsulating data and related operations.
- **Pass by Value**: In Go, structs are passed by value, making copies of the data. This means changes to a struct in one part of the code will not inadvertently affect other parts.

Creating an instance of a struct is straightforward. You can initialize a struct by assigning values to its fields using a composite literal as shown below:

```
person1 := Person{
    FirstName: "John",
    LastName: "Doe",
    Age: 30,
}
```

By utilizing composite literals, you explicitly specify the names of the fields being initialized, enhancing clarity and reducing the risk of mistakes.

It is also possible to initialize a struct without explicitly stating field names. However, it should be done cautiously, particularly with larger structs or during maintenance, as it relies on the order of fields which may change over time:

```
person2 := Person{"Jane", "Smith", 25}
```

To access or modify a field within a struct, the dot (.) operator is used. Here is an example illustrating both access and modification of struct fields:

```
fmt.Println(person1.FirstName) // Accessing the FirstName field; Output: "John"
```

```
person1.Age = 31 // Modifying the Age field to 31
```

Structs may also be used to define methods, which enables associating functions specifically with types. This is particularly useful for encapsulating related operations and behaviors within the same entity:

```
func (p Person) FullName() string {
    return p.FirstName + " " + p.LastName
}
```

Here, FullName is a method associated with the Person struct, which returns the full name of the person by combining the FirstName and LastName fields.

By utilizing structs in this manner, the design and structure of data are both improved significantly, promoting a clear, logical, and maintainable codebase. As we continue through this chapter, we will delve deeper into defining, creating, and manipulating structs, including advanced topics such as embedded structs, methods, and interfaces to fully leverage Go's robust type system.

7.2 Defining and Creating Structs

Structs in Go are composite data types that group variables or data fields into a single entity. They provide a way to encapsulate and organize related data, making the code more modular and maintainable. A struct declaration defines a named type with a collection of fields, each with its own name and type.

```
type Person struct {
    Name string
    Age int
    Address string
}
```

Listing 7.1: Struct Definition

In the above example, we define a struct named Person with three fields: Name, Age, and Address.

To create an instance of a struct, we use the struct literal notation, which initializes a struct by listing the field values in the order in which they are defined:

```
p1 := Person{"Alice", 30, "123 Cherry Lane"}
```

Listing 7.2: Creating a Struct Instance

Here, p1 is an instance of the Person struct with the Name as "Alice", Age as 30, and Address as "123 Cherry Lane".

Alternatively, to improve code readability and flexibility, we can use named fields when creating a struct instance. This method allows the fields to be listed in any order and makes it clear which value corresponds to which field:

```
p2 := Person{
    Name: "Bob",
    Age: 25,
    Address: "456 Maple Street",
}
```

Listing 7.3: Creating a Struct Instance with Named Fields

When using named field initialization, fields that are omitted will take the zero value of their type.

```
p3 := Person{
    Name: "Charlie",
    Age: 40,
}
```

Listing 7.4: Creating a Struct with Partial Initialization

In this case, p3.Address will be the zero value for a string, which is an empty string.

It is also possible to create pointers to structs. Pointers can be used to avoid copying the entire struct when passing it around and allow for modification of the struct from different parts of the code.

```
p4 := &Person{
    Name: "Diana",
    Age: 28,
    Address: "789 Elm Avenue",
}
```

Listing 7.5: Creating a Pointer to a Struct

A pointer to the Person struct is created using the & operator. The p4 variable now holds the address of the struct instance.

To access and modify struct fields through a pointer, Go provides automatic dereferencing. This means you can use the dot notation directly on the pointer to access or change the field values.

```
fmt.Println(p4.Name) // Output: Diana
p4.Age = 29
fmt.Println(p4.Age) // Output: 29
```

Listing 7.6: Accessing Fields via a Struct Pointer

Beyond creating instances using literals, struct instances can also be created using the new function. The new function allocates memory for a given type and returns a pointer to it.

```
p5 := new(Person)
p5.Name = "Ethan"
p5.Age = 22
p5.Address = "321 Pine Road"
```

Listing 7.7: Creating a Struct Instance with new Function

The p5 variable holds a pointer to a newly created Person struct.

When working with structs, attention should be given to the size and layout of the data. Go stores fields in the order they are defined, which can have implications for memory alignment and performance. For example, grouping fields of similar type can reduce padding and make the struct more memory-efficient.

Consider a struct with reordered fields to minimize padding:

```
type OptimizedPerson struct {
    Age int
    Name string
    Address string
}
```

Listing 7.8: Struct Optimization Example

By placing the int field first, followed by the string fields, the memory layout might become more optimal, depending on the underlying architecture's alignment requirements.

To summarize, defining and creating structs in Go involves declaring the struct type with a collection of fields and then creating instances using literals, named fields, pointers, or the new function. Proper attention to the order and types of fields ensures efficient memory utilization.

7.3 Struct Fields and Tags

A struct in Go is a composite data type that groups together variables under a single name for better modularity and data organization. A struct comprises fields, each with its own name and type. Understanding struct fields and tags is essential since they form the core of how structs manage and manipulate data.

Defining Struct Fields

To define a struct, use the type keyword followed by the struct name and the struct keyword. Inside the struct, each field is declared with a name and a data type.

```
type Person struct {
    FirstName string
    LastName string
    Age int
}
```

In this example, the Person struct has three fields: FirstName, LastName, and Age. The FirstName and LastName fields are of type string, and the Age field is of type int.

Accessing and Modifying Struct Fields

Once a struct is defined, you can create an instance (also called a struct value) and access or modify its fields using the dot notation. Whether in composite literals, individual field assignments, or function calls, the dot notation remains straightforward and intuitive.

Creating an instance of a struct:

```
var p1 Person
p1.FirstName = "John"
p1.LastName = "Doe"
p1.Age = 30

fmt.Println(p1.FirstName) // Output: John
```

You can also use a composite literal to initialize a struct with field values:

```
p2 := Person{
    FirstName: "Jane",
    LastName: "Smith",
    Age: 25,
}
fmt.Println(p2)
```

The output will display the struct with its fields initialized accordingly.

```
{Jane Smith 25}
```

Struct Tags

Struct tags in Go provide metadata about struct fields. They are commonly used in the context of JSON encoding and decoding, database interactions, and more. Struct tags are defined by placing a string literal after the field type. The string literal contains key-value pairs conventionally separated by spaces.

For example, where JSON encoding is concerned, the encoding/json package uses struct tags to map struct fields to JSON keys:

```
type Person struct {
    FirstName string 'json:"first_name"'
    LastName string 'json:"last_name"'
    Age int 'json:"age"'
}
```

In this updated Person struct, the JSON field names are specified in the tags. When encoding a Person struct to JSON, the specified names in the tags are used:

```
import (
    "encoding/json"
    "fmt"
)

func main() {
    p := Person{
        FirstName: "John",
        LastName: "Doe",
        Age: 30,
    }

    jsonData, _ := json.Marshal(p)
    fmt.Println(string(jsonData))
}
```

Output after marshaling the struct to JSON format:

```
{"first_name":"John","last_name":"Doe","age":30}
```

Struct tags can carry multiple key-value pairs. For instance, combining JSON encoding instructions and database field annotations:

```
type Person struct {
```

```
    FirstName string `json:"first_name" db:"first_name"`
    LastName string `json:"last_name" db:"last_name"`
    Age int `json:"age" db:"age"`
}
```

In this example, when working with a database package like sqlx, the db tags guide the package in mapping struct fields to database columns.

Struct tags in Go have a defined syntax and best practices as outlined in the Go documentation: - The struct tag string must be a space-separated list of key:"value" pairs. - Values must be surrounded by double quotes. - Keys within a struct tag cannot contain spaces.

Given these rules, struct tags become essential in tasks involving serialization and deserialization, offering concise ways to align struct fields with external data schemas.

By mastering struct fields and tags, you enhance your capability in defining and manipulating data structures that seamlessly integrate with various libraries and frameworks. Proper utilization of struct tags also ensures clear, maintainable, and effective code when interfacing with external data formats and storage systems.

7.4 Accessing and Modifying Struct Fields

Struct fields in Go can be accessed and modified directly using dot notation. This process is paramount for leveraging the encapsulated data within structs, allowing for efficient and organized data management. When you create an instance of a struct, you can manipulate its fields smoothly, given that you understand the scope and permissions associated with each field.

Consider the following example of a simple struct definition and instantiation:

```
type Person struct {
    Name string
    Age int
}

func main() {
    var person Person
    person.Name = "Alice"
    person.Age = 30
}
```

In this example, the struct Person has two fields: Name and Age. These fields are of type string and int, respectively. When an instance of the struct is created and assigned to the variable person, the fields can be accessed and modified using the dot notation.

person.Name = "Alice" assigns the value "Alice" to the Name field of the person instance. Similarly, person.Age = 30 assigns the value 30 to the Age field.

Accessing the fields works similarly:

```
fmt.Println(person.Name) // Output: Alice
fmt.Println(person.Age) // Output: 30
```

Field access can be subject to struct type's export rules. Only exported fields (those starting with an uppercase letter) are accessible from other packages, whereas non-exported fields (lowercase letter) can only be accessed within the same package.

For example:

```
type Employee struct {
    id int // non-exported field
    Name string // exported field
}

func main() {
    var emp Employee
    // emp.id = 1001 // this would cause a compilation error if accessed outside the
         package
    emp.Name = "Bob"
}
```

In this script, Employee has a non-exported field id and an exported field Name. Direct access to id outside of its defining package would result in a compilation error.

Fields nested within embedded structs can also be accessed using dot notation:

```
type Address struct {
    City, State string
}

type User struct {
    Name string
    Address // embedded struct
}

func main() {
    var user User
    user.Name = "Carol"
    user.Address.City = "New York"
    user.Address.State = "NY"

    // Alternative shortcut for accessing embedded fields
```

```
    user.City = "Los Angeles"
    user.State = "CA"
}
```

In the above example, Address is an embedded struct within User, and its fields, City and State, can be accessed directly via user.Address.City or user.Address.State. Moreover, because Address is embedded, you can access these fields as if they were part of the User struct itself, using user.City and user.State.

Modifying fields through pointers ensures changes persist across function calls:

```
func UpdateAge(person *Person, newAge int) {
    person.Age = newAge
}

func main() {
    person := Person{Name: "Dave", Age: 25}
    UpdateAge(&person, 26)
    fmt.Println(person.Age) // Output: 26
}
```

Here, the function UpdateAge takes a pointer to a Person struct and an integer newAge. The function modifies the Age field of the person instance via the pointer. This ensures the age update in the main function persists after UpdateAge is called.

Field access through slices of structs follows a similar pattern:

```
type Product struct {
    Name string
    Price float64
}

func main() {
    products := []Product{
        {"Laptop", 999.99},
        {"Smartphone", 599.99},
    }

    fmt.Println(products[0].Name) // Output: "Laptop"
    fmt.Println(products[1].Price) // Output: 599.99

    products[0].Price = 899.99 // Modify the price of the first product
    fmt.Println(products[0].Price) // Output: 899.99
}
```

Here, a slice of Product structs is created and initialized. Accessing and modifying their fields can be achieved using indexing and dot notation, as shown.

Ensuring thread-safe access to struct fields might necessitate the use of synchronization primitives such as mutexes from the sync package.

Billions of reads should be protected by locks to avoid race conditions:

```
import (
    "fmt"
    "sync"
)

type Counter struct {
    mu sync.Mutex
    count int
}

func (c *Counter) Increment() {
    c.mu.Lock()
    c.count++
    c.mu.Unlock()
}

func (c *Counter) Value() int {
    c.mu.Lock()
    defer c.mu.Unlock()
    return c.count
}

func main() {
    counter := Counter{}
    var wg sync.WaitGroup

    for i := 0; i < 1000; i++ {
        wg.Add(1)
        go func() {
            defer wg.Done()
            counter.Increment()
        }()
    }

    wg.Wait()
    fmt.Println(counter.Value()) // Output: 1000
}
```

In this example, the Counter struct encapsulates a count integer field and a sync.Mutex. The Increment method locks the mutex, increments the count, and then unlocks it; Value method also ensures safe concurrent access with a lock. This pattern is essential for maintaining accuracy in concurrent executions.

7.5 Embedded Structs and Composition

In Go, embedding structs within other structs provides a flexible way to achieve code reuse and composition. This mechanism allows a struct to include fields from another struct, implicitly granting it a subset of the original struct's capabilities. Embedding promotes modularity and cleaner design by facilitating the creation of composite structs without resorting to inheritance, which is not present in Go.

Consider the following example to understand the concept of embedded structs:

```
package main

import "fmt"

type Address struct {
    Street string
    City string
    State string
}

type Person struct {
    Name string
    Age int
    Address // Embedded struct
}

func main() {
    p := Person{
        Name: "John Doe",
        Age: 30,
        Address: Address{
            Street: "123 Elm Street",
            City: "Gotham",
            State: "NY",
        },
    }

    fmt.Println(p.Name)
    fmt.Println(p.Street) // Accessing embedded struct field directly
}
```

In this example, the Person struct embeds the Address struct. This implies that a Person instance has an Address instance as a part of itself, and the fields of Address can be accessed directly through a Person instance. Note the direct access to Street within main, even though it belongs to the embedded Address struct.

Embedding is particularly beneficial when creating composite types that inherit behaviors and properties without explicit inheritance. When an embedded struct is specified without a field name, access to its fields is simplified, as shown in the example above.

Let's examine another scenario where embedding brings more functionality:

```
package main
```

```
import "fmt"

type Animal struct {
    Name string
    Species string
}

func (a Animal) Speak() {
    fmt.Printf("%s is a %s\n", a.Name, a.Species)
}

type Dog struct {
    Animal // Embedded struct
    Breed string
}

func (d Dog) Bark() {
    fmt.Printf("%s the %s barks!\n", d.Name, d.Breed)
}

func main() {
    d := Dog{
        Animal: Animal{
            Name: "Buddy",
            Species: "Canine",
        },
        Breed: "Golden Retriever",
    }

    d.Speak() // Method from embedded struct
    d.Bark() // Method specific to Dog
}
```

In this case, the Dog struct embeds the Animal struct. The Dog struct can directly utilize the Speak method defined for Animal. This embedding approach allows simple composition of types while reusing the logic encapsulated in the Animal struct.

It is crucial to understand that in the context of embedding, methods with the same name in both the embedded struct and the embedding struct result in method shadowing. The method in the embedding struct overrides the method in the embedded struct. Consider the following example:

```
package main

import "fmt"

type Base struct{}
```

```
func (Base) Describe() {
    fmt.Println("This is the base struct.")
}

type Derived struct {
    Base // Embedded struct
}

func (Derived) Describe() {
    fmt.Println("This is the derived struct.")
}

func main() {
    d := Derived{}
    d.Describe() // Calls Derived's Describe method
    d.Base.Describe() // Calls Base's Describe method
}
```

Here, the Derived struct has its own Describe method, which shadows the Describe method of the Base struct. However, by explicitly referencing the embedded struct, it's still possible to call the shadowed method using d.Base.Describe().

When using embedded structs, constructor functions can ensure proper initialization of composite structs:

```
package main

import "fmt"

type Point struct {
    X, Y int
}

type Circle struct {
    Point // Embedded struct
    Radius int
}

func NewCircle(x, y, radius int) *Circle {
    return &Circle{
        Point: Point{X: x, Y: y},
        Radius: radius,
    }
}

func main() {
    c := NewCircle(5, 7, 10)
    fmt.Printf("Circle at (%d, %d) with radius %d\n", c.X, c.Y, c.Radius)
}
```

The NewCircle function initializes both the embedded Point struct and the Circle struct itself. This method ensures that all fields are consistently and correctly set upon creation.

Embedded structs and composition stand out as powerful features in Go for constructing complex types with clearly organized and reusable code components. These concepts extend the capabilities of your structs, enabling sophisticated data modeling while maintaining simplicity and readability.

7.6 Introduction to Methods

In Go, a method is essentially a function with a special receiver argument. This receiver is a type that is either a struct or a named type. Methods allow attaching functionality to types, enabling us to define behaviors associated with instances of these types. By designing thoughtful methods, we endow our types with expressive and reusable behaviors, facilitating encapsulation and code organization.

To define a method in Go, we use the following syntax:

```
func (receiver_type Receiver) methodName(parameters) returnType {
    // function body
}
```

Here, receiver_type specifies the type to which the method is associated, Receiver acts as the receiver variable within the method, methodName is the name of the method, and the parameters and returnType define the input parameters and return type of the method, respectively.

Consider the following example:

```
package main

import (
    "fmt"
)

type Rectangle struct {
    length, width float64
}

// Method to calculate the area of a Rectangle
func (r Rectangle) Area() float64 {
    return r.length * r.width
}
```

```
func main() {
    rect := Rectangle{length: 5, width: 3}
    fmt.Println("Area of rectangle:", rect.Area())
}
```

In this example, the Rectangle struct has an Area method defined on it. The receiver type is Rectangle, and the receiver variable is r. The Area method simply multiplies the length and width fields of the Rectangle struct to compute the area. When we create an instance of Rectangle in the main function and call rect.Area(), it executes the method defined.

Methods enhance the expressiveness of our types by permitting operations to be defined directly on the instances of those types. Additionally, when we import packages or utilize types from libraries, we can commonly call methods associated with those types.

To further illustrate, we can create methods on named types:

```
package main

import (
    "fmt"
)

type Celsius float64

func (c Celsius) Fahrenheit() float64 {
    return float64(c*9/5 + 32)
}

func main() {
    tempC := Celsius(25)
    fmt.Println("Temperature in Fahrenheit:", tempC.Fahrenheit())
}
```

In this example, Celsius is a named type based on float64, and we define a Fahrenheit method that converts the temperature from Celsius to Fahrenheit. The method leverages the Celsius receiver type for conversion operations.

Methods also allow us to manipulate complex data structures efficiently. By defining relevant methods, operations on those data structures become more intuitive and readable.

Methods can have pointer receivers or value receivers. A pointer receiver allows the method to modify the receiver's value, whereas a value receiver works with a copy of the receiver's value. A decision on whether to use a pointer or a value receiver depends on the desired functionality and efficiency considerations.

Consider a method with a pointer receiver:

```
package main

import (
    "fmt"
)

type Counter struct {
    value int
}

// Method with pointer receiver to increment the counter
func (c *Counter) Increment() {
    c.value++
}

func main() {
    counter := Counter{value: 0}
    counter.Increment()
    fmt.Println("Counter value:", counter.value)
}
```

In this example, the Counter struct has an Increment method with a pointer receiver *Counter. This allows the method to modify the value field of Counter directly, leading to the updated value when we call counter.Increment().

Understanding methods in Go is pivotal for building fluent and maintainable APIs. Methods encapsulate behaviors associated with types and enable developers to define highly cohesive and coherent interfaces. As you use and define methods, it is important to consider the receiver type—whether using a value or pointer receiver—based on the requirements and efficiency of your program.

7.7 Defining and Calling Methods

In Go, methods are functions with a special receiver argument. Defining methods on a type can enhance the utility of that type by associating said methods directly with it. To define a method, specify the receiver argument in the method declaration. The receiver appears between the func keyword and the method name.

Essentially, the receiver argument behaves like an implicit first parameter of the method, which denotes the instance of the type that the method operates on. Receivers can be either value receivers or pointer receivers, and choosing one over the other has significant implications on method behavior and efficiency.

To create a method in Go, consider a simple struct representing a rectangle:

```
type Rectangle struct {
    Width, Height float64
}
```

To define a method that calculates the area of the rectangle, use a receiver of type Rectangle:

```
func (r Rectangle) Area() float64 {
    return r.Width * r.Height
}
```

Now, the 'Area' method is associated with the Rectangle type and can be called on any instance of Rectangle. Here is how you create an instance of Rectangle and call the Area method:

```
rect := Rectangle{Width: 5, Height: 10}
area := rect.Area()
fmt.Println("Area:", area)
```

The output is:

```
Area: 50
```

Go supports methods with pointer receivers. A pointer receiver takes a pointer to the instance of the struct, which allows the method to modify the struct's fields directly. Here is an example method to scale a rectangle:

```
func (r *Rectangle) Scale(factor float64) {
    r.Width *= factor
    r.Height *= factor
}
```

When using a pointer receiver, the method can alter the receiver's values. To demonstrate, consider:

```
rect := Rectangle{Width: 5, Height: 10}
rect.Scale(2)
fmt.Println("Scaled Rectangle:", rect)
```

The output is:

```
Scaled Rectangle: {Width: 10 Height: 20}
```

Value receivers use a copy of the original value, and hence, modifications within the method do not affect the original value. Choosing between pointer and value receivers depends on the method's requirements. Pointer receivers are advisable when the method needs to mutate the receiver, or to avoid copying large struct values, enhancing performance.

The type of the receiver distinguishes between functions and methods. Compare the method definition with its equivalent function using an explicit receiver parameter:

```
func Area(r Rectangle) float64 {
    return r.Width * r.Height
}
```

This 'Area' function uses an explicit receiver parameter. However, it is called differently:

```
rect := Rectangle{Width: 5, Height: 10}
area := Area(rect)
fmt.Println("Area:", area)
```

Using methods enhances readability and encapsulates the behavior tightly with data structures. Methods provide clearer, more intuitive syntax for operations specific to a type and support the definition of custom types that behave like built-ins.

For example, you can define a string representation of the Rectangle struct:

```
func (r Rectangle) String() string {
    return fmt.Sprintf("Rectangle [Width: %.2f, Height: %.2f]", r.Width, r.Height)
}
```

The fmt package calls this String method when using the %v format verb. You can now directly print an instance of Rectangle:

```
rect := Rectangle{Width: 5, Height: 10}
fmt.Println(rect)
```

The output is:

```
Rectangle [Width: 5.00, Height: 10.00]
```

Adopting methods yields better-organized code that adheres to Go's design principles of simplicity and efficiency. Methods provide a mechanism for creating behavior-rich types essential for building scalable and maintainable applications.

7.8 Pointer Receivers vs. Value Receivers

In Go, methods can be associated with either pointer receivers or value receivers. Understanding the differences and appropriate usage of pointer receivers versus value receivers is crucial for writing efficient and correct Go programs. This section delves into the distinctions between these types of receivers, how they affect method behavior, and their implications on performance and design.

Definitions

A value receiver in a method operates on a copy of the original value. This means that any modification made to the receiver inside the method does not affect the original value. A pointer receiver, on the other hand, holds the memory address of the value. Consequently, any modification made to a pointer receiver impacts the original value since the method works with the actual memory address.

Syntax

The syntax for defining methods with value receivers and pointer receivers is slightly different. Here's how it is done:

```
type Vertex struct {
    X, Y float64
}

// Method with value receiver
func (v Vertex) Abs() float64 {
    return math.Sqrt(v.X*v.X + v.Y*v.Y)
}
```

Listing 7.9: Method with Value Receiver

```
type Vertex struct {
    X, Y float64
}

// Method with pointer receiver
func (v *Vertex) Scale(f float64) {
    v.X = v.X * f
    v.Y = v.Y * f
}
```

Listing 7.10: Method with Pointer Receiver

Behavioral Differences

To understand the behavioral differences, consider the following example:

```
package main

import (
    "fmt"
    "math"
)

type Vertex struct {
    X, Y float64
}

func (v Vertex) Abs() float64 {
    return math.Sqrt(v.X*v.X + v.Y*v.Y)
}

func (v *Vertex) Scale(f float64) {
    v.X = v.X * f
    v.Y = v.Y * f
}

func main() {
    v := Vertex{3, 4}
    fmt.Println(v.Abs()) // Output: 5
    v.Scale(2) // Modify the original v since Scale method uses a pointer receiver
    fmt.Println(v) // Output: {6, 8}
}
```

```
Output:
5
{6, 8}
```

In the above example, calling v.Abs() does not alter the state of v, since Abs() method has a value receiver. However, v.Scale(2) modifies the original v because Scale() method has a pointer receiver.

When to Use Value Receivers

Value receivers are typically used when the method does not need to modify the underlying data of the receiver. They are particularly useful for immutable types or when dealing with small structs because value receivers do not involve the overhead of pointers. For example, it's common to use value receivers for methods related to fmt.Stringer interface implementations or other read-only properties.

```
type Point struct {
    X, Y int
}

// Method with value receiver
func (p Point) String() string {
    return fmt.Sprintf("(%d, %d)", p.X, p.Y)
}
```

Listing 7.11: Read-Only Method with Value Receiver

When to Use Pointer Receivers

Pointer receivers should be used if the method needs to modify the receiver's value. They are also necessary to avoid copying large structs when calling the method, thus improving performance. This is particularly beneficial for methods that encapsulate expensive operations.

```
type Counter struct {
    Value int
}

// Method with pointer receiver
func (c *Counter) Increment() {
    c.Value++
}
```

Listing 7.12: Mutable Method with Pointer Receiver

Moreover, pointer receivers are essential when implementing methods for interfaces that require pointer receiver methods.

Considerations for Choosing Receivers

Choosing between pointer receivers and value receivers depends on:

- **Modification Requirement**: If the method needs to modify the receiver, use a pointer receiver.
- **Performance Concerns**: For large structs, use pointer receivers to avoid the cost of copying the value.
- **Consistency**: If some methods modify the state of the receiver, consider using pointer receivers for all methods of that type for consistency.
- **Interface Implementation**: Ensure the method signature

matches the interface requirement, which may necessitate using pointer receivers.

Examples of Applying Pointer and Value Receivers

To see these concepts in practice, consider the following struct and its methods:

```
type Rectangle struct {
    Width, Height float64
}

// Area calculates and returns the area of the rectangle (read-only operation)
func (r Rectangle) Area() float64 {
    return r.Width * r.Height
}

// Resize adjusts the dimensions of the rectangle (modifying operation)
func (r *Rectangle) Resize(factor float64) {
    r.Width *= factor
    r.Height *= factor
}
```

Usage of these methods would demonstrate their different impacts:

```
func main() {
    rect := Rectangle{10, 5}
    fmt.Println(rect.Area()) // Output: 50
    rect.Resize(2)
    fmt.Println(rect.Area()) // Output: 200 (after resizing)
}
```

```
Output:
50
200
```

Conclusively, selecting between pointer receivers and value receivers is crucial in determining the method's impact on the receiver's data and overall program efficiency. Through understanding and applying these concepts, Go programmers can write more predictable and performant code.

7.9 Method Sets

In Go, a method set is a collection of methods bound to a specific type. Each type can have a distinct method set, and these methods can be called using instances of the type or pointers to those instances. Understanding method sets is essential for effective use of Go's type system, especially when dealing with interfaces.

A type's method set determines the methods that can be called on an instance of that type. This concept is crucial when types are used with interfaces because a type implements an interface if its method set includes all the methods defined by the interface. Here, we will delve into how method sets work for different types and their implications.

To illustrate this, let us define a custom type:

```
type MyStruct struct {
    Field int
}
```

Next, we will define two methods for this type; one with a value receiver and the other with a pointer receiver.

```
func (ms MyStruct) ValueReceiver() {
    fmt.Println("Value receiver called. Field:", ms.Field)
}

func (ms *MyStruct) PointerReceiver() {
    fmt.Println("Pointer receiver called. Field:", ms.Field)
}
```

In the above code, ValueReceiver is a method with a value receiver, meaning it can be called on a value of type MyStruct. Conversely, PointerReceiver is a method with a pointer receiver and can only be called on a pointer to MyStruct.

Method sets differ for value types and pointer types based on the types of methods defined. For a value type T, the method set includes all methods with receivers of type T. For a pointer type *T, the method set includes all methods with receivers of type T and *T.

Let's explicitly explore the method sets for our example MyStruct and *MyStruct.

Example: Method Set for Value Type MyStruct

For the value type MyStruct, the method set includes:

- ValueReceiver()

Thus, you can call the method with a value of MyStruct:

```
ms := MyStruct{Field: 10}
```

```
ms.ValueReceiver() // This will work
```

However, calling PointerReceiver directly on a value of MyStruct will result in a compilation error:

```
ms.PointerReceiver() // This will not work, causes a compilation error
```

Example: Method Set for Pointer Type *MyStruct

For the pointer type *MyStruct, the method set includes:

- ValueReceiver()
- PointerReceiver()

Hence, you can call both methods when using a pointer to MyStruct:

```
pms := &MyStruct{Field: 20}
pms.ValueReceiver() // This will work
pms.PointerReceiver() // This will also work
```

Compilation and Execution Output

Here's the complete program to demonstrate method sets in Go:

```
package main

import "fmt"

type MyStruct struct {
    Field int
}

func (ms MyStruct) ValueReceiver() {
    fmt.Println("Value receiver called. Field:", ms.Field)
}

func (ms *MyStruct) PointerReceiver() {
    fmt.Println("Pointer receiver called. Field:", ms.Field)
}

func main() {
    ms := MyStruct{Field: 10}
    ms.ValueReceiver()
    // ms.PointerReceiver() // Uncommenting this line will cause compilation
        error

    pms := &MyStruct{Field: 20}
    pms.ValueReceiver()
    pms.PointerReceiver()
}
```

Executing this code will generate the following output:

```
Value receiver called. Field: 10
Value receiver called. Field: 20
Pointer receiver called. Field: 20
```

This behavior demonstrates that a method with a pointer receiver can be invoked on a pointer but not a value, while a method with a value receiver can be invoked on both a value and a pointer.

By examining and understanding method sets, we pave the way for the clear implementation of interfaces in Go. Mastery of this concept ensures that types are correctly designed and capable of fulfilling the requirements of the interfaces they need to adhere to.

7.10 Interface in Go

Interfaces in Go provide a mechanism to specify the behavior of objects through method sets. An interface, by definition, is a type that comprises a collection of method signatures. By implementing these methods, any type can satisfy the interface, enabling polymorphism. This section covers the foundational aspects of interfaces, their significance, and their practical application in Go programming.

Interfaces are declared using the type keyword followed by the interface name and the keyword interface. The general syntax is as follows:

```
type InterfaceName interface {
    MethodName1(param1 paramType1, ...) returnType1
    MethodName2(param1 paramType1, ...) returnType2
    // more method signatures
}
```

Consider an example interface Shape that defines methods for calculating area and perimeter:

```
type Shape interface {
    Area() float64
    Perimeter() float64
}
```

To implement this interface, a type must define all methods declared in the interface. For instance, here we implement the Shape interface with a Rectangle and a Circle struct.

```
type Rectangle struct {
```

```
    Width, Height float64
}

func (r Rectangle) Area() float64 {
    return r.Width * r.Height
}

func (r Rectangle) Perimeter() float64 {
    return 2 * (r.Width + r.Height)
}
```

```
type Circle struct {
    Radius float64
}

func (c Circle) Area() float64 {
    return math.Pi * c.Radius * c.Radius
}

func (c Circle) Perimeter() float64 {
    return 2 * math.Pi * c.Radius
}
```

In this example, both Rectangle and Circle have methods Area() and Perimeter() and thus satisfy the Shape interface. This allows instances of these types to be used interchangeably where the Shape interface is expected.

Interface Usage Example:

```
func printShapeDetails(s Shape) {
    fmt.Printf("Area: %f\n", s.Area())
    fmt.Printf("Perimeter: %f\n", s.Perimeter())
}

func main() {
    r := Rectangle{Width: 3, Height: 4}
    c := Circle{Radius: 5}

    shapes := []Shape{r, c}

    for _, shape := range shapes {
        printShapeDetails(shape)
    }
}
```

```
Area: 12.000000
Perimeter: 14.000000
Area: 78.539816
Perimeter: 31.415927
```

Interfaces are fundamental to achieving polymorphism in Go. By relying on method signatures rather than specific types, functions can accept and operate on any type that implements the interface. This flexibility allows for more general and reusable code.

Beyond single interface implementations, it is possible to compose interfaces, enabling complex behaviors to be described succinctly. For example, consider the following interfaces:

```
type Drawable interface {
    Draw()
}

type Resizable interface {
    Resize(factor float64)
}

type GraphicsObject interface {
    Drawable
    Resizable
}
```

Here, GraphicsObject is composed of both Drawable and Resizable interfaces, meaning any type that satisfies GraphicsObject must implement methods from both included interfaces.

It's also pertinent to understand that in Go, there's no explicit declaration to implement an interface. The type implicitly implements the interface by providing the necessary methods. This implicit satisfaction contrasts with languages that require explicit interface declarations.

Empty interfaces, interface{}, can hold values of any type, making them extremely versatile. However, their use should be carefully considered to maintain type safety and clarity.

Type assertions and type switches are powerful tools for working with interfaces and extracting the underlying concrete types.

Type Assertion Example:

```
var i interface{} = "hello"

s := i.(string)
fmt.Println(s)
```

```
hello
```

Type Switch Example:

```
func doSomething(i interface{}) {
    switch v := i.(type) {
    case int:
        fmt.Printf("Twice %d is %d\n", v, v*2)
    case string:
        fmt.Printf("%q is %d bytes long\n", v, len(v))
    default:
        fmt.Printf("I don't know about type %T!\n", v)
    }
}
```

```
Twice 21 is 42
"hello" is 5 bytes long
I don't know about type float64!
```

Interfaces in Go provide a robust system for defining and fulfilling contracts in code, enabling polymorphism, composability, and high levels of abstraction. The seamless integration of interfaces into Go's type system is a cornerstone feature that empowers developers to write flexible and maintainable programs.

7.11 Polymorphism with Interfaces

Polymorphism is a core concept in object-oriented programming that allows for entities to be processed in multiple forms. In Go, polymorphism is primarily achieved through the use of interfaces. By defining methods in interfaces and having types implement these methods, Go enables a high degree of flexibility and modularity in code design. Understanding polymorphism with interfaces is essential for writing idiomatic and maintainable Go code.

To begin, an interface in Go specifies a set of method signatures. A type fulfills this interface if it implements these methods. Unlike other programming languages, Go interfaces are satisfied implicitly, meaning there is no need for explicit declarations.

Consider the following example:

```
type Speaker interface {
    Speak() string
}
```

Here, the Speaker interface is defined with a single method, Speak, that returns a string. Any type that implements the Speak method with the exact signature fulfills the Speaker interface.

For instance, let us define two types, Person and Robot, both of which implement the Speak method:

```
type Person struct {
    Name string
}

func (p Person) Speak() string {
    return "Hello, my name is " + p.Name
}

type Robot struct {
    Model string
}

func (r Robot) Speak() string {
    return "Greetings, I am model " + r.Model
}
```

In this example, Person and Robot both implement the Speak method. Thus, both types fulfill the Speaker interface.

To demonstrate polymorphism, we can write a function that accepts a Speaker interface and utilizes the Speak method:

```
func Announce(s Speaker) {
    fmt.Println(s.Speak())
}
```

We can call this function using either a Person or a Robot type as an argument, showcasing polymorphic behavior:

```
p := Person{Name: "Alice"}
r := Robot{Model: "RX-78"}

Announce(p) // Output: Hello, my name is Alice
Announce(r) // Output: Greetings, I am model RX-78
```

```
Hello, my name is Alice
Greetings, I am model RX-78
```

This example clearly illustrates how polymorphism allows the Announce function to work with different types that implement the Speaker interface.

Another powerful feature of Go interfaces is that they can be composed of other interfaces. This allows for the creation of more complex types. Consider the following example where we have an Announcement interface that includes both the Speaker and Greeting interfaces:

```
type Greeting interface {
    Greet() string
}

type Announcement interface {
    Speaker
    Greeting
}
```

Any type that implements both Speak and Greet methods satisfies the Announcement interface. For example:

```
type Conference struct {
    EventName string
}

func (c Conference) Speak() string {
    return "Welcome to " + c.EventName
}

func (c Conference) Greet() string {
    return "We are pleased to have you here."
}

func MakeAnnouncement(a Announcement) {
    fmt.Println(a.Speak())
    fmt.Println(a.Greet())
}
```

Now, let's instantiate a Conference struct and use it with MakeAnnouncement function:

```
conf := Conference{EventName: "GoCon"}

MakeAnnouncement(conf)
```

```
Welcome to GoCon
We are pleased to have you here.
```

This example demonstrates the compositional capabilities of Go interfaces, allowing more complex behavior to be defined and reused.

Additionally, Go's type assertion and type switches enable further leveraging of polymorphism. Type assertions are used to extract the underlying concrete value from an interface type. Here's an example:

```
var s Speaker = Person{Name: "Bob"}

if p, ok := s.(Person); ok {
```

```
    fmt.Println("This is a person:", p.Name)
}
```

In this case, the code checks if the Speaker is of type Person and then accesses the person's name.

Type switches can handle multiple types within a single block:

```
func DescribeSpeaker(s Speaker) {
    switch v := s.(type) {
    case Person:
        fmt.Println("Person named:", v.Name)
    case Robot:
        fmt.Println("Robot model:", v.Model)
    default:
        fmt.Println("Unknown Speaker")
    }
}
```

Using DescribeSpeaker with different types comes through as follows:

```
DescribeSpeaker(p) // Output: Person named: Alice
DescribeSpeaker(r) // Output: Robot model: RX-78
```

```
Person named: Alice
Robot model: RX-78
```

In these ways, polymorphism—enabled through interfaces—grants Go programs a structured and type-safe method of achieving dynamic behavior while adhering to static typing principles. This harnessing of polymorphic capabilities aids in creating extensible and maintainable code.

7.12 Use Cases and Best Practices for Structs and Methods

Structs and methods are fundamental components of the Go programming language, supporting the organization and manipulation of complex data. Efficient use of structs and methods in Go enhances code readability, maintainability, and performance. This section provides exemplary use cases and outlines best practices.

Structs in Go are advantageous for:

- **Modeling Real-World Entities**: By encapsulating attributes of real-world entities, structs provide a method to represent data models ranging from simple entities, such as a Person, to more complex entities, like Transaction or Account.

- **Data Aggregation**: Structs facilitate the aggregation of related data under a single unit, therefore simplifying data management, access, and manipulation.
- **Custom Data Types**: Creating custom data types using structs allows for domain-specific representations and validations, enhancing type safety and code clarity.

To elaborate on the aforementioned points, consider how structs can be used to model a simple Person entity:

```
type Person struct {
    FirstName string
    LastName string
    Age int
    Address Address
}

type Address struct {
    Street string
    City string
    ZipCode string
}
```

In the above example, Person encapsulates an Address, demonstrating how struct fields can themselves be other structs, facilitating a hierarchical data representation.

Methods in Go, associated with struct types, offer a mechanism to define behaviors on those types. Some core use cases include:

- **Encapsulation of Behavior**: Methods enable encapsulation of business logic within struct definitions. For instance, a method to display the full name of a Person can be created as follows:

```
func (p Person) FullName() string {
    return p.FirstName + " " + p.LastName
}
```

- **State Mutation**: Methods can be used to alter the state of a struct. Implementing pointer receivers allows methods to modify the original struct, important for operations that require updating the struct's fields.

```
func (p *Person) Birthday() {
    p.Age++
}
```

- **Interface Implementation**: Methods allow structs to implement interfaces, enabling polymorphism. For example, should multiple types implement a Stringer interface with a String() method, they can be used interchangeably in functions that accept this interface.

When working with structs and methods in Go, certain best practices should be adhered to:

- **Use Pointer Receivers for Large Structs**: For structs that are large or will be frequently modified, use pointer receivers to avoid performance overhead associated with copying.
- **Exported Fields and Methods**: Clearly differentiate between exported and unexported fields and methods. Exported components should start with a capital letter and be used sparingly to maintain data encapsulation.
- **Avoid Method Overloading**: Unlike some other programming languages, Go does not support method overloading. Emphasize distinguishing method purposes clearly to avoid confusion.
- **Nil Receivers**: Gracefully handle cases where receiver pointers are nil, particularly common in interface implementations.
- **Documentation and Naming Conventions**: Ensure that methods and struct fields are well-documented. Follow consistent naming conventions to enhance code readability and comprehension.

These practices integrate into a comprehensive strategy for Go development, ensuring that structs and methods are employed effectively, harnessing their full potential while maintaining code quality. The practical application of these concepts can be seen in scenarios such as managing user accounts, processing transactions, and representing complex hierarchical data structures.

Chapter 8

Concurrency in Go

This chapter explores concurrency in Go, focusing on the use of goroutines and channels. It explains how to create and manage goroutines, and how to perform channel operations, including buffered and unbuffered channels, channel directions, and the select statement for multiplexing. Synchronization primitives like WaitGroups and mutexes are also covered, along with common concurrency patterns and best practices to avoid pitfalls in concurrent programming.

8.1 Introduction to Concurrency

Concurrency is an essential concept in programming, particularly in Go, where it forms the backbone of the language's approach to modern software design. Concurrency allows different parts of a program to execute independently while sharing the same resources, enhancing efficiency and responsiveness. Understanding concurrency helps developers build scalable, high-performance applications that can handle multiple tasks simultaneously, without compromising reliability or performance.

In Go, concurrency is primarily managed through goroutines and channels. Before diving into the specifics of goroutines and channels, it is crucial to understand the foundational principles of concurrency itself—including the challenges it presents and the techniques used to manage it effectively.

Concurrent vs. Parallel Execution: Although often used interchangeably, concurrency and parallelism are distinct concepts. Concurrency involves multiple tasks making progress within overlapping periods. It doesn't necessarily require them to run simultaneously but rather allows for the program to manage multiple tasks effectively by interleaving their execution. Parallelism, on the other hand, is a subset of concurrency where tasks are executed exactly at the same time, typically on multi-core processors. Concurrency provides an illusion of parallelism which suffices for achieving significant improvements in throughput and responsiveness in many applications.

Challenges in Concurrency: Implementing concurrency can introduce several challenges such as race conditions, deadlocks, and resource contention. A race condition occurs when the output of a program depends on the timing of uncontrollable events like thread scheduling. Deadlocks happen when two or more goroutines wait indefinitely for each other to release resources, thus halting program execution. Resource contention arises when multiple goroutines compete for the same resource, leading to inefficiencies and potential program errors.

Managing Concurrency in Go: Go addresses these concurrency issues by providing robust features like goroutines and channels which simplify the development of concurrent applications. Goroutines are lightweight threads managed by the Go runtime, making it feasible to run thousands of them simultaneously without significant overhead. Channels in Go serve as conduits through which goroutines communicate and synchronize, ensuring safe and predictable data sharing.

The following Go code snippet demonstrates the creation and invocation of a basic goroutine:

```
package main

import (
    "fmt"
    "time"
)

func sayHello() {
    fmt.Println("Hello, Goroutine!")
}

func main() {
    go sayHello() // Initiates a new goroutine
    time.Sleep(time.Second) // Allows time for goroutine to complete
}
```

In this example, the sayHello function is executed concurrently with the main function. The go keyword precedes the function call, effectively creating a new goroutine. The time.Sleep function is used here to prevent the main function from exiting before the goroutine has had the chance to execute.

Data Synchronization: One of the key aspects of concurrency in Go is data synchronization. To prevent race conditions, channels are frequently used to synchronize data access among goroutines. Go's standard library offers additional synchronization primitives such as sync.WaitGroup and sync.Mutex to help manage complexity in concurrent programs.

Here is an example illustrating the use of sync.WaitGroup to wait for multiple goroutines to finish:

```
package main

import (
    "fmt"
    "sync"
)

func worker(id int, wg *sync.WaitGroup) {
    fmt.Printf("Worker %d starting\n", id)
    // Simulate work
    fmt.Printf("Worker %d done\n", id)
    wg.Done() // Notify that the goroutine is finished
}

func main() {
    var wg sync.WaitGroup

    for i := 1; i <= 3; i++ {
        wg.Add(1) // Increment the counter
        go worker(i, &wg)
    }

    wg.Wait() // Wait for all goroutines to finish
    fmt.Println("All workers completed.")
}
```

This code uses a sync.WaitGroup to ensure the main function waits for all worker goroutines to complete before printing "All workers completed." The wg.Add(1) method increases the counter for each goroutine, and wg.Done() decrements it when a goroutine finishes. wg.Wait() blocks until the counter drops back to zero, signifying that all goroutines have completed their tasks.

Conclusion: Concurrency is an imperative skill in Go programming, as it enables efficient and scalable application design. By comprehending the differences between concurrency and parallelism and recognizing the challenges, developers can leverage Go's concurrency primitives to design robust, high-performance software. In the following sections, we will delve deeper into the intricacies of goroutines, channels, and synchronization primitives, expanding on the fundamental concepts introduced here. This will equip you with the knowledge needed to master concurrency in Go, ensuring your applications can handle multiple tasks seamlessly and efficiently.

8.2 Goroutines: Lightweight Threads

Goroutines are a fundamental building block for achieving concurrency in Go. They are essentially lightweight threads managed by the Go runtime, designed to be more efficient than traditional operating system threads in terms of memory and initialization time. This section will delve into the concept of goroutines, explaining their creation, execution, and effective utilization.

To create a goroutine, the go keyword is used followed by a function call. This function then runs concurrently with the calling code. Here is a basic example:

```
package main

import (
    "fmt"
    "time"
)

func sayHello() {
    fmt.Println("Hello, Goroutine!")
}

func main() {
    go sayHello()
    time.Sleep(1 * time.Second)
    fmt.Println("Main function")
}
```

In this example, the sayHello function is executed as a goroutine. The main function calls go sayHello(), which runs the sayHello function concurrently. The main function then sleeps for one second to allow the goroutine to complete before the program exits. Without the time.Sleep, the main function might exit before the goroutine has a chance to run, due to the nature of the Go runtime.

Goroutines are more efficient than traditional threads because they use a segmented stack that grows and shrinks as needed, which typically starts at a small size (e.g., 2KB). The Go runtime multiplexes thousands of goroutines onto a smaller number of operating system threads. This contrasts with traditional threads that often start with a fixed stack size (typically 1MB), consuming more memory resources.

A key aspect of goroutines is their ability to handle concurrent operations without explicit synchronization mechanisms such as locks. This is achieved through channels, which we will discuss in subsequent sections. However, for now, it's important to understand how goroutines manage their execution.

Goroutines can be executed as anonymous functions, providing more flexibility. Here is an example that shows the usage of an anonymous function:

```
package main

import (
    "fmt"
    "time"
)

func main() {
    go func() {
        fmt.Println("Hello from an anonymous goroutine!")
    }()
    time.Sleep(1 * time.Second)
    fmt.Println("Main function")
}
```

In this case, an anonymous function is defined and immediately invoked with the go keyword, creating a goroutine that prints a message. As before, a sleep timer is used to ensure the goroutine has time to execute before the main function exits.

Goroutines can also take arguments, either through a named function or an anonymous function. This enables more dynamic handling of concurrent tasks. For example, consider the following modification to incorporate arguments:

```
package main

import (
    "fmt"
```

```
    "time"
)

func task(id int) {
    fmt.Printf("Task %d is running\n", id)
}

func main() {
    for i := 1; i <= 5; i++ {
        go task(i)
    }

    time.Sleep(1 * time.Second)
    fmt.Println("Main function")
}
```

This program spawns five goroutines, each printing its respective task ID. The loop in the main function calls go task(i) for i values from 1 to 5. Each goroutine runs the task function concurrently with the others.

Care needs to be taken with variable scope inside anonymous functions within goroutines to avoid unintended consequences. Here's a common pitfall:

```
package main

import (
    "fmt"
    "time"
)

func main() {
    for i := 1; i <= 5; i++ {
        go func() {
            fmt.Printf("Task %d is running\n", i)
        }()
    }

    time.Sleep(1 * time.Second)
    fmt.Println("Main function")
}
```

In this example, it might seem like each goroutine should print its respective task ID. However, due to the closure property of the anonymous function, it captures the variable i, not its value at the time of the goroutine creation. As a result, all goroutines might print the same final value of i, which is 6 in this case. The correct approach is to pass the loop variable as an argument to the anonymous function:

```
package main
```

```
import (
    "fmt"
    "time"
)

func main() {
    for i := 1; i <= 5; i++ {
        go func(id int) {
            fmt.Printf("Task %d is running\n", id)
        }(i)
    }

    time.Sleep(1 * time.Second)
    fmt.Println("Main function")
}
```

By passing i as an argument to the anonymous function, each goroutine receives the correct task ID.

Understanding and effectively utilizing goroutines is crucial for writing concurrent programs in Go. Their lightweight nature, combined with the Go runtime's efficient management, allows developers to build scalable and high-performance applications with relative ease.

8.3 Creating and Managing Goroutines

In Go, goroutines are the cornerstone of concurrent programming. They are lightweight threads managed by the Go runtime and can be created efficiently with minimal overhead. To create a goroutine, the go keyword is used before a function call. The function runs concurrently with the calling function, allowing multiple functions to execute simultaneously.

To illustrate the creation of a goroutine, consider the following simple example:

```
package main

import (
    "fmt"
)

func printMessage(message string) {
    fmt.Println(message)
}
```

```
func main() {
    go printMessage("Hello, Goroutine!")
    fmt.Println("Hello, main!")
}
```

In this example, the printMessage function is invoked as a goroutine using the go keyword. Consequently, it runs concurrently with the main function. The output of this program can vary depending on the execution timing of the goroutines, as shown in the following possible outputs:

```
Hello, main!
Hello, Goroutine!
```

Or alternatively:

```
Hello, Goroutine!
Hello, main!
```

Managing goroutines involves ensuring that they complete their tasks correctly and that resources are shared without conflicts. One way to manage goroutines is by using synchronization primitives, such as WaitGroups.

Using WaitGroups

The sync package in Go provides a WaitGroup type to synchronize multiple goroutines. A WaitGroup waits for a collection of goroutines to finish executing. The main goroutine can block and wait for other goroutines to complete by calling WaitGroup.Wait(). Consider the following example:

```
package main

import (
    "fmt"
    "sync"
)

func printMessage(message string, wg *sync.WaitGroup) {
    defer wg.Done()
    fmt.Println(message)
}

func main() {
    var wg sync.WaitGroup

    messages := []string{"Hello", "Concurrency", "in", "Go"}

    for _, message := range messages {
```

```
        wg.Add(1)
        go printMessage(message, &wg)
    }

    wg.Wait()
    fmt.Println("All goroutines finished.")
}
```

In this example, a WaitGroup is used to wait for all goroutines to complete. The WaitGroup counter is incremented with wg.Add(1) for each goroutine and each goroutine calls wg.Done() using defer to decrease the counter. The main function waits for all goroutines to complete by calling wg.Wait(), ensuring that the program does not exit prematurely.

Anonymous Function Goroutines

In addition to named functions, goroutines can be created with anonymous functions. Anonymous functions are useful for cases where the function logic is not reused. Here is an example of creating goroutines with anonymous functions:

```
package main

import (
    "fmt"
    "sync"
)

func main() {
    var wg sync.WaitGroup

    messages := []string{"Hello", "Concurrency", "with", "Anonymous", "
        Functions"}

    for _, message := range messages {
        wg.Add(1)
        go func(msg string) {
            defer wg.Done()
            fmt.Println(msg)
        }(message)
    }

    wg.Wait()
    fmt.Println("All anonymous goroutines finished.")
}
```

In this example, each goroutine is launched using an anonymous function. The message parameter is passed to the anonymous function to prevent capturing the loop variable which could lead to unexpected behavior due to the inherent concurrency in the loop.

Handling Goroutine Panics

Goroutines, like normal functions, can panic. However, if a goroutine panics, it will not cause the entire program to terminate. Instead, the runtime handles the panic within the goroutine. To handle panics within a goroutine, a recover mechanism can be employed. This ensures that the goroutine can handle its own errors gracefully without affecting other goroutines or the main program flow. Here is an illustrative example:

```
package main

import (
    "fmt"
    "sync"
)

func safePrint(message string, wg *sync.WaitGroup) {
    defer func() {
        if r := recover(); r != nil {
            fmt.Println("Recovered in safePrint:", r)
        }
        wg.Done()
    }()
    if message == "" {
        panic("Empty message")
    }
    fmt.Println(message)
}

func main() {
    var wg sync.WaitGroup

    messages := []string{"Hello", "", "Concurrent", "Go"}

    for _, message := range messages {
        wg.Add(1)
        go safePrint(message, &wg)
    }

    wg.Wait()
    fmt.Println("All safePrint goroutines finished.")
}
```

In this example, each goroutine runs safePrint and any potential panic is recovered by the anonymous function deferred within safePrint. This practice isolates errors and maintains the stability of the concurrent execution.

Effectively creating and managing goroutines is crucial for harnessing the power of concurrency in Go. The use of synchronization primitives such as WaitGroup, anonymous function-based goroutines, and panic handling mechanisms are essential techniques in achieving reliable and robust concurrent programs.

8.4 Introduction to Channels

Channels serve as critical conduits for communication between goroutines in Go, enabling a clean and effective means to synchronize operations and share data. A channel in Go is a typed conduit through which you can send and receive values of a specific type, using the channel operator <-. Channels provide a way for one goroutine to send data to another goroutine, effectively facilitating communication and coordination.

The declaration of channels is carried out using the make function, as demonstrated in the following code snippet:

```
ch := make(chan int)
```

In this example, ch is a channel capable of transporting integer values. Channels, much like other types in Go, impose strict type constraints, disallowing the transfer of values of incompatible types.

Communication over a channel occurs through the use of the channel operator <-, which enables both sending and receiving of values. To send a value to a channel, you might write:

```
ch <- 42
```

Here, the integer value 42 is sent into the channel ch. The receiving end can be managed as follows:

```
value := <-ch
```

This operation extracts a value from the channel ch and assigns it to the variable value. The send and receive operations are blocking; the send operation blocks until another goroutine is ready to receive from the channel, and vice versa. This property ensures synchronization between the sending and receiving goroutines.

Creating a simple example involving channels to illustrate their use might look as follows:

```
package main
```

```
import (
    "fmt"
)

func main() {
    // Create a new channel for sending integer values
    ch := make(chan int)

    // Start a new goroutine that sends a value into the channel
    go func() {
        ch <- 42
    }()

    // Receive the value from the channel and print it
    value := <-ch
    fmt.Println(value)
}
```

When this program executes, the main goroutine initiates the channel and starts a new goroutine that promptly sends the integer value 42 into the channel. The main goroutine then waits for a value to be made available on the channel and, upon receiving it, prints out the value. The synchronization here is implicit and inherent to the behavior of channels.

Channels can also be used to convey more complex data structures, including slices, maps, or even custom defined struct types. Declaring a channel for a custom struct can be done as follows:

```
type Task struct {
    id string
    description string
}

taskChannel := make(chan Task)
```

With a Task channel, we can send and receive Task structs between goroutines. This flexibility makes channels a powerful feature for concurrency in Go.

Channels can be either buffered or unbuffered. In unbuffered channels, a send operation is blocked until another goroutine performs a receive on that channel. Buffered channels, however, allow sending goroutines to proceed without waiting, provided the buffer is not full. The declaration of a buffered channel involves specifying the buffer capacity:

```
bufferedCh := make(chan int, 10)
```

In this scenario, bufferedCh is a channel with a buffer capacity of 10 integers. Sending to a buffered channel occurs without blocking until the buffer is full. Similarly, receiving from a buffered channel occurs without blocking until the buffer is empty.

An example utilizing a buffered channel could appear as follows:

```
package main

import "fmt"

func main() {
    // Create a buffered channel with a capacity of 2
    ch := make(chan int, 2)

    // Send values to the buffered channel
    ch <- 1
    ch <- 2

    // Receive and print values from the buffered channel
    fmt.Println(<-ch)
    fmt.Println(<-ch)
}
```

This example sends two integers into a buffered channel with a capacity of 2, and then receives and prints these integers. The buffered channel allows sending both integers without waiting, before performing the receive operations.

Channels are equipped with the ability to be closed, signaling that no additional values will be sent on the channel. This operation is achieved using the close function:

```
close(ch)
```

Closing a channel retrieves any remaining values from receiving operations. A closed channel can still be read, returning zero values for the channel's type until it is empty.

The for range construct can be used to iterate over values received from a channel until it is closed:

```
package main

import "fmt"

func main() {
    ch := make(chan int, 5)

    for i := 0; i < 5; i++ {
```

```
        ch <- i
    }
    close(ch)

    for value := range ch {
        fmt.Println(value)
    }
}
```

When executed, this program creates a buffered channel, sends five integers, closes the channel, and iterates over the channel, printing each received value.

8.5 Channel Operations

In Go, channels provide a means for goroutines to communicate with each other and synchronize their execution. Channels are typed conduits through which you can send and receive values with the channel operator <-. This section explores the fundamental operations on channels, including sending, receiving, closing channels, and checking the state of a channel.

```
ch := make(chan int)
```

Sending Values to a Channel: To send a value to a channel, use the channel operator <- followed by the value you want to send. The sending goroutine will block until the value is received by another goroutine.

```
ch <- 42
```

This code snippet creates a channel ch of type int and sends the number 42 into the channel. The sending action will only complete when the value has been received from the channel.

Receiving Values from a Channel: To receive a value from a channel, use the channel operator <- placed before the channel. The receiving goroutine will block until a value is sent to the channel.

```
value := <- ch
```

This code snippet receives a value from the channel ch and assigns it to the variable value.

Closing a Channel: A channel can be closed using the close() function.

Closing a channel is a signal that no more values will be sent on this channel. Receivers can still receive any values already sent on the channel. After all values have been received, further receives will return the zero value of the channel's type and false as the second value to indicate that no more values will be sent.

```
close(ch)
```

This function call closes the channel ch. Attempting to send values on a closed channel results in a panic.

Non-blocking Channel Operations: Sometimes, you may need to perform channel operations without blocking. This can be achieved through the use of the select statement with a default clause.

```
select {
case msg := <-ch:
    fmt.Println("Received", msg)
default:
    fmt.Println("No message received")
}
```

In this snippet, if there's a message available in ch, it will be received and printed. If not, the default case will execute, printing a message indicating that no value was received.

Checking if a Channel is Closed: You can check if a channel is closed by attempting to read from it. When a channel is closed and empty, receiving from it returns the zero value of the channel's type and false as the second result.

```
value, ok := <-ch
if !ok {
    fmt.Println("Channel is closed")
}
```

Here, value receives the value from the channel, and ok is false if the channel is closed. If ok is false, it indicates that the channel ch is closed.

Range over Channels: You can use the range keyword to receive values from a channel until it is closed.

```
for v := range ch {
    fmt.Println("Received:", v)
}
```

This loop will continue to receive values from the channel ch until it is closed. It's a convenient pattern for reading from channels where the sender knows exactly when no more values will be sent.

Effective use of channels allows for writing concurrent programs that are both clear and efficient. When used correctly, channels enable safe communication and coordination between goroutines without the need for explicit locks or condition variables.

8.6 Buffered vs. Unbuffered Channels

Channels in Go provide a mechanism for goroutines to communicate with each other and synchronize their execution. Understanding the difference between buffered and unbuffered channels is crucial for leveraging Go's concurrency model effectively.

Unbuffered channels block the sender until the receiver is available to receive the data, ensuring synchronous communication between goroutines. This exact blocking behavior is fundamental for many concurrency patterns, especially when synchronization is a priority.

To create an unbuffered channel, we utilize the make function without specifying a buffer capacity:

```
ch := make(chan int)
```

In the following example, we illustrate the behavior of an unbuffered channel:

```
package main

import (
    "fmt"
)

func main() {
    ch := make(chan int)

    // Goroutine to send data
    go func() {
        ch <- 42
        fmt.Println("Sent 42")
    }()

    // Receiving data
    value := <-ch
    fmt.Println("Received", value)
}
```

```
function main
Output:
Sent 42
Received 42
```

In this example, the sending goroutine is blocked until the main goroutine is ready to receive the value 42 from the channel, demonstrating synchronous communication.

Buffered channels, on the other hand, allow the sender to proceed without waiting for the receiver as long as there is space in the channel buffer. This allows for asynchronous communication and can improve performance by decoupling the goroutines.

To create a buffered channel, the buffer capacity is specified as the second argument to the make function:

```
ch := make(chan int, 2)
```

Here, we create a buffered channel with a capacity of 2. The sending operation will only block if the buffer is full. The following example demonstrates buffered channel behavior:

```
package main

import (
    "fmt"
)

func main() {
    ch := make(chan int, 2)

    ch <- 1
    fmt.Println("Sent 1")
    ch <- 2
    fmt.Println("Sent 2")

    // Buffered channel allows sending without blocking
    go func() {
        ch <- 3
        fmt.Println("Sent 3 in goroutine")
    }()

    value1 := <-ch
    fmt.Println("Received", value1)
    value2 := <-ch
    fmt.Println("Received", value2)
    value3 := <-ch
    fmt.Println("Received", value3)
}
```

```
Output:
Sent 1
Sent 2
Sent 3 in goroutine
Received 1
Received 2
Received 3
```

Although data was sent to the channel in a separate goroutine, the values were stored in the buffer, allowing the sender to proceed immediately without waiting for the receiver.

One must manage the buffer size carefully to avoid potential deadlocks. For example, consider the following scenario:

```go
package main

import (
    "fmt"
)

func main() {
    ch := make(chan int, 1)

    ch <- 1
    fmt.Println("Sent 1")
    ch <- 2
    fmt.Println("Sent 2")
}
```

This program will deadlock because the buffer can only hold one value, and there is no receiver available to consume the data, resulting in the second send operation blocking indefinitely.

Managing channel buffers involves assessing the expected communication patterns and load between goroutines. For example, a producer-consumer pattern will often benefit from a properly sized buffer, supporting smooth data flow between producing and consuming goroutines.

In summary, the choice between buffered and unbuffered channels depends on the synchronization requirements and performance characteristics of the application. Unbuffered channels provide guaranteed synchronization at the expense of potential blocking, while buffered channels offer improved throughput by allowing asynchronous communication, though they require careful management to avoid deadlocks and ensure consistency.

8.7 Channel Direction and Usage

Channels in Go can be utilized to pass data between goroutines safely. By leveraging the type system in Go, it is possible to specify the direction of a channel, enhancing the expressiveness and safety of the code. The direction of a channel can be defined as 'send-only', 'receive-only', or 'bidirectional'. This section will delve into the semantics and usage, emphasizing best practices that should be adhered to for efficient concurrent programming.

A bidirectional channel is the default form when a channel is instantiated using the make function. This type of channel allows both sending and receiving data. For instance:

```
ch := make(chan int)
```

A send-only channel restricts operations to sending data into the channel. Declaring such a channel involves using the chan<- type. For example:

```
var sendOnlyCh chan<- int
sendOnlyCh = make(chan int)
```

Conversely, a receive-only channel restricts operations to receiving data from the channel, using the <-chan type:

```
var receiveOnlyCh <-chan int
receiveOnlyCh = make(chan int)
```

The following example demonstrates how to create a function that accepts a send-only channel:

```
func sender(out chan<- int) {
    out <- 42
}
```

In contrast, a function that accepts a receive-only channel can be written as shown below:

```
func receiver(in <-chan int) {
    val := <-in
    fmt.Println(val)
}
```

When working with channels, it is advantageous to define the direction explicitly in function signatures. This discipline aids in preventing accidental misuse, ensuring clearer and safer code. Consider the following complete program to illustrate this:

```
package main

import "fmt"

func sender(out chan<- int) {
    out <- 42
}

func receiver(in <-chan int) {
    val := <-in
    fmt.Println(val)
}

func main() {
    ch := make(chan int)
    go sender(ch)
    go receiver(ch)
}
```

The sender function sends an integer value into the channel and the receiver function retrieves and prints it. The main function initiates the goroutines, demonstrating the transfer of data through directional channels.

It is essential to understand that channel directionality ensures that the senders and receivers are well-defined and used correctly. For instance, assigning a receive-only channel to a send-only variable will result in a compilation error. This kind of type safety helps to avoid race conditions and deadlocks that can arise from inadvertent channel misuse.

```
prog.go:16: cannot use ch (type <-chan int) as type chan<- int in argument to sender
```

Another important aspect of channel usage is to ensure proper closure of channels. Closing a channel signals to all receivers that no more data will be sent on that channel. The close function achieves this. It is typically invoked by the goroutine responsible for sending data. Here is an example demonstrating channel closure and range iteration over channel values:

```
func generator(out chan<- int) {
    for i := 0; i < 5; i++ {
        out <- i
    }
    close(out)
}

func main() {
    ch := make(chan int)
    go generator(ch)

    for val := range ch {
        fmt.Println(val)
```

```
    }
}
```

In the example above, the generator function sends five integers into the channel and then closes it. The main function ranges over the channel, receiving values until it is closed.

Channel directionality, thoughtful use, and proper termination are pivotal concepts for mastering Go concurrency patterns. These elements ensure that data flows correctly between goroutines while maintaining program integrity and preventing common concurrency issues. As you harness these practices, you will find that Go's channel mechanism provides a robust and flexible foundation for concurrent programming tasks.

8.8 Select Statement for Multiplexing

The select statement in Go is a powerful feature used to manage multiple channels and handle their operations simultaneously. The select statement allows a goroutine to wait on multiple communication operations, effectively multiplexing the input across multiple channels. This section delves into the mechanics of the select statement, providing a detailed examination of its syntax, usage, and practical applications in concurrent Go programs.

select works similarly to a switch statement but is designed specifically for channels. Each case in a select statement must be a communication operation involving a channel. One notable feature of the select statement is that it picks a channel operation that can proceed and executes the associated statements. If multiple channels are ready, one case is selected randomly.

The syntax of the select statement is straightforward:

```
select {
case <-ch1:
    // code to execute when ch1 is ready to receive
case msg := <-ch2:
    // code to execute when ch2 is ready to receive with message msg
case ch3 <- msg:
    // code to execute when ch3 is ready to send message msg
default:
    // code to execute when no other cases are ready
}
```

A more detailed example is shown below to illustrate its application. Consider a scenario where a function receives and processes data from multiple channels representing different sources.

```
package main

import (
    "fmt"
    "time"
)

func main() {
    ch1 := make(chan int)
    ch2 := make(chan int)

    go func() {
        time.Sleep(1 * time.Second)
        ch1 <- 1
    }()

    go func() {
        time.Sleep(2 * time.Second)
        ch2 <- 2
    }()

    for i := 0; i < 2; i++ {
        select {
        case msg1 := <-ch1:
            fmt.Println("Received from ch1:", msg1)
        case msg2 := <-ch2:
            fmt.Println("Received from ch2:", msg2)
        }
    }
}
```

Here, the program creates two channels, ch1 and ch2, and launches two goroutines to send data to these channels after a delay. The select statement in the main goroutine waits for data from either channel and prints the received message. Since the operations are asynchronous, the actual sequence in which the messages are printed may vary, depending on which channel becomes ready first.

The default case in a select statement executes if none of the communication operations are ready. This feature is useful for implementing non-blocking communication or timeout mechanisms. Consider the following example where we use a select statement to implement a timeout for receiving from a channel:

```
package main
```

```
import (
    "fmt"
    "time"
)

func main() {
    ch := make(chan int)

    go func() {
        time.Sleep(3 * time.Second)
        ch <- 1
    }()

    select {
    case msg := <-ch:
        fmt.Println("Received:", msg)
    case <-time.After(2 * time.Second):
        fmt.Println("Timeout")
    }
}
```

In this example, the time.After function creates a channel that sends a value after the specified duration. The select statement waits for either a message from the ch channel or a timeout event. If the timeout occurs first, the program prints "Timeout". If the message arrives first, it prints the received message. This pattern is commonly used to handle scenarios where operations should complete within a certain period.

It is crucial to note that both case and default cases are evaluated only once at the time the select statement is reached. This means that you cannot rely on select statements to dynamically adapt to changes in channel states that occur after the select is entered. Instead, they provide a snapshot of the channel states at the moment of execution.

```
package main

import (
    "fmt"
    "time"
)

func main() {
    ch1 := make(chan string)
    ch2 := make(chan string)
    done := make(chan bool)

    // Goroutine to send data to ch1
    go func() {
        time.Sleep(2 * time.Second)
        ch1 <- "Hello from ch1"
```

```
    }()

    // Goroutine to send data to ch2
    go func() {
        time.Sleep(1 * time.Second)
        ch2 <- "Hello from ch2"
    }()

    go func() {
        select {
        case msg1 := <-ch1:
            fmt.Println(msg1)
        case msg2 := <-ch2:
            fmt.Println(msg2)
        case <-time.After(3 * time.Second):
            fmt.Println("Timeout")
        }
        done <- true
    }()

    <-done
}
```

In this example, the select statement within the second goroutine waits for messages from either ch1 or ch2, or a timeout event, and sends a completion signal to the done channel once any case is fulfilled. The program prints the message from whichever channel sends first or a timeout message if neither channel sends within 3 seconds.

One common pattern is using select within an infinite loop to continuously listen to multiple channels. The following example demonstrates this:

```
package main

import (
    "fmt"
    "time"
)

func main() {
    ch1 := make(chan string)
    ch2 := make(chan string)

    go func() {
        for {
            time.Sleep(1 * time.Second)
            ch1 <- "ping"
        }
    }()
```

```
    go func() {
        for {
            time.Sleep(2 * time.Second)
            ch2 <- "pong"
        }
    }()

    go func() {
        for {
            select {
            case msg1 := <-ch1:
                fmt.Println(msg1)
            case msg2 := <-ch2:
                fmt.Println(msg2)
            }
        }
    }()

    // Run indefinitely
    select {}
}
```

This program consists of three goroutines. Two of them periodically send the strings "ping" and "pong" to ch1 and ch2, respectively. The third goroutine continuously listens for messages from these channels using a select statement and prints the received values. The main function uses a select statement with an empty block to run indefinitely, ensuring the goroutines continue execution.

Understanding and mastering the select statement allows Go programmers to efficiently manage multiple concurrent channel operations and implement sophisticated communication patterns. As we continue through this chapter, these principles and techniques will form a foundation for more advanced concurrency constructs and paradigms.

8.9 Syncing Goroutines with WaitGroups

In concurrent programming, managing the execution order and synchronization of multiple goroutines is an essential aspect to ensure that concurrent processes interact correctly and avoid race conditions. The WaitGroup type provided by the Go sync package is a synchronization primitive that helps coordinate the commencement and completion of goroutines. This section delves into the usage of WaitGroup, demonstrating how to properly initialize, manage, and ensure synchronization across multiple goroutines.

To begin using WaitGroup, import the sync package:

```
import (
    "sync"
)
```

A WaitGroup waits for a collection of goroutines to finish. It operates by counting the number of goroutines to wait on, decrementing for each goroutine that completes. The fundamental methods associated with WaitGroup are Add, Done, and Wait:

- Add(delta int): Increases or decreases the wait group counter by delta.
- Done(): Decrements the wait group counter by one. This method should be called as a deferred function in the executing goroutine.
- Wait(): Blocks until the wait group counter reaches zero, i.e., all goroutines complete their execution.

Consider the following example illustrating the basic use of WaitGroup to sync multiple goroutines:

```
package main

import (
    "fmt"
    "sync"
    "time"
)

func worker(id int, wg *sync.WaitGroup) {
    defer wg.Done() // Decrements counter when goroutine completes
    fmt.Printf("Worker %d starting\n", id)
    time.Sleep(time.Second) // Simulate time-consuming task
    fmt.Printf("Worker %d done\n", id)
}

func main() {
    var wg sync.WaitGroup

    for i := 1; i <= 3; i++ {
        wg.Add(1) // Increment counter to track this goroutine
        go worker(i, &wg)
    }

    wg.Wait() // Block until all goroutines complete
    fmt.Println("All workers done")
}
```

```
Worker 1 starting
Worker 2 starting
Worker 3 starting
Worker 1 done
Worker 2 done
Worker 3 done
All workers done
```

- wg.Add(1) increments the wait group counter by one for each goroutine created.
- worker(i, &wg), each worker function runs as a separate goroutine, taking the wait group as an argument.
- defer wg.Done() ensures that the goroutine will signal completion regardless of how the goroutine exits.
- wg.Wait() blocks the main function from exiting until all goroutines have called Done().

Using WaitGroup prevents race conditions where the main function might exit before all goroutines have completed. To extend the aforementioned example, consider incorporating error handling or complex computations in the workers.

```
package main

import (
    "errors"
    "fmt"
    "sync"
)

func task(id int, wg *sync.WaitGroup, errChan chan error) {
    defer wg.Done()
    if id == 3 {
        errChan <- errors.New("error from task 3")
        return
    }
    fmt.Printf("Task %d completed successfully\n", id)
}

func main() {
    var wg sync.WaitGroup
    errChan := make(chan error, 3)

    for i := 1; i <= 3; i++ {
        wg.Add(1)
        go task(i, &wg, errChan)
    }
```

```
    go func() {
        wg.Wait()
        close(errChan)
    }()

    for err := range errChan {
        if err != nil {
            fmt.Println("Error received:", err)
        }
    }
}
```

```
Task 1 completed successfully
Task 2 completed successfully
Error received: error from task 3
```

In this example:

- errChan channel is used to collect and report errors from goroutines.
- &wg and errChan are shared resources between the main function and the worker goroutines.
- An anonymous goroutine waits on wg.Wait() and closes the errChan channel, ensuring the main function can range over the channel to handle errors after all tasks have completed.

To summarize the importance of WaitGroup:

- It facilitates the synchronization of goroutines, ensuring safe and efficient concurrent execution.
- Proper usage of WaitGroup involves correct incrementing, decrementing, and awaiting completion to avoid leaks, race conditions, or premature termination.
- Enhancing WaitGroup with channels allows more sophisticated inter-goroutine communication and error handling, contributing to robust concurrent program design.

8.10 Mutexes and Other Synchronization Primitives

In concurrent programming, synchronization primitives are essential tools that help manage the interaction between multiple goroutines accessing shared resources. Among the primitives provided by Go, mutexes stand out as a fundamental mechanism for achieving mutual exclusion, ensuring that only one goroutine can access a particular section of code or data at any given time. This prevents race conditions and maintains data integrity.

The Go sync package offers a number of synchronization primitives, with Mutex being one of the most commonly used. In addition to Mutex, there are other primitives like RWMutex, Cond, and Once. Each primitive serves specific use cases and provides different mechanisms for synchronizing goroutines.

- Mutex: Provides mutual exclusion, ensuring a block of code can be executed by only one goroutine at a time.
- RWMutex: A reader-writer mutex that allows multiple readers or one writer at a time.
- Cond: A condition variable that allows goroutines to wait for or broadcast events.
- Once: Ensures a piece of code is executed only once across multiple goroutines.

Using Mutex for Mutual Exclusion

A Mutex is a simple locking mechanism used to protect shared data from being accessed simultaneously by multiple goroutines. Below is an example illustrating the use of Mutex in a concurrent Go program:

```
package main

import (
    "fmt"
    "sync"
)

type SafeCounter struct {
    mu sync.Mutex
    count int
}
```

```
func (sc *SafeCounter) Increment() {
    sc.mu.Lock()
    sc.count++
    sc.mu.Unlock()
}

func (sc *SafeCounter) Value() int {
    sc.mu.Lock()
    defer sc.mu.Unlock()
    return sc.count
}

func main() {
    sc := SafeCounter{}

    var wg sync.WaitGroup
    for i := 0; i < 1000; i++ {
        wg.Add(1)
        go func() {
            defer wg.Done()
            sc.Increment()
        }()
    }

    wg.Wait()
    fmt.Printf("Count: %d\n", sc.Value())
}
```

Listing 8.1: Using Mutex for mutual exclusion

In this example, SafeCounter contains a count field which is protected by a sync.Mutex. The Increment method locks the mutex before modifying count and unlocks it afterward. This guarantees mutual exclusion, ensuring that only one goroutine can increment the counter at any time.

Reader-Writer Mutex: RWMutex

While Mutex guarantees exclusive access to shared resources, there are scenarios where multiple reads may safely execute concurrently as long as there are no writes. For this purpose, Go provides a reader-writer mutex (RWMutex) through the sync package.

```
package main

import (
    "fmt"
    "sync"
)

type ReadWriteCounter struct {
    mu sync.RWMutex
```

```
    count int
}

func (rwc *ReadWriteCounter) Increment() {
    rwc.mu.Lock()
    rwc.count++
    rwc.mu.Unlock()
}

func (rwc *ReadWriteCounter) Value() int {
    rwc.mu.RLock()
    defer rwc.mu.RUnlock()
    return rwc.count
}

func main() {
    rwc := ReadWriteCounter{}
    var wg sync.WaitGroup

    // Incrementing the counter
    for i := 0; i < 1000; i++ {
        wg.Add(1)
        go func() {
            defer wg.Done()
            rwc.Increment()
        }()
    }

    // Reading the counter
    for i := 0; i < 1000; i++ {
        wg.Add(1)
        go func() {
            defer wg.Done()
            fmt.Printf("Count: %d\n", rwc.Value())
        }()
    }

    wg.Wait()
}
```

Listing 8.2: Using RWMutex for concurrent reads

The RWMutex allows for fine-grained locking by differentiating between read (shared) and write (exclusive) locks. In the ReadWriteCounter type, the Increment method uses mu.Lock() to prevent concurrent writes, whereas the Value method uses mu.RLock() to allow concurrent reads.

Condition Variables: Cond

A condition variable (Cond) enables goroutines to wait for certain conditions to become true. This is useful when goroutines need to block until some event occurs, such as waiting for a resource to become available.

```
package main

import (
    "fmt"
    "sync"
)

type Queue struct {
    items []int
    cond *sync.Cond
}

func (q *Queue) Enqueue(item int) {
    q.cond.L.Lock()
    q.items = append(q.items, item)
    q.cond.Signal()
    q.cond.L.Unlock()
}

func (q *Queue) Dequeue() int {
    q.cond.L.Lock()
    for len(q.items) == 0 {
        q.cond.Wait()
    }
    item := q.items[0]
    q.items = q.items[1:]
    q.cond.L.Unlock()
    return item
}

func main() {
    q := Queue{cond: sync.NewCond(&sync.Mutex{})}
    var wg sync.WaitGroup

    // Producer
    go func() {
        for i := 0; i < 10; i++ {
            wg.Add(1)
            q.Enqueue(i)
            wg.Done()
        }
    }()

    // Consumer
    go func() {
        for i := 0; i < 10; i++ {
            wg.Add(1)
            item := q.Dequeue()
            fmt.Println(item)
            wg.Done()
        }
```

```
    }()

    wg.Wait()
}
```

Listing 8.3: Using Condition Variables

In this example, a Queue is protected by a sync.Cond. Enqueue adds an item to the queue and signals any waiting goroutines. Dequeue waits for items to be available and then retrieves them. The condition variable is used to signal and wait within critical sections locked by a Mutex.

Single Execution: Once

The sync.Once type is used to ensure a piece of code runs only once, regardless of the number of times it is called by multiple goroutines. This can be useful for one-time initialization tasks.

```
package main

import (
    "fmt"
    "sync"
)

var once sync.Once

func initOnce() {
    fmt.Println("Initializing...")
}

func main() {
    var wg sync.WaitGroup

    for i := 0; i < 5; i++ {
        wg.Add(1)
        go func() {
            defer wg.Done()
            once.Do(initOnce)
        }()
    }

    wg.Wait()
}
```

Listing 8.4: Using sync.Once

In this code, the initOnce function will be called exactly once, regardless of how many goroutines attempt to call once.Do(initOnce). This is ensured by the sync.Once mechanism.

Each of these synchronization primitives plays a vital role in building robust concurrent Go programs by offering tools to control access to shared resources and coordination among goroutines. They help avoid common pitfalls such as race conditions, ensuring data consistency and program correctness.

8.11 Common Concurrency Patterns

Concurrency patterns are essential in Go programming as they offer structured ways to manage execution and communication between goroutines. Efficient use of these patterns enables better utilization of resources, maintenance of code readability, and avoidance of common concurrency pitfalls. This section delves into the prevalent concurrency patterns in Go, illustrating their usage with examples.

Worker Pool Pattern

The Worker Pool pattern, or Goroutine Pool, is useful when you have multiple tasks to be executed concurrently but want to limit the number of goroutines running at the same time. This is often required to control resource usage or to avoid exhausting system resources.

```
package main

import (
    "fmt"
    "sync"
)

// Worker function
func worker(id int, jobs <-chan int, results chan<- int, wg *sync.WaitGroup) {
    defer wg.Done()
    for j := range jobs {
        fmt.Println("worker", id, "started job", j)
        results <- j * 2
        fmt.Println("worker", id, "finished job", j)
    }
}

func main() {
    const numJobs = 5
    const numWorkers = 3

    jobs := make(chan int, numJobs)
    results := make(chan int, numJobs)
    var wg sync.WaitGroup
```

```
    // Starting worker goroutines
    for w := 1; w <= numWorkers; w++ {
        wg.Add(1)
        go worker(w, jobs, results, &wg)
    }

    // Sending jobs to the workers
    for j := 1; j <= numJobs; j++ {
        jobs <- j
    }
    close(jobs)

    // Waiting for all workers to finish
    wg.Wait()
    close(results)

    // Collecting results
    for result := range results {
        fmt.Println("result", result)
    }
}
```

func main() initializes channels for jobs and results, and uses a sync.WaitGroup to wait for all workers to finish. Each worker function processes jobs and returns results, demonstrating a controlled use of goroutines.

Pipeline Pattern

The Pipeline pattern allows the transformation of data through a series of stages, where each stage is a separate goroutine. Data flows between stages via channels, thereby decoupling each step of processing.

```
package main

import (
    "fmt"
)

// Function to generate numbers
func gen(nums ...int) <-chan int {
    out := make(chan int)
    go func() {
        for _, n := range nums {
            out <- n
        }
        close(out)
    }()
    return out
}
```

```
// Function to square numbers
func sq(in <-chan int) <-chan int {
    out := make(chan int)
    go func() {
        for n := range in {
            out <- n * n
        }
        close(out)
    }()
    return out
}

func main() {
    // Setting up the pipeline
    c := gen(2, 3, 4)
    out := sq(c)

    // Consuming the squared results
    for n := range out {
        fmt.Println(n)
    }
}
```

This example illustrates a simple pipeline where gen generates numbers and passes them to the sq function, which squares each number. Results flow through channels and are processed independently by goroutines.

Fan-Out, Fan-In Pattern

The Fan-Out, Fan-In pattern is useful when tasks can be decomposed into several concurrent sub-tasks (fan-out) whose results are then aggregated (fan-in).

```
package main

import (
    "fmt"
    "sync"
)

// Fan-out function to double numbers
func double(num int, out chan<- int, wg *sync.WaitGroup) {
    defer wg.Done()
    out <- num * 2
}

func main() {
    nums := []int{1, 2, 3, 4, 5}
    out := make(chan int, len(nums))
```

```
    var wg sync.WaitGroup
    for _, num := range nums {
        wg.Add(1)
        go double(num, out, &wg)
    }

    wg.Wait()
    close(out)

    // Fan-in to aggregate results
    for result := range out {
        fmt.Println(result)
    }
}
```

In this case, the double function is run in separate goroutines to concurrently double numbers, demonstrating the Fan-Out process. The results are then aggregated using the Fan-In pattern by collecting from the output channel.

Select Statement for Timeout and Cancellation

In concurrent programs, there are situations where goroutines need to be terminated after a certain duration or upon receiving a cancellation signal. This can be achieved using the select statement.

```
package main

import (
    "fmt"
    "time"
)

func main() {
    ch := make(chan string)

    go func() {
        time.Sleep(2 * time.Second)
        ch <- "result from goroutine"
    }()

    select {
    case res := <-ch:
        fmt.Println(res)
    case <-time.After(1 * time.Second):
        fmt.Println("timeout")
    }
}
```

The select statement waits for communication on the ch channel; however, if no communication occurs within the specified timeout duration (1 second), it proceeds with the timeout case, demonstrating a graceful handling of timeouts.

Or-Done Channel

The Or-Done channel is a pattern that helps signal the completion or termination of goroutines, facilitating clean and managed exits from concurrent activities.

```
package main

import (
    "fmt"
)

// Or-Done function
func orDone(done, c <-chan interface{}) <-chan interface{} {
    valStream := make(chan interface{})
    go func() {
        defer close(valStream)
        for {
            select {
            case <-done:
                return
            case v, ok := <-c:
                if !ok {
                    return
                }
                select {
                case valStream <- v:
                case <-done:
                }
            }
        }
    }()
    return valStream
}

func main() {
    done := make(chan interface{})
    dataStream := make(chan interface{})

    go func() {
        dataStream <- "some data"
        close(dataStream)
    }()

    for val := range orDone(done, dataStream) {
        fmt.Println(val)
    }
```

```
    // Assuming some condition here to close the 'done' channel
    close(done)
}
```

The orDone function wraps the dataStream with a done channel, allowing for clean exits once done is closed. This pattern ensures controlled termination when certain conditions are met.

These patterns enable scalable, maintainable, and resource-efficient concurrency in Go programs. Each pattern should be chosen based on the specific needs and constraints of the task at hand. Employing these patterns effectively contributes to robust and concurrent Go applications.

8.12 Concurrency Best Practices and Avoiding Pitfalls

When writing concurrent programs in Go, adhering to best practices and being aware of common pitfalls is essential to ensure efficient and bug-free execution. The following practices and considerations will help to optimize the performance and correctness of your concurrent Go applications.

- **Understand the Concurrency Model:** Before diving into concurrent programming, it is crucial to understand Go's concurrency model, which is based on goroutines and channels. This model is distinct from traditional threading models used in other languages.
- **Use Goroutines Wisely:** While goroutines are lightweight, they aren't free in terms of memory and resource consumption. Launching an excessive number of goroutines can exhaust system resources, leading to performance degradation or crashes. Use profiling tools to monitor the number of active goroutines and ensure optimal resource utilization.

```
package main

import (
    "log"
    "runtime"
    "time"
)
```

```
func main() {
    for {
        log.Printf("Active Goroutines: %d\n", runtime.NumGoroutine())
        time.Sleep(1 * time.Second)
    }
}
```

Listing 8.5: Monitor Active Goroutines

- **Avoid Blocking Operations in Goroutines:** Blocking operations, such as I/O or computation-heavy tasks, should be handled carefully in goroutines. These operations can block the scheduler, leading to reduced concurrency levels. Use channels to offload blocking tasks or consider separating such operations into distinct goroutines.
- **Channel Utilization:** Channels are powerful for communication between goroutines, but they must be used judiciously. Always close channels when they are no longer needed to prevent resource leaks. Never close a channel from multiple goroutines, and avoid sending on a closed channel, which will cause a panic.

```
package main

import "fmt"

func main() {
    ch := make(chan int)
    go func() {
        for i := 0; i < 5; i++ {
            ch <- i
        }
        close(ch)
    }()

    for val := range ch {
        fmt.Println(val)
    }
}
```

Listing 8.6: Proper Channel Closure

- **Use Select for Multiplexing:** The select statement provides a way to wait on multiple channel operations. It is highly useful for implementing timeouts, default cases, and handling multiple channels efficiently.

```
package main
```

```
import (
    "fmt"
    "time"
)

func main() {
    ch1 := make(chan int)
    ch2 := make(chan int)

    go func() {
        time.Sleep(2 * time.Second)
        ch1 <- 1
    }()

    go func() {
        time.Sleep(1 * time.Second)
        ch2 <- 2
    }()

    select {
    case val := <-ch1:
        fmt.Println("Received from channel 1:", val)
    case val := <-ch2:
        fmt.Println("Received from channel 2:", val)
    case <-time.After(3 * time.Second):
        fmt.Println("Timeout reached")
    }
}
```

Listing 8.7: Using Select for Multiplexing

- **Avoid Deadlocks:** Deadlocks occur when two or more goroutines are waiting for each other to release resources, resulting in a standstill. Be careful with the order of locks and channel operations to avoid circular dependencies.

- **Employ Atomic Operations and Mutexes:** For shared data that requires synchronization, use sync/atomic for simple counters or flags and sync.Mutex for more complex critical sections. Using these primitives allows you to prevent race conditions and ensure data integrity.

```
package main

import (
    "fmt"
    "sync"
)

func main() {
```

```
    var mu sync.Mutex
    counter := 0

    var wg sync.WaitGroup
    wg.Add(2)

    go func() {
        defer wg.Done()
        mu.Lock()
        counter++
        mu.Unlock()
    }()

    go func() {
        defer wg.Done()
        mu.Lock()
        counter++
        mu.Unlock()
    }()

    wg.Wait()
    fmt.Println("Counter:", counter)
}
```

Listing 8.8: Using Mutex for Concurrent Access

- **Leverage Context Package:** The context package is essential for controlling the lifecycle of goroutines, particularly for canceling goroutines or setting timeouts and deadlines. This practice improves resource management and responsiveness.

```
package main

import (
    "context"
    "fmt"
    "time"
)

func main() {
    ctx, cancel := context.WithTimeout(context.Background(), 3*time.
        Second)
    defer cancel()

    go func() {
        select {
        case <-ctx.Done():
            fmt.Println("Goroutine terminated:", ctx.Err())
        }
    }()

    time.Sleep(5 * time.Second)
```

```
}
```

Listing 8.9: Using Context for Lifecycle Management

- **Avoid Shared State Where Possible:** Minimize shared state among goroutines to reduce complexity and the likelihood of race conditions. Instead, pass data through channels, which provides a safer and more controlled communication mechanism.

Mastering these best practices and being mindful of potential concurrency pitfalls will significantly contribute to the robustness and performance of your Go applications. Concurrency in Go, when handled correctly, can lead to highly efficient and scalable programs.

Chapter 9

Error Handling

This chapter addresses error handling in Go, starting with the basics of the error interface and how to use it. It covers creating custom errors, error wrapping with fmt.Errorf, and handling errors within functions. The chapter also delves into deferred error handling with defer, and the panic and recover mechanism. It concludes with best practices and common error handling patterns to ensure robust and resilient code.

9.1 Introduction to Error Handling

Effective error handling is a fundamental aspect of writing robust and resilient software. In the Go programming language, error handling is implemented in a manner that encourages explicit, clear, and concise code. Unlike traditional error handling mechanisms in other languages, which might rely heavily on exceptions, Go adopts a more explicit approach by using the `error` interface. This section will provide a comprehensive overview of the basics of error handling in Go, laying the foundation for more advanced concepts covered in subsequent sections.

Errors in Go are represented by the built-in `error` type, which is an interface. The `error` interface contains a single method, `Error()`, which returns a string describing the error:

```
type error interface {
    Error() string
```

```
}
```

Listing 9.1: The error Interface

Any type that implements this interface can be used as an error. Go follows a pattern where functions and methods return an error value as the last return value to indicate if an operation was successful or if an error occurred. Consider the following example:

```
package main

import (
    "errors"
    "fmt"
)

func divide(a, b float64) (float64, error) {
    if b == 0 {
        return 0, errors.New("division by zero")
    }
    return a / b, nil
}
func main() {
    result, err := divide(4, 0)
    if err != nil {
        fmt.Println("Error:", err)
    } else {
        fmt.Println("Result:", result)
    }
}
```

Listing 9.2: Basic Error Return Pattern

In this example, the divide function attempts to divide a by b. If b is zero, it returns an error indicating "division by zero". Otherwise, it returns the result of the division and a nil error. The main function demonstrates how to check for and handle this error.

To create custom error messages, Go provides the errors package with the New function, which generates a simple error value with a specified message. Additionally, the fmt package offers the Errorf function for formatted error messages:

```
package main

import (
    "errors"
    "fmt"
)
```

```
func divide(a, b float64) (float64, error) {
    if b == 0 {
        return 0, fmt.Errorf("cannot divide %f by zero", a)
    }
    return a / b, nil
}

func main() {
    result, err := divide(4, 0)
    if err != nil {
        fmt.Println("Error:", err)
    } else {
        fmt.Println("Result:", result)
    }
}
```

Listing 9.3: Custom Error Messages

In this modified version, the divide function uses fmt.Errorf to include contextual information in the error message. This improves the usefulness of the error for debugging purposes.

Handling errors in a consistent manner is key to writing maintainable code. A common pattern in Go is to check for errors immediately after a function call and handle them appropriately. This minimizes the risk of overlooking errors and ensures that exceptional conditions are addressed promptly:

```
package main

import (
    "fmt"
    "io/ioutil"
)

func readFile(filename string) (string, error) {
    data, err := ioutil.ReadFile(filename)
    if err != nil {
        return "", err
    }
    return string(data), nil
}

func main() {
    content, err := readFile("nonexistent.txt")
    if err != nil {
        fmt.Println("Error:", err)
    } else {
        fmt.Println("File Content:", content)
    }
}
```

Listing 9.4: Consistent Error Handling Pattern

Here, the readFile function attempts to read the contents of a file. If reading the file fails, it immediately returns the error. The main function then checks this error and prints an appropriate message.

Understanding the importance of nil in error handling is also essential. In Go, returning a nil error signifies that the function executed successfully. Conversely, a non-nil error indicates a problem that must be addressed. Hence, it is critical to maintain this convention to avoid confusing the function's consumers.

Equipped with the foundation of error handling concepts in Go, we are prepared to explore more sophisticated techniques and best practices in the following sections.

9.2 Errors in Go: The Basics

Error handling in Go is a critical aspect of robust software engineering. Go, often referred to as Golang, treats errors as distinct from exceptions, aiming for simplicity and explicitness. This section focuses on foundational concepts, enabling a nuanced understanding of how Go approaches error handling.

At the core of Go's error handling is the error type, which is an interface type. The error interface is defined in the builtin package as follows:

```
type error interface {
    Error() string
}
```

Here, the error interface contains a single method, Error(), which returns a string. Any type that implements this method could potentially be used as an error.

To generate an error in Go, a common practice is to use the errors package, which provides support for creating and testing error conditions. The New function from the errors package can be used to instantiate a new error:

```
import "errors"

func main() {
    err := errors.New("an error occurred")
```

```
    if err != nil {
        fmt.Println(err)
    }
}
```

In this example, errors.New creates a new error with the specified message. The program subsequently checks if the error is non-nil, a common idiom in Go, before printing the error message.

When handling errors, functions in Go often return an error as their last return value, providing a straightforward method for error transmission. Consider the following function which attempts to read a file:

```
import (
    "fmt"
    "os"
)

func readFile(filename string) (string, error) {
    file, err := os.Open(filename)
    if err != nil {
        return "", err
    }
    defer file.Close()

    stat, err := file.Stat()
    if err != nil {
        return "", err
    }

    data := make([]byte, stat.Size())
    _, err = file.Read(data)
    if err != nil {
        return "", err
    }

    return string(data), nil
}
```

This function readFile attempts to open a file and read its contents. Each step checks for potential errors and returns early if an error is encountered, making the flow of error handling explicit. Notice the use of defer to ensure that the file is closed, which mitigates potential resource leaks even if an error occurs.

Error-handling conventions in Go emphasize clarity and explicitness. This approach contrasts with languages that use exceptions, where handling might inadvertently obscure the control flow. The design goals of Go's errors are to keep error handling straightforward by making code paths and error handling explicit, improving overall code maintainability and readability.

Consider a function designed to perform a simple division, which also needs to handle potential errors such as division by zero. Here's a practical example:

```
import "fmt"

func divide(a, b float64) (float64, error) {
    if b == 0 {
        return 0, errors.New("cannot divide by zero")
    }
    return a / b, nil
}

func main() {
    result, err := divide(4.0, 0.0)
    if err != nil {
        fmt.Println("Error:", err)
        return
    }
    fmt.Println("Result:", result)
}
```

In the divide function, we check if the divisor b is zero before performing the division. If b is zero, the function returns an error using errors.New. When calling this function, the error is checked and handled appropriately.

Returning errors as values makes it possible for the caller to explicitly handle these errors. This paradigm necessitates disciplined error checking by the programmer but endows them with complete control over error management.

Error handling in Go is not just about ensuring correctness but also about enhancing code readability and maintainability. Go's error handling convention encourages developers to write graceful error handling mechanisms without added complexities of try-catch blocks or exception hierarchies. This design philosophy aligns with Go's overarching principles aimed at simplicity and clarity in system-level programming.

Understanding these fundamentals prepares readers for more advanced error handling techniques, including custom error types, error wrapping, and deferred handling strategies, which will be elaborated on in subsequent sections.

9.3 Using the error Interface

The error interface in Go is a built-in interface used to represent error conditions. The standard error interface is defined in the Go programming language's core library as follows:

```
type error interface {
    Error() string
}
```

This interface has a single method, Error(), which returns a string describing the error. Any type that implements this method is considered to be an error type and can be used wherever an error is expected.

To illustrate this, consider the standard library's use of error. The errors package in Go provides a simple way to create error values. The errors.New function returns an error that formats as the given text:

```
package main

import (
    "errors"
    "fmt"
)

func main() {
    err := errors.New("an error occurred")
    if err != nil {
        fmt.Println(err)
    }
}
```

This program creates a new error with the message "an error occurred" and prints it using fmt.Println, which internally calls the Error() method to convert the error into a string. The output is:

```
an error occurred
```

Custom Errors

You can create custom error types by implementing the Error() method. This approach allows you to add more context and functionality to your error messages.

```
package main

import (
    "fmt"
```

```
)

type MyError struct {
    When string
    What string
}

func (e *MyError) Error() string {
    return fmt.Sprintf("%s: %s", e.When, e.What)
}

func run() error {
    return &MyError{
        When: "Now",
        What: "Something went wrong",
    }
}

func main() {
    if err := run(); err != nil {
        fmt.Println(err)
    }
}
```

In this example, MyError is a struct with two fields: When and What. The Error() method returns a formatted string containing these fields. The run function returns an instance of MyError, and the main function checks for and prints the error if it exists. The output is:

```
Now: Something went wrong
```

Type Assertions

Type assertions can be used to access the underlying concrete value of an error. This technique is particularly useful when you need to handle specific types of errors differently.

```
package main

import (
    "fmt"
)

func doSomething() error {
    return &MyError{
        When: "Later",
        What: "Another error",
    }
}

func main() {
```

```
    err := doSomething()
    if myErr, ok := err.(*MyError); ok {
        fmt.Printf("Custom error: %s\n", myErr)
    } else {
        fmt.Printf("Generic error: %s\n", err)
    }
}
```

In this example, the doSomething function returns a MyError error type. Using a type assertion, we check if the error returned by doSomething is of type *MyError. If so, we print a custom message; otherwise, we print a generic error message. The output is:

```
Custom error: Later: Another error
```

Error Comparisons

Errors can be compared using the errors.Is function. This function helps to determine whether an error is equal to a specific error. The errors package also provides an errors.As function, which checks if an error can be assigned to the target via type assertion.

```
package main

import (
    "errors"
    "fmt"
)

var ErrNotFound = errors.New("not found")

func findSomething() error {
    return ErrNotFound
}

func main() {
    err := findSomething()
    if errors.Is(err, ErrNotFound) {
        fmt.Println("Error is ErrNotFound")
    } else {
        fmt.Println("Different error")
    }
}
```

Here, ErrNotFound is a predefined error. The findSomething function returns this error. In the main function, errors.Is is used to compare the returned error with ErrNotFound. If they match, a specific message is printed; otherwise, a different message is printed. The output is:

```
Error is ErrNotFound
```

Implementing and utilizing the error interface in Go programs is fundamental for robust error handling. It allows fine-grained control over error propagation and facilitates informative error reporting, enhancing the overall code reliability and maintainability.

9.4 Creating Custom Errors

In Go, creating custom errors allows for more expressive error handling and better encapsulation of specific error conditions relevant to your application domain. This section covers the process of defining and using custom errors in a structured and practical manner.

To define a custom error, you typically create a new type that implements the error interface. The error interface in Go is quite simple and requires just one method:

```
type error interface {
    Error() string
}
```

The custom error type can be any Go type, but it's most common to use a struct to provide more context with your errors. Let's create a custom error type, MyError, which includes additional context like an error code.

```
package main

import (
    "fmt"
)

// MyError is a custom error type that includes an error code and message.
type MyError struct {
    Code int
    Message string
}

// Error implements the error interface for MyError.
func (e *MyError) Error() string {
    return fmt.Sprintf("Error %d: %s", e.Code, e.Message)
}

// NewMyError is a constructor for creating a new MyError.
func NewMyError(code int, message string) error {
    return &MyError{
        Code: code,
        Message: message,
```

```
    }
}

func main() {
    err := NewMyError(404, "resource not found")
    if err != nil {
        fmt.Println(err)
    }
}
```

Execution of the above code will produce the following output:

```
Error 404: resource not found
```

This custom error, MyError, provides a more detailed description and can carry additional information such as an error code. To utilize this custom error effectively, it is essential to handle it appropriately within your functions.

Consider the following function that simulates an attempt to access a resource by ID, potentially returning a MyError if the resource is not found:

```
package main

import (
    "fmt"
)

// GetResourceByID simulates resource retrieval and returns a custom error if not
    found.
func GetResourceByID(id int) (string, error) {
    if id == 42 {
        return "The Answer to the Ultimate Question of Life, the Universe, and
            Everything", nil
    }
    return "", NewMyError(404, "resource not found")
}

func main() {
    id := 42
    resource, err := GetResourceByID(id)
    if err != nil {
        if myErr, ok := err.(*MyError); ok {
            fmt.Printf("Custom error: Code %d, Message %s\n", myErr.Code,
                myErr.Message)
        } else {
            fmt.Println("Generic error:", err)
        }
        return
    }
```

```
    fmt.Println("Resource:", resource)
}
```

Execution will yield the following output for two scenarios, 'id := 42' and 'id := 41' (resource not found):

```
Resource: The Answer to the Ultimate Question of Life, the Universe, and Everything

Custom error: Code 404, Message resource not found
```

This example demonstrates how to work with, interpret, and display custom errors. The construction of a custom error using the NewMyError function allows for easy initialization and ensures that the error adheres to a consistent structure.

An additional technique involves using error constants for common error types while allowing for error comparison. Here's an illustration:

```
package main

import (
    "errors"
    "fmt"
)

// Predefined error for resource not found.
var ErrResourceNotFound = errors.New("resource not found")

// FetchResource simulates resource retrieval, returning predefined errors.
func FetchResource(id int) (string, error) {
    if id == 42 {
        return "Life, Universe, Everything", nil
    }
    return "", ErrResourceNotFound
}

func main() {
    id := 41
    resource, err := FetchResource(id)
    if err != nil {
        if errors.Is(err, ErrResourceNotFound) {
            fmt.Println("Checked predefined error: resource not found")
        } else {
            fmt.Println("Generic error:", err)
        }
        return
    }
    fmt.Println("Resource:", resource)
}
```

Output for the above execution will be:

```
Checked predefined error: resource not found
```

This method is advantageous for common error conditions, establishing uniform error values that can be easily compared using the errors.Is function.

Creating custom errors in Go is an essential practice for managing complex error scenarios. By leveraging custom types, constructor functions, and predefined error constants, you achieve informative, maintainable, and predictable error handling within your codebase.

9.5 Error Wrapping with fmt.Errorf

Error handling in Go is a fundamental skill that often involves creating well-defined error messages that can be easily understood and traced. The fmt.Errorf function plays a crucial role in this process by enabling the wrapping of errors. Wrapping errors means adding contextual information to the error message before passing it up the call stack. This helps in understanding where the error occurred and what caused it, making debugging more efficient.

fmt.Errorf is a function in the fmt package that provides formatted I/O similar to fmt.Print, but it returns an error value. Commonly used for wrapping existing errors with additional context, fmt.Errorf supports format specifiers, allowing you to include both static text and dynamic values in the error message.

```
package main

import (
    "fmt"
    "errors"
)

func openFile(filename string) error {
    if filename == "" {
        return errors.New("filename cannot be empty")
    }
    // Imagine logic to open file here
    return nil
}

func processFile(filename string) error {
    err := openFile(filename)
```

```
    if err != nil {
        return fmt.Errorf("failed to open %s: %w", filename, err)
    }
    // Additional processing logic
    return nil
}
func main() {
    err := processFile("")
    if err != nil {
        fmt.Println(err)
    }
}
```

In the example above, the processFile function calls openFile and checks if it returns an error. If an error is encountered, fmt.Errorf is used to add context by including the filename and wrapping the original error. The wrapped error is then returned. The %w verb in fmt.Errorf is used to wrap the original error, which allows for error unwrapping and inspection with the errors package.

```
failed to open : filename cannot be empty
```

The output shows the contextual error message generated by fmt.Errorf. This error message includes both the high-level action (failed to open) and the root cause (filename cannot be empty). Such detailed error messages are invaluable for debugging.

Error Unwrapping

Go's errors package provides utilities to unwrap and inspect wrapped errors. The errors.Unwrap function returns the result of calling the Unwrap method on an error (if the error implements Unwrap). This allows you to retrieve the original error wrapped by fmt.Errorf.

```
package main

import (
    "fmt"
    "errors"
)

func openFile(filename string) error {
    if filename == "" {
        return errors.New("filename cannot be empty")
    }
    // Imagine logic to open file here
    return nil
}
```

```
func processFile(filename string) error {
    err := openFile(filename)
    if err != nil {
        return fmt.Errorf("failed to open %s: %w", filename, err)
    }
    return nil
}

func main() {
    err := processFile("")
    if err != nil {
        fmt.Println(err)
        unwrappedErr := errors.Unwrap(err)
        fmt.Println(unwrappedErr)
    }
}
```

```
failed to open : filename cannot be empty
filename cannot be empty
```

The unwrapped error, displayed by errors.Unwrap, exposes the root cause of the issue, separate from the contextual information added by fmt.Errorf.

Using errors.Is and errors.As

In addition to errors.Unwrap, the errors package offers the errors.Is and errors.As functions, which enable more advanced error inspection. The errors.Is function checks if an error is equivalent to a target error, including through any wrapping. The errors.As function attempts to cast an error to a specific type.

```
package main

import (
    "fmt"
    "errors"
)

var ErrEmptyFilename = errors.New("filename cannot be empty")

func openFile(filename string) error {
    if filename == "" {
        return ErrEmptyFilename
    }
    // Imagine logic to open file here
    return nil
}
```

```
func processFile(filename string) error {
    err := openFile(filename)
    if err != nil {
        return fmt.Errorf("failed to open %s: %w", filename, err)
    }
    return nil
}

func main() {
    err := processFile("")
    if err != nil {
        fmt.Println(err)
        if errors.Is(err, ErrEmptyFilename) {
            fmt.Println("Error is due to an empty filename.")
        }
        var e *os.PathError
        if errors.As(err, &e) {
            fmt.Printf("Path error: %+v\n", e)
        }
    }
}
```

```
failed to open : filename cannot be empty
Error is due to an empty filename.
```

In this example, errors.Is checks if the wrapped error is equivalent to ErrEmptyFilename, allowing targeted error handling. errors.As can be used to determine if the error is of a specific type, though it's not demonstrated fully here as os.PathError is unrelated to this case. These functions significantly enhance error handling capabilities by providing sophisticated inspection methods for wrapped errors.

9.6 Handling Errors in Functions

Handling errors in functions is a fundamental aspect of programming in Go. Error handling ensures that when a function encounters an issue, it can notify the calling code appropriately. Let's delve into the principles and techniques for handling errors effectively within functions.

In Go, functions that perform operations which could result in an error typically return an error as their last return value. This convention enables the caller to check for errors and handle them accordingly. Here is a basic example:

```
package main
```

```
import (
    "errors"
    "fmt"
)

func divide(a, b float64) (float64, error) {
    if b == 0 {
        return 0, errors.New("division by zero")
    }
    return a / b, nil
}

func main() {
    result, err := divide(4, 0)
    if err != nil {
        fmt.Println("Error:", err)
        return
    }
    fmt.Println("Result:", result)
}
```

In this example, the divide function checks if the divisor b is zero. If so, it returns an error created with errors.New. Otherwise, it returns the result of the division and nil to indicate the absence of an error.

When calling this function in the main, we must always check if err is nil before using the result. This practice helps to ensure that errors are caught and handled appropriately.

The errors package provides basic error handling primitives, but Go 1.13 introduced the fmt.Errorf function, which supports formatted error messages. Here is an enhanced version using fmt.Errorf:

```
package main

import (
    "fmt"
)

func divide(a, b float64) (float64, error) {
    if b == 0 {
        return 0, fmt.Errorf("cannot divide %v by zero", a)
    }
    return a / b, nil
}

func main() {
    result, err := divide(4, 0)
    if err != nil {
        fmt.Println("Error:", err)
        return
```

```
    }
    fmt.Println("Result:", result)
}
```

Here, fmt.Errorf allows us to include the operand a in the error message, providing more context to the caller. This technique becomes particularly useful for debugging complex issues.

In addition to checking for nil errors, another common pattern is to print the error and return from the function immediately if an error is encountered. This pattern is often referred to as "early return" and keeps the code clean and readable.

Let's consider a more complex example where multiple functions return errors, and the caller function needs to handle these:

```
package main

import (
    "errors"
    "fmt"
)

func readConfig() (string, error) {
    return "", errors.New("failed to read config")
}

func connectDatabase() error {
    return errors.New("database connection failed")
}

func startServer() error {
    return nil
}

func startApplication() error {
    config, err := readConfig()
    if err != nil {
        return fmt.Errorf("startApplication: %w", err)
    }
    fmt.Println("Config:", config)

    err = connectDatabase()
    if err != nil {
        return fmt.Errorf("startApplication: %w", err)
    }

    err = startServer()
    if err != nil {
        return fmt.Errorf("startApplication: %w", err)
    }
```

```
    return nil
}

func main() {
    err := startApplication()
    if err != nil {
        fmt.Println("Error starting application:", err)
        return
    }
    fmt.Println("Application started successfully")
}
```

In this example, startApplication aggregates errors from three different operations: reading a configuration, connecting to a database, and starting a server. If any operation fails, it wraps the error with additional context using fmt.Errorf and the %w format verb.

Errors should propagate up the call stack until they can be handled appropriately. In the main function, we handle the error by checking if it is nil and printing a suitable message. This pattern facilitates structured error handling and improves code maintainability.

Proper error handling in functions is crucial for developing reliable software systems. Always ensure that errors are checked and managed correctly, providing meaningful messages to assist in diagnosing issues and debugging.

9.7 Deferred Error Handling with defer

The defer statement in Go is used to postpone the execution of a function or a method until the surrounding function returns. This is particularly useful for resource cleanup tasks such as closing files, network connections, or database transactions. When implementing error handling, defer helps ensure that necessary cleanup code runs even if an error occurs.

Consider a typical use case of defer in file handling. The following example demonstrates how to open a file and ensure it gets closed even if an error occurs during the file operations:

```
package main

import (
    "fmt"
    "os"
```

```
)

func main() {
    file, err := os.Open("example.txt")
    if err != nil {
        fmt.Println("Error opening file:", err)
        return
    }
    defer file.Close()

    // Read or write operations on the file
    // Any error handling code
}
```

The defer file.Close() statement ensures that the file is closed when main() function returns, regardless of whether an error occurs during file operations.

Deferred functions are executed in last-in-first-out order. This is especially beneficial when multiple resources need to be cleaned up. Consider the following example involving multiple deferred calls:

```
package main

import (
    "fmt"
    "os"
)

func main() {
    fmt.Println("Start")
    file1, err := os.Open("file1.txt")
    if err != nil {
        fmt.Println("Error opening file1:", err)
        return
    }
    defer file1.Close()

    file2, err := os.Open("file2.txt")
    if err != nil {
        fmt.Println("Error opening file2:", err)
        return
    }
    defer file2.Close()

    fmt.Println("Performing file operations")
}
```

In this scenario, file2.Close() will be called before file1.Close() because file2.Close() was deferred after file1.Close().

One common pattern in Go is to use defer for error logging or recovery. The following example demonstrates a function that uses defer to handle resource cleanup and additional error logging:

```
package main

import (
    "fmt"
    "os"
)

func processFile(filename string) {
    file, err := os.Open(filename)
    if err != nil {
        fmt.Println("Error opening file:", err)
        return
    }
    defer func() {
        if cerr := file.Close(); cerr != nil {
            fmt.Println("Error closing file:", cerr)
        }
    }()

    // File processing code, possibly inducing an error
    _, err = file.Stat()
    if err != nil {
        fmt.Println("Error stating file:", err)
        return
    }

    // Additional file processing code
}

func main() {
    processFile("example.txt")
}
```

In this example, the deferred function ensures that any error occurring while closing the file is appropriately logged. This pattern ensures robustness, especially when dealing with multiple potential points of error within a function.

Deferred error handling can also be used in conjunction with the recover function to handle panics gracefully, preventing the program from crashing unexpectedly. The following example illustrates this approach:

```
package main

import (
    "fmt"
)
```

```
func main() {
    defer func() {
        if r := recover(); r != nil {
            fmt.Println("Recovered from panic:", r)
        }
    }()

    panic("An unexpected error occurred")
    fmt.Println("This line will not be executed")
}
```

Here, the deferred function uses recover to catch any panic that occurs within main. As a result, the program doesn't crash; instead, it prints the message "Recovered from panic: An unexpected error occurred".

To summarize, defer is a powerful mechanism in Go for ensuring resource cleanup and handling post-execution tasks. Its application in error handling is critical for writing robust and resilient code, enabling developers to manage errors and resources efficiently. It is vital to understand the sequential order of deferred function calls and to use defer strategically within functions to cover all potential error scenarios.

9.8 Panic and Recover Mechanism

The panic and recover mechanism in Go is designed for managing unexpected conditions and errors that cannot be handled gracefully during execution. While Go's philosophy emphasizes error management through explicit return values, panic and recover provide additional control for exceptional situations.

Panic is a built-in function that stops the normal execution of the current goroutine. When a panic occurs, the function in which the panic call resides will cease to execute, and control will be transferred to the nearest deferred function. If the deferred function contains a call to recover, it can halt the panic, thus resuming normal execution and allowing the programmer to handle the error.

The panic function accepts an argument of any type that can describe the error or unexpected situation. Here's a basic example of a panic:

```
package main

import "fmt"

func main() {
```

```
    fmt.Println("Starting the program...")
    panic("A severe error occurred: Division by zero")
    fmt.Println("This line will not be printed, as panic stops the execution.")
}
```

When this program is executed, the output will be:

```
Starting the program...
panic: A severe error occurred: Division by zero

goroutine 1 [running]:
main.main()
    /path/to/source.go:6 +0x49
exit status 2
```

The output shows that the execution stops where the panic was called, and the error message is printed. It is important to understand that panic should not be used for regular error handling but for situations that are truly unexpected and irrecoverable.

Recover is a built-in function that can regain control of a panicking goroutine. It stops the panic and returns the value passed to the call of panic. Recover can only be called within a deferred function. Here's an example demonstrating the use of recover:

```
package main

import "fmt"

func main() {
    defer func() {
        if r := recover(); r != nil {
            fmt.Println("Recovered from panic:", r)
        }
    }()

    fmt.Println("Starting the program...")
    panic("A severe error occurred: Division by zero")
    fmt.Println("This line will not be printed, as panic stops the execution.")
}
```

Executing this code will result in:

```
Starting the program...
Recovered from panic: A severe error occurred: Division by zero
```

In this example, the deferred function recovers from the panic and prints the recovered message. Once recovered, the program exits the deferred function and continues execution after the defer statement. However, if no recover is called, the program will terminate as demonstrated in the earlier example.

Consider the following more complex example where panic and recover can be used to handle errors occurring within a nested function call hierarchy:

```
package main

import (
    "fmt"
)

func main() {
    defer func() {
        if r := recover(); r != nil {
            fmt.Println("Recovered in main:", r)
        }
    }()
    fmt.Println("Calling functionA...")
    functionA()
    fmt.Println("Returned normally from functionA.")
}

func functionA() {
    defer func() {
        if r := recover(); r != nil {
            fmt.Println("Recovered in functionA:", r)
        }
    }()
    fmt.Println("Calling functionB...")
    functionB()
    fmt.Println("Returned normally from functionB.")
}

func functionB() {
    fmt.Println("Inside functionB...")
    panic("Panic in functionB")
}
```

The output of running this program is:

```
Calling functionA...
Calling functionB...
Inside functionB...
Recovered in functionA: Panic in functionB
Returned normally from functionA.
Recovered in main: Panic in functionA
```

This example demonstrates how the control flow changes with panic and recover. When a panic occurs in functionB, the deferred function within functionA catches the panic and recovers from it, allowing functionA to return normally. The normal flow is then continued back to main, where another deferred function recovers from any remaining panic, preserving the overall program's execution flow.

Importantly, using panic and recover judiciously is crucial. Overusing them can lead to code that is difficult to understand and maintain. Best practices suggest reserving panic for truly exceptional circumstances—for instance, when a program encounters an invalid state that it cannot handle at runtime.

Understanding the proper use of panic and recover fortifies the developer's ability to create robust and resilient applications. It augments traditional error handling methods with a mechanism to manage unexpected failures gracefully, thereby enhancing the stability of the software system.

9.9 Best Practices for Error Handling

Error handling plays a crucial role in enhancing the robustness and maintainability of Go programs. Adhering to best practices ensures that errors are managed predictably, facilitating debugging and maintaining code quality. Below is a comprehensive look at several best practices when managing errors in Go.

1. Return Errors to Callers

In Go, the idiomatic way to handle errors is to return them to the caller. This practice leverages the built-in capabilities of Go functions, which can return multiple values. Typically, an operation that might produce an error should return two values: the result of the operation and an error. For instance:

```
func divide(a, b float64) (float64, error) {
    if b == 0 {
        return 0, fmt.Errorf("cannot divide by zero")
    }
    return a / b, nil
}
```

Here, fmt.Errorf is used to generate an error, and it is returned alongside the result. The caller can then handle the error appropriately.

2. Handle Errors Immediately

It is best to handle errors at the point where they occur or at the earliest possible opportunity. By doing so, the context of the error remains clear, making it easier to understand and debug the issue. Handling errors immediately also reduces the cognitive load required to reason about how far the error might propagate before it gets handled.

For example:

```
result, err := divide(4, 0)
if err != nil {
    log.Fatalf("error: %v", err)
}
fmt.Println(result)
```

In this snippet, the error is checked and handled right after the call to divide, ensuring that subsequent logic only executes if no error occurred.

3. Provide Context in Errors

When creating or returning an error, it is vital to include as much context as possible. This helps in tracing the source and nature of the error more efficiently. To provide context, you can wrap errors or create descriptive error messages.

```
err := fmt.Errorf("processing file: %v", originalError)
```

The contextual information ("processing file") makes the error message more informative, aiding in debugging.

4. Use Sentinel Errors Appropriately

Sentinel errors are predefined, immutable error values used to represent specific error conditions. While they are useful for checking against specific error conditions, overuse can lead to tightly coupled code that is hard to maintain. Use sentinel errors judiciously and prefer error wrapping for adding context.

```
var ErrNotFound = errors.New("not found")

func findValue(key string) (string, error) {
    if key == "" {
        return "", ErrNotFound
    }
    // ...
}
```

ErrNotFound can be used for comparison by the caller to check if a specific error condition occurred.

5. Avoid Using Panic for Error Handling

Using panic for error handling is generally discouraged in Go, as it is meant for unexpected, non-recoverable conditions. The panic function disrupts the normal flow of control and should be reserved for truly exceptional states. Prefer returning errors instead.

```
func readFile(filename string) ([]byte, error) {
    data, err := ioutil.ReadFile(filename)
    if err != nil {
        return nil, fmt.Errorf("could not read file %s: %v", filename, err)
    }
    return data, nil
}
```

This function returns an error rather than calling panic.

6. Group Error Handling Logic

For readability and maintainability, group your error handling logic together. When possible, this can be consolidated in the main execution flow or in specific utility functions that handle common error cases.

```
func processFile(filename string) error {
    data, err := readFile(filename)
    if err != nil {
        return fmt.Errorf("processing file %s: %v", filename, err)
    }

    // process data...

    return nil
}

func main() {
    if err := processFile("data.txt"); err != nil {
        log.Fatalf("Error: %v", err)
    }
}
```

By grouping error-handling code together into a single responsibility function, the main function becomes clean and straightforward.

7. Leverage the errors Package

The errors package introduced in Go 1.13 provides a suite of new functions to deal with errors more effectively, such as errors.Is, errors.As, and errors.Unwrap. These functions enable better handling and inspection of wrapped errors.

```
if errors.Is(err, ErrNotFound) {
```

```
    fmt.Println("The specified resource was not found.")
}
```

Using these functions helps to create more understandable and inspectable error handling.

8. Centralize Error Logging

For larger applications, centralizing error logging can make it easier to maintain consistent logging behavior and simplify debugging. Implement a dedicated logging function or utility to handle all error logging in a consistent format.

```
func logError(err error) {
    if err != nil {
        log.Printf("ERROR: %v", err)
    }
}
```

9. Test Error Conditions

Testing error conditions is as crucial as testing successful code paths. Write tests that specifically trigger and verify the behavior under erroneous conditions. Use techniques like table-driven tests to ensure comprehensive coverage.

```
func TestDivide(t *testing.T) {
    tests := []struct {
        a, b float64
        want float64
        err error
    }{
        {4, 2, 2, nil},
        {4, 0, 0, ErrDivideByZero},
    }

    for _, tt := range tests {
        got, err := divide(tt.a, tt.b)
        if got != tt.want || !errors.Is(err, tt.err) {
            t.Errorf("divide(%f, %f) = (%f, %v); want (%f, %v)",
                tt.a, tt.b, got, err, tt.want, tt.err)
        }
    }
}
```

By following these best practices in error handling, you can write more reliable and maintainable Go programs with clear and effective error management.

9.10 Common Error Handling Patterns

In Go, handling errors consistently and effectively is crucial for maintaining robust and maintainable code. This section explores common error handling patterns employed in Go programming, offering detailed mechanisms to enhance error management and ensure clearer, more understandable code.

One of the foundational patterns in Go is error propagation. This involves returning errors from functions when something goes wrong. A common idiom for this is the immediate check-return pattern, where functions return errors as soon as they are detected, allowing the caller to handle them appropriately.

```
func readFile(fileName string) error {
    file, err := os.Open(fileName)
    if err != nil {
        return fmt.Errorf("failed to open file: %w", err)
    }
    defer file.Close()
    _, err = io.Copy(os.Stdout, file)
    if err != nil {
        return fmt.Errorf("failed to read file: %w", err)
    }
    return nil
}
```

Listing 9.5: Immediate Check-Return Pattern Example

In this example, the function readFile performs error checking immediately after every operation that could fail, making it clear where and why a failure occurred.

Another common pattern is grouping multiple error checks using a consistently styled block. This is often done to simplify and streamline error handling, especially when multiple operations could fail within a single function.

```
func processFiles(files []string) error {
    for _, fileName := range files {
        file, err := os.Open(fileName)
        if err != nil {
            return fmt.Errorf("cannot open file %s: %w", fileName, err)
        }
        defer file.Close()

        err = process(file)
        if err != nil {
            return fmt.Errorf("error processing file %s: %w", fileName, err)
```

```
        }
    }
    return nil
}
```

Listing 9.6: Grouped Error Checking Pattern Example

In this pattern, error checks are grouped logically within repeated operations, making the code more readable and manageable.

A widespread pattern in Go is the use of sentinel errors. These are predefined errors that the code returns under specific conditions. The errors package in Go provides functions to create sentinel errors.

```
var ErrNotFound = errors.New("resource not found")

func findResource(id string) (Resource, error) {
    if id == "" {
        return Resource{}, ErrNotFound
    }
    // Perform operations to find the resource
    return resource, nil
}
```

Listing 9.7: Sentinel Errors Example

Using sentinel errors like ErrNotFound makes it easier for the caller to identify and handle specific error conditions.

Error wrapping with fmt.Errorf is another technique utilized to provide more context when returning errors. By wrapping the error, the programmer can add additional information about where the error occurred or the state of the program when the error was detected.

```
func computeValue(input int) (int, error) {
    if input < 0 {
        return 0, fmt.Errorf("input value %d is invalid: %w", input,
            ErrInvalidInput)
    }
    // Perform computations
    return result, nil
}
```

Listing 9.8: Error Wrapping Example

In this case, the error returned with fmt.Errorf carries more comprehensive context, aiding in debugging and error tracing.

The idiom of handling errors at boundary locations is pivotal in Go. Boundary locations refer to the points where an operation interacts with external systems or components, such as file systems, network connections, or databases. Handling errors at these boundaries ensure that internal state management remains clean and predictable.

```
func fetchDataFromAPI(apiURL string) ([]byte, error) {
    response, err := http.Get(apiURL)
    if err != nil {
        return nil, fmt.Errorf("failed to fetch data: %w", err)
    }
    defer response.Body.Close()

    body, err := io.ReadAll(response.Body)
    if err != nil {
        return nil, fmt.Errorf("failed to read response body: %w", err)
    }
    return body, nil
}
```

Listing 9.9: Boundary Error Handling Example

Here, errors are handled directly at the point where HTTP requests and responses are dealt with, ensuring that any issues are managed where they arise.

Handling errors alongside logging is an effective approach to monitor the application's behavior. It's common to log errors before returning them, providing a traceable record of what went wrong.

```
func loadConfiguration(filePath string) (*Config, error) {
    file, err := os.Open(filePath)
    if err != nil {
        log.Printf("error opening config file %s: %v", filePath, err)
        return nil, fmt.Errorf("unable to open configuration file: %w", err)
    }
    defer file.Close()

    // Read and parse the configuration
    return config, nil
}
```

Listing 9.10: Logging Error Example

The log statements offer insights into error occurrences which is invaluable for troubleshooting in production environments.

A more sophisticated pattern involves using custom error types to represent different error conditions within a program. This approach enables richer error details and more precise error handling.

```
type ValidationError struct {
    Field string
```

```
    Message string
}

func (e *ValidationError) Error() string {
    return fmt.Sprintf("validation error on %s: %s", e.Field, e.Message)
}

func validate(data map[string]string) error {
    for field, value := range data {
        if value == "" {
            return &ValidationError{Field: field, Message: "cannot be empty"}
        }
    }
    return nil
}
```

Listing 9.11: Custom Error Types Example

Custom error types like ValidationError provide the flexibility to add fields and methods specific to the error being modeled, facilitating more granular error management.

These patterns aid in writing informative, maintainable, and reliable Go code by promoting consistency in error handling, underscoring the significance of thorough error management practices.

Chapter 10

Standard Library and Packages

This chapter provides an overview of Go's standard library, highlighting key packages that handle common tasks. It covers working with strings, file I/O, error handling, and various data structures. The chapter also explores time and date operations, networking, HTTP handling, and concurrency utilities. Additionally, it discusses parsing JSON, building command-line applications, and managing temporary files, demonstrating the versatility and power of Go's built-in packages.

10.1 Introduction to Go's Standard Library

The Go programming language comes equipped with a comprehensive standard library that supports a wide array of programming tasks, ranging from basic operations like string manipulation and file handling to more advanced functions such as networking, concurrency control, and web server implementation. This section offers an overview of the core components of Go's standard library, providing the foundational knowledge required for mastering the intricacies of the language.

The standard library is vast, encompassing various packages that address different needs. These packages allow developers to write robust, efficient, and high-performance applications. To better understand the structure and utility of Go's standard library, we will explore key packages and their functionalities.

strings and strconv Packages: The strings package provides various functions to manipulate UTF-8 encoded strings, such as substring search, case conversion, and string splitting or joining. The strconv package is used for conversions to and from string representations of basic data types.

os and ioutil Packages: File input/output operations are handled through the os and ioutil packages. The os package provides the interface to operating system functionality, including file and directory manipulation, whereas ioutil contains utility functions for simpler file operations like reading and writing files.

errors and fmt Packages: Error handling is a critical aspect of Go programming. The errors package provides simple error handling primitives, and the fmt package is used for formatted I/O, including error message generation.

container Package: This package offers implementations of standard data structures such as heaps, lists, and ring buffers. These are essential for constructing more complex data management solutions.

time Package: The time package provides functionality for measuring and displaying time. It includes capabilities for time manipulation, formatting, and parsing of time-related data.

net Package: The net package encompasses functionality for network I/O, allowing the creation and use of network clients and servers, handling TCP and UDP connections, and performing domain name resolution.

net/http Package: Building upon net, the net/http package facilitates the creation and management of HTTP clients and servers. This package is instrumental in developing web applications and services.

sync and atomic Packages: Concurrency is a pillar of Go. The sync package includes synchronization primitives like mutexes and wait groups, while the atomic package provides low-level atomic memory primitives essential for concurrent programming.

encoding/json Package: JSON parsing and generation are crucial for many modern applications. The encoding/json package enables the seamless conversion between Go objects and JSON data interchange format.

flag Package: Command-line interfaces (CLIs) are frequently used for automation and tooling. The flag package supports the definition and parsing of command-line flags.

ioutil Package: In addition to its role in file handling, the ioutil package also provides functions for creating temporary files and directories, simplifying tasks requiring non-permanent storage.

To illustrate the practicality of Go's standard library, consider the following example where we read a file and process its content as a string. We will then convert this string into two types of data using the strconv package.

```
// Sample program illustrating file reading and string conversion using Go's
    standard library.

package main

import (
    "fmt"
    "io/ioutil"
    "os"
    "strconv"
)

func main() {
    // Reading a file content
    data, err := ioutil.ReadFile("example.txt")
    if err != nil {
        fmt.Println("File reading error", err)
        return
    }

    fileContent := string(data)
    fmt.Println("File content:", fileContent)

    // Example of string conversion
    if intValue, err := strconv.Atoi(fileContent); err == nil {
        fmt.Println("Converted integer:", intValue)
    } else {
        fmt.Println("Error converting string to integer:", err)
    }

    if floatValue, err := strconv.ParseFloat(fileContent, 64); err == nil {
        fmt.Println("Converted float:", floatValue)
    } else {
        fmt.Println("Error converting string to float:", err)
    }
}
```

The file example.txt should exist in the same directory, containing numeric string data for conversion. Running the program will read the content of the file, output it, and attempt to convert the string into an integer and a floating-point number respectively.

```
File content: 123.45
Converted integer: Error converting string to integer: strconv.Atoi: parsing "123.45": invalid syntax
Converted float: 123.45
```

This example underscores the ease with which Go's standard library allows us to handle file input, perform string manipulations, and execute type conversions, demonstrating the library's flexibility and utility in real-world scenarios. An in-depth understanding and efficient use of these packages is essential for any Go programmer aiming to write clean, maintainable, and efficient code.

10.2 Working with Strings: strings and strconv Packages

Go's standard library offers robust support for string manipulation through the strings and strconv packages. These packages provide a multitude of functions for handling a variety of string operations and conversions between strings and other data types. Understanding how to leverage these packages effectively is essential for performing text processing and data transformation tasks in Go.

The strings package contains functions for manipulating and analyzing UTF-8 encoded strings. This package covers common operations such as comparing, splitting, trimming, and modifying strings. Here is an example showcasing some fundamental functionalities of the strings package:

```
package main

import (
    "fmt"
    "strings"
)

func main() {
    sample := "Go is an open source programming language."

    // Checking if the string contains a specific substring
    fmt.Println(strings.Contains(sample, "open")) // true

    // Counting occurrences of a substring
    fmt.Println(strings.Count(sample, "g")) // 3
```

```
    // HasPrefix and HasSuffix
    fmt.Println(strings.HasPrefix(sample, "Go")) // true
    fmt.Println(strings.HasSuffix(sample, "language.")) // true

    // Changing string case
    fmt.Println(strings.ToUpper(sample)) // "GO IS AN OPEN SOURCE
        PROGRAMMING LANGUAGE."
    fmt.Println(strings.ToLower(sample)) // "go is an open source programming
        language."

    // Splitting a string into substrings
    words := strings.Split(sample, " ")
    fmt.Println(words)
}
```

Outputs:

```
true
3
true
true
GO IS AN OPEN SOURCE PROGRAMMING LANGUAGE.
go is an open source programming language.
[Go is an open source programming language.]
```

strings.Contains checks if a string sample contains the substring "open". The strings.Count function counts the number of non-overlapping instances of g in the given string. strings.HasPrefix and strings.HasSuffix check for specific substrings at the beginning and end of the string, respectively. The strings.ToUpper and strings.ToLower functions return a copy of the string converted to upper or lower case. Finally, strings.Split splits the string into all substrings separated by the delimiter, returning a slice of substrings.

Moreover, the strings package includes functions like Join, which concatenates slice elements into a single string separated by a specified delimiter, and TrimSpace, which removes all leading and trailing whitespace:

```
package main

import (
    "fmt"
    "strings"
)

func main() {
    words := []string{"Go", "is", "fun"}
```

```
    // Joining a slice of strings
    fmt.Println(strings.Join(words, " ")) // "Go is fun"

    // Trimming whitespace characters
    padded := " Hello, Go! "
    fmt.Println(strings.TrimSpace(padded)) // "Hello, Go!"
}
```

Outputs:

```
Go is fun
Hello, Go!
```

The strconv package is used for conversions between strings and other basic data types such as integers, floating-point numbers, and booleans. Key functions in the strconv package include Atoi, Itoa, ParseFloat, FormatFloat, ParseBool, and FormatBool.

The following examples illustrate the fundamental conversions using strconv:

```
package main

import (
    "fmt"
    "strconv"
)

func main() {
    // Converting string to integer
    str := "42"
    num, err := strconv.Atoi(str)
    if err != nil {
        fmt.Println(err)
    } else {
        fmt.Println(num) // 42
    }

    // Converting integer to string
    numStr := strconv.Itoa(42)
    fmt.Println(numStr) // "42"

    // Converting string to float
    floatStr := "3.1415926535"
    floatNum, err := strconv.ParseFloat(floatStr, 64)
    if err != nil {
        fmt.Println(err)
    } else {
        fmt.Println(floatNum) // 3.1415926535
    }
```

```
    // Converting float to string
    floatToStr := strconv.FormatFloat(3.1415926535, 'f', -1, 64)
    fmt.Println(floatToStr) // "3.1415926535"

    // Converting string to boolean
    boolStr := "true"
    boolVal, err := strconv.ParseBool(boolStr)
    if err != nil {
        fmt.Println(err)
    } else {
        fmt.Println(boolVal) // true
    }

    // Converting boolean to string
    boolToStr := strconv.FormatBool(true)
    fmt.Println(boolToStr) // "true"
}
```

Outputs:

```
42
42
3.1415926535
3.1415926535
true
true
```

strconv.Atoi converts a string to an integer (int), while strconv.Itoa performs the reverse operation, converting an integer to a string. The strconv.ParseFloat and strconv.FormatFloat functions work similarly for floating-point numbers, allowing specification of precision and format. For boolean values, strconv.ParseBool converts a string representation to a boolean, and strconv.FormatBool converts a boolean to its string representation.

The strings and strconv packages empower developers to execute a wide range of string operations and transformations, providing tools necessary for efficient and effective text processing in Go. The computational efficiency and extensive functionalities make these packages indispensable for general programming tasks involving strings.

10.3 File I/O: os and ioutil Packages

When developing applications in Go, interacting with the file system can be a common task. The Go standard library provides robust and straightforward tools for file I/O operations through the os and ioutil packages. This section will delve into the methods and functions provided by these packages, examining their usage in practical scenarios.

os package offers low-level functions and types to interact with the operating system, including file and directory manipulation. We will cover fundamental functionalities such as reading from and writing to files, managing file permissions, and handling file paths.

To begin with, consider the task of reading a file's content. Utilizing the os package, a file can be opened using the os.Open() function, which returns a file descriptor and potentially an error, as illustrated below:

```
import (
    "os"
    "fmt"
)

func main() {
    file, err := os.Open("example.txt")
    if err != nil {
        fmt.Println("Error opening file:", err)
        return
    }
    defer file.Close()

    // Further file processing
}
```

In this code, the os.Open() function attempts to open "example.txt". If unsuccessful, it returns an error. The defer statement ensures that the file is closed when the surrounding function returns, thus preventing resource leaks.

Reading the file's content can be done using various methods like file.Read(), which reads bytes into a slice, or more conveniently using the bufio package, as shown:

```
import (
    "bufio"
    "os"
    "fmt"
)

func main() {
    file, err := os.Open("example.txt")
    if err != nil {
        fmt.Println("Error opening file:", err)
        return
    }
    defer file.Close()
```

```
    scanner := bufio.NewScanner(file)
    for scanner.Scan() {
        fmt.Println(scanner.Text())
    }
    if err := scanner.Err(); err != nil {
        fmt.Println("Error reading file:", err)
    }
}
```

In this snippet, bufio.NewScanner() creates a scanner to read the file line-by-line, enhancing performance and simplicity.

For writing to a file, os.Create() can be used, which truncates the file if it already exists or creates it if it does not:

```
import (
    "os"
    "fmt"
)

func main() {
    file, err := os.Create("example.txt")
    if err != nil {
        fmt.Println("Error creating file:", err)
        return
    }
    defer file.Close()

    _, err = file.WriteString("Hello, World!\n")
    if err != nil {
        fmt.Println("Error writing to file:", err)
    }
}
```

Here, os.Create ensures that example.txt is available for writing, and file.WriteString() writes the specified string to the file.

Moving on to the ioutil package, it offers utility functions that simplify file reading and writing. For instance, reading a file's entire content into memory is seamlessly handled by ioutil.ReadFile():

```
import (
    "io/ioutil"
    "fmt"
)

func main() {
    content, err := ioutil.ReadFile("example.txt")
    if err != nil {
        fmt.Println("Error reading file:", err)
```

```
        return
    }
    fmt.Println(string(content))
}
```

This function reads the file into a byte slice, reducing the need for byte-by-byte or line-by-line processing. Similarly, ioutil.WriteFile() facilitates writing a byte slice to a file with specific permissions:

```
import (
    "io/ioutil"
    "os"
    "fmt"
)

func main() {
    content := []byte("Hello, World!\n")
    err := ioutil.WriteFile("example.txt", content, 0644)
    if err != nil {
        fmt.Println("Error writing to file:", err)
    }
}
```

Here, ioutil.WriteFile() writes the byte slice to example.txt with 0644 permissions, denoting readable and writable by the owner, and readable by others.

File manipulation tasks like renaming or removing files can be achieved using the os.Rename() and os.Remove() functions, respectively:

```
import (
    "os"
    "fmt"
)

func main() {
    err := os.Rename("example.txt", "new_example.txt")
    if err != nil {
        fmt.Println("Error renaming file:", err)
    }

    err = os.Remove("new_example.txt")
    if err != nil {
        fmt.Println("Error removing file:", err)
    }
}
```

These functions provide straightforward interfaces for renaming and deleting files.

The os package also includes methods for retrieving and modifying file information through os.Stat() and os.Chmod():

```
import (
    "os"
    "fmt"
)

func main() {
    info, err := os.Stat("example.txt")
    if err != nil {
        fmt.Println("Error getting file information:", err)
        return
    }
    fmt.Println("File Name:", info.Name())
    fmt.Println("Is Directory:", info.IsDir())
    fmt.Println("File Size:", info.Size())

    err = os.Chmod("example.txt", 0755)
    if err != nil {
        fmt.Println("Error changing file permissions:", err)
    }
}
```

In this code, os.Stat() retrieves file metadata, while os.Chmod() modifies the file's permissions.

Understanding both the os and ioutil packages enables efficient handling of file I/O operations, providing the foundation for developing a wide array of Go applications.

10.4 Error Handling: errors and fmt Packages

In Go, error handling is a critical aspect of writing robust and maintainable code. Unlike some other languages that use exceptions, Go uses explicit error handling through returned values. The errors and fmt packages are fundamental in this context.

The errors package in Go provides a simple mechanism for error handling by defining an error type, which is an interface. The error interface consists of a single method:

```
type error interface {
    Error() string
}
```

This implies that any type that implements the Error() method, returning a string, satisfies the error interface. A common pattern for creating errors is using the errors.New function, which returns an error with the specified message.

Here's a basic example of creating and handling an error:

```
package main

import (
    "errors"
    "fmt"
)

func mightFail(shouldFail bool) error {
    if shouldFail {
        return errors.New("something went wrong")
    }
    return nil
}

func main() {
    err := mightFail(true)
    if err != nil {
        fmt.Println("Error encountered:", err)
    } else {
        fmt.Println("Operation succeeded")
    }
}
```

```
Error encountered: something went wrong
```

The mightFail function returns an error if the input parameter is true. In the main function, we check the returned error. If it is not nil, we handle the error by printing it. Otherwise, we proceed as usual.

The fmt package provides formatting functions that are widely used for error handling. The fmt.Errorf function is particularly useful for creating formatted error messages. This function is analogous to errors.New, but it allows formatted strings, enabling more descriptive error messages.

Here's an example of using fmt.Errorf:

```
package main

import (
    "fmt"
)
```

```
func divide(a, b float64) (float64, error) {
    if b == 0 {
        return 0, fmt.Errorf("cannot divide by zero: %v / %v", a, b)
    }
    return a / b, nil
}

func main() {
    result, err := divide(4, 0)
    if err != nil {
        fmt.Println(err)
    } else {
        fmt.Println("Result:", result)
    }
}
```

```
cannot divide by zero: 4 / 0
```

In this example, the divide function attempts to divide a by b. If b is zero, it returns an error using fmt.Errorf with a formatted message. In the main function, we handle the error by checking if err is not nil and then printing the error message.

To build more sophisticated error handling, Go supports custom error types by creating types that implement the error interface. This method helps encapsulate more context about the error.

Here is an example of a custom error type:

```
package main

import (
    "fmt"
)

type DivideError struct {
    Dividend float64
    Divisor float64
}

func (e *DivideError) Error() string {
    return fmt.Sprintf("cannot divide %v by %v", e.Dividend, e.Divisor)
}

func divide(a, b float64) (float64, error) {
    if b == 0 {
        return 0, &DivideError{a, b}
    }
    return a / b, nil
}
```

```
func main() {
    result, err := divide(4, 0)
    if err != nil {
        fmt.Println("Error:", err)
    } else {
        fmt.Println("Result:", result)
    }
}
```

```
Error: cannot divide 4 by 0
```

In this example, DivideError is a custom error type that includes the dividend and divisor as fields. The Error() method provides a detailed error message. The divide function returns a DivideError when a division by zero is attempted. In the main function, the error is handled similarly to previous examples.

By leveraging these powerful features of the errors and fmt packages, Go developers can implement comprehensive, clear, and informative error handling.

10.5 Data Structures: container Package

The container package in Go's standard library provides advanced data structure implementations that underpin many common algorithms and operations. This package ensures efficient operations for stacks, lists, and heap-based priority queues. It includes three primary subpackages: container/list, container/ring, and container/heap.

container/list: This sub-package implements a doubly linked list, allowing traversal in both directions. Each element in the list is of type ListElement, structured as follows:

```
type Element struct {
    next, prev *Element
    list *List
    Value interface{}
}
```

A new linked list is created using the New function:

```
list := list.New()
```

To manipulate the list, several methods are available:

- PushBack(value interface{}) *Element: Adds a value at the end of the list. - PushFront(value interface{}) *Element: Adds a value at the beginning of the list. - InsertAfter(value interface{}, mark *Element) *Element: Inserts a value after a specified element. - InsertBefore(value interface{}, mark *Element) *Element: Inserts a value before a specified element.

Example usage:

```
package main

import (
    "container/list"
    "fmt"
)

func main() {
    l := list.New()
    l.PushBack(1)
    l.PushBack(2)
    l.PushFront(0)

    for e := l.Front(); e != nil; e = e.Next() {
        fmt.Println(e.Value)
    }
}
```

Upon execution, this will produce:

```
0
1
2
```

container/ring: This sub-package implements a circular list or ring buffer. Each ring element points to the next and previous elements, creating a closed loop. The ring's zero value is a one-element ring. As such, to initialize a ring of size n, you use:

```
r := ring.New(n)
```

Populating and manipulating the ring requires methods such as:

- Link(s *Ring) *Ring: Connects ring s after r and returns the modified ring. - Unlink(n int) *Ring: Removes the n elements from the ring starting at r.next.

Example demonstrating a ring traversal:

```
package main
```

```
import (
    "container/ring"
    "fmt"
)

func main() {
    r := ring.New(3)

    // Populate ring with values: 1, 2, 3
    for i := 1; i <= r.Len(); i++ {
        r.Value = i
        r = r.Next()
    }

    r.Do(func(p interface{}) {
        fmt.Println(p.(int))
    })
}
```

Upon execution, this will produce:

```
1
2
3
```

container/heap: This sub-package enables the creation and maintenance of a heap (priority queue). A heap is a specialized tree-based data structure that satisfies the heap property. In a max heap, for any given node C, if P is a parent node of C, then the value of P is greater than or equal to the value of C. A min heap is the opposite.

To use container/heap, one must create a type that implements the heap.Interface:

```
package main

import (
    "container/heap"
    "fmt"
)

type IntHeap []int

func (h IntHeap) Len() int { return len(h) }
func (h IntHeap) Less(i, j int) bool { return h[i] < h[j] }
func (h IntHeap) Swap(i, j int) { h[i], h[j] = h[j], h[i] }

func (h *IntHeap) Push(x interface{}) {
    *h = append(*h, x.(int))
}
```

```
func (h *IntHeap) Pop() interface{} {
    old := *h
    n := len(old)
    x := old[n-1]
    *h = old[0 : n-1]
    return x
}

func main() {
    h := &IntHeap{2, 1, 5}
    heap.Init(h)
    heap.Push(h, 3)
    fmt.Printf("minimum: %d\n", (*h)[0])
    for h.Len() > 0 {
        fmt.Printf("%d ", heap.Pop(h))
    }
}
```

Upon execution, this will produce:

```
minimum: 1
1 2 3 5
```

These examples illustrate the power and flexibility of the container package when working with advanced data structures in Go. The container package provides efficient and robust implementations of commonly used data structures that can significantly simplify the development of complex algorithms and applications.

10.6 Time and Date: time Package

The time package in Go's standard library provides comprehensive functionality for working with dates and times. This package is essential for applications that require time measurement, scheduling, and even timezone computation. The time package allows for the representation, formatting, and parsing of time values, adjusting times for time zones, measuring the passage of time, and performing arithmetic on time durations.

One of the fundamental types in the time package is Time, representing an instant in time with nanosecond precision. The current time can be obtained using the Now function:

```
package main

import (
```

```
    "fmt"
    "time"
)

func main() {
    currentTime := time.Now()
    fmt.Println("Current time:", currentTime)
}
```

```
Current time: 2023-10-01 12:34:56.789123456 +0000 UTC
```

Time values can be constructed using the Date function, which takes parameters for year, month, day, hour, minute, second, and nanosecond:

```
specifiedTime := time.Date(2023, time.October, 1, 12, 34, 56, 789123456, time.UTC)
fmt.Println("Specified time:", specifiedTime)
```

```
Specified time: 2023-10-01 12:34:56.789123456 +0000 UTC
```

Time instances offer various methods for extracting components of the time. For example:

```
year := currentTime.Year()
month := currentTime.Month()
day := currentTime.Day()
hour := currentTime.Hour()
minute := currentTime.Minute()
second := currentTime.Second()

fmt.Printf("Year: %d, Month: %s, Day: %d\n", year, month, day)
fmt.Printf("Hour: %d, Minute: %d, Second: %d\n", hour, minute, second)
```

```
Year: 2023, Month: October, Day: 1
Hour: 12, Minute: 34, Second: 56
```

Formatting and parsing time strings are facilitated by the Format and Parse methods. Format uses a reference time, Mon Jan 2 15:04:05 MST 2006, to define the layout:

```
layout := "2006-01-02 15:04:05"
formattedTime := currentTime.Format(layout)
fmt.Println("Formatted time:", formattedTime)
```

```
Formatted time: 2023-10-01 12:34:56
```

To parse a string into a Time value, the same layout reference is used:

```
parsedTime, err := time.Parse(layout, "2023-10-01 12:34:56")
if err != nil {
    fmt.Println("Error parsing time:", err)
}
fmt.Println("Parsed time:", parsedTime)
```

```
Parsed time: 2023-10-01 12:34:56 +0000 UTC
```

For time zones, the Location type represents a geographic time zone. You can use the LoadLocation function to get the location information and adjust times accordingly:

```
location, err := time.LoadLocation("America/New_York")
if err != nil {
    fmt.Println("Error loading location:", err)
}
nycTime := currentTime.In(location)
fmt.Println("New York time:", nycTime)
```

```
New York time: 2023-10-01 08:34:56.789123456 -0400 EDT
```

Duration arithmetic can be performed using the Add, Sub, and AddDate methods. The Duration type represents elapsed time in nanoseconds:

```
duration := time.Hour * 2
futureTime := currentTime.Add(duration)
fmt.Println("Future time (2 hours later):", futureTime)

durationBetween := futureTime.Sub(currentTime)
fmt.Println("Duration between times:", durationBetween)

nextYear := currentTime.AddDate(1, 0, 0)
fmt.Println("Next year:", nextYear)
```

```
Future time (2 hours later): 2023-10-01 14:34:56.789123456 +0000 UTC
Duration between times: 2h0m0s
Next year: 2024-10-01 12:34:56.789123456 +0000 UTC
```

Timers and tickers are used for async operations. NewTimer and NewTicker provide channels that send time events:

```
timer := time.NewTimer(2 * time.Second)
<-timer.C
fmt.Println("Timer expired")

ticker := time.NewTicker(1 * time.Second)
for i := 0; i < 3; i++ {
    <-ticker.C
    fmt.Println("Ticker ticked")
}
ticker.Stop()
```

```
Timer expired
Ticker ticked
Ticker ticked
Ticker ticked
```

In dealing with concurrency, these time-related mechanisms are critical for implementing intervals and delays. Effective use of the time package enhances the robustness of your Go application by providing precise control over temporal aspects.

10.7 Networking: net Package

The net package in Go provides a portable interface for network I/O, including TCP/IP, UDP, domain name resolution, and Unix domain sockets. This section explores the various functionalities within the net package, demonstrating how to create and manage network connections effectively.

net.Dial is the cornerstone function for client-side connections. It establishes a connection to an address on a named network.

```go
package main

import (
    "fmt"
    "net"
    "os"
)

func main() {
    conn, err := net.Dial("tcp", "golang.org:80")
    if err != nil {
        fmt.Println("Error: ", err)
        os.Exit(1)
    }
    fmt.Fprintf(conn, "GET / HTTP/1.0\r\n\r\n")
    buf := make([]byte, 1024)
    n, _ := conn.Read(buf)
    fmt.Println(string(buf[:n]))
    conn.Close()
}
```

Listing 10.1: Client-side connection using net.Dial

net.Dial takes two parameters: the network type and the address. In this example, the network type is tcp, and the address consists of a hostname and port number. The standard data transfer protocols supported include tcp, udp, ip, and unix.

For server-side applications, the net.Listen function creates servers that wait for connections.

```
package main

import (
    "fmt"
    "net"
    "os"
)

func main() {
    ln, err := net.Listen("tcp", ":8080")
    if err != nil {
        fmt.Println("Error: ", err)
        os.Exit(1)
    }
    for {
        conn, err := ln.Accept()
        if err != nil {
            fmt.Println("Error: ", err)
            continue
        }
        go handleConnection(conn)
    }
}

func handleConnection(conn net.Conn) {
    buf := make([]byte, 1024)
    n, _ := conn.Read(buf)
    fmt.Println(string(buf[:n]))
    conn.Write([]byte("HTTP/1.0 200 OK\r\n\r\nHello, World!"))
    conn.Close()
}
```

Listing 10.2: Server-side connection using net.Listen

In the server example, a TCP listener is created on port 8080. The ln.Accept function waits for and returns the next connection. Each connection is handled concurrently using a goroutine to maintain responsiveness.

The net package also provides the DialTimeout, DialTCP, DialUDP, and DialUnix functions for more specialized network connections, allowing for precise control over connection timeouts and protocol behavior.

For UDP connections, one can use net.ListenPacket to create a listening endpoint for packet-oriented protocols.

```
package main

import (
    "fmt"
    "net"
)

func main() {
    addr := net.UDPAddr{
        Port: 8081,
        IP: net.ParseIP("127.0.0.1"),
    }
    conn, err := net.ListenPacket("udp", addr.String())
    if err != nil {
        fmt.Println("Error: ", err)
        return
    }
    defer conn.Close()

    buf := make([]byte, 1024)
    for {
        n, addr, err := conn.ReadFrom(buf)
        if err != nil {
            fmt.Println("Error: ", err)
            continue
        }
        fmt.Println("Received ", string(buf[:n]), " from ", addr)
        conn.WriteTo([]byte("Hello from server"), addr)
    }
}
```

Listing 10.3: UDP connection using net.ListenPacket

In this UDP example, the listening endpoint is created using net.ListenPacket, and the ReadFrom method is used to read data from the connection, taking note of the source address for the response.

Network interfaces and addresses can be managed using the net.Interface and net.Addr types. These provide methods for listing available network interfaces and addresses, useful in more complex networking scenarios.

```
package main

import (
    "fmt"
    "net"
)

func main() {
    interfaces, err := net.Interfaces()
```

```
    if err != nil {
        fmt.Println("Error: ", err)
        return
    }
    for _, i := range interfaces {
        fmt.Println("Interface: ", i.Name)
        addrs, err := i.Addrs()
        if err != nil {
            fmt.Println("Error: ", err)
            continue
        }
        for _, addr := range addrs {
            fmt.Println(" Addr: ", addr.String())
        }
    }
}
```

Listing 10.4: Listing network interfaces and addresses

The net.LookupHost and net.LookupIP functions perform domain name resolution, converting names to IP addresses and vice versa.

```
package main

import (
    "fmt"
    "net"
)

func main() {
    ips, err := net.LookupIP("golang.org")
    if err != nil {
        fmt.Println("Error: ", err)
        return
    }
    for _, ip := range ips {
        fmt.Println("IP address: ", ip)
    }
}
```

Listing 10.5: Domain name resolution using net.LookupHost

Each of these functionalities within the net package enables robust, efficient network programming. The package abstracts many complexities of network communication, allowing developers to build both simple and sophisticated networked applications. Proper error handling and concurrency control are vital in these scenarios to ensure reliable and high-performance applications.

10.8 HTTP Handling: net/http Package

The net/http package in Go is essential for developing web servers and clients. This package provides fundamental HTTP client and server implementations, along with useful utilities for parsing URLs, handling requests and responses, and managing headers. Understanding how to leverage this package effectively is crucial for building robust web applications in Go.

HTTP Servers

To create an HTTP server, you need to define request handlers that implement the http.Handler interface. The most common approach is to use the http.HandleFunc() function, which allows you to associate a URL path with a handler function. Consider the following example:

```
package main

import (
    "fmt"
    "net/http"
)

func helloHandler(w http.ResponseWriter, r *http.Request) {
    fmt.Fprintf(w, "Hello, World!")
}

func main() {
    http.HandleFunc("/", helloHandler)
    http.ListenAndServe(":8080", nil)
}
```

In this example, http.HandleFunc("/") associates the root URL path with the helloHandler function. The server listens on port 8080, and when a request is made to the root path, helloHandler is called. The function writes "Hello, World!" to the response writer.

HTTP Handlers and Multiplexers

The http.Handle and http.HandleFunc functions allow associating custom handlers with URL paths. However, for more flexible routing, you might use the http.ServeMux type. An http.ServeMux is an HTTP request multiplexer that matches the URL of each incoming request against a list of registered patterns and calls the handler for the pattern that most closely matches the URL.

Consider the following extended example:

```
package main

import (
    "fmt"
    "net/http"
)

func helloHandler(w http.ResponseWriter, r *http.Request) {
    fmt.Fprintf(w, "Hello, World!")
}

func goodbyeHandler(w http.ResponseWriter, r *http.Request) {
    fmt.Fprintf(w, "Goodbye, World!")
}

func main() {
    mux := http.NewServeMux()
    mux.HandleFunc("/hello", helloHandler)
    mux.HandleFunc("/goodbye", goodbyeHandler)

    http.ListenAndServe(":8080", mux)
}
```

In this code, the http.NewServeMux() function creates a new request multiplexer. We then register two handlers. Requests to /hello are handled by helloHandler, and requests to /goodbye are handled by goodbyeHandler. The http.ListenAndServe(":8080", mux) function starts the server with this custom multiplexer.

HTTP Clients

The net/http package also provides a powerful set of tools for making HTTP requests. The http.Get, http.Post, and http.PostForm functions are convenient high-level functions for making HTTP requests.

Here is an example of an HTTP GET request:

```
package main

import (
    "fmt"
    "io/ioutil"
    "net/http"
)

func main() {
    resp, err := http.Get("http://example.com")
    if err != nil {
```

```
        fmt.Println("Error:", err)
        return
    }
    defer resp.Body.Close()

    body, err := ioutil.ReadAll(resp.Body)
    if err != nil {
        fmt.Println("Error reading response:", err)
        return
    }
    fmt.Println(string(body))
}
```

In this example, http.Get("http://example.com") makes an HTTP GET request to the specified URL. The defer resp.Body.Close() statement ensures that the response body is properly closed after reading. The ioutil.ReadAll(resp.Body) function reads the entire response body, and fmt.Println(string(body)) prints the response.

Custom HTTP Requests

For more control over HTTP requests, you can use the http.NewRequest function to create an http.Request object, and then use an http.Client to send the request. Consider the following example:

```
package main

import (
    "fmt"
    "net/http"
    "strings"
)

func main() {
    client := &http.Client{}
    req, err := http.NewRequest("POST", "http://example.com", strings.
        NewReader("name=value"))
    if err != nil {
        fmt.Println("Error creating request:", err)
        return
    }
    req.Header.Set("Content-Type", "application/x-www-form-urlencoded")

    resp, err := client.Do(req)
    if err != nil {
        fmt.Println("Error making request:", err)
        return
    }
```

```
    defer resp.Body.Close()

    body, err := ioutil.ReadAll(resp.Body)
    if err != nil {
        fmt.Println("Error reading response:", err)
        return
    }
    fmt.Println(string(body))
}
```

In this example, http.NewRequest("POST", "http://example.com", strings.NewReader("name=value")) creates a new POST request with the body "name=value". The header "Content-Type" is set to "application/x-www-form-urlencoded". The client.Do(req) function sends the request, and the response is read and printed similarly to the previous example.

Working with JSON

Handling JSON is a common requirement when working with HTTP APIs. The encoding/json package, combined with net/http, makes this process straightforward. The following example demonstrates how to create a simple web server that responds with JSON data:

```
package main

import (
    "encoding/json"
    "net/http"
)

type Response struct {
    Message string `json:"message"`
}

func jsonHandler(w http.ResponseWriter, r *http.Request) {
    response := Response{Message: "Hello, JSON!"}
    w.Header().Set("Content-Type", "application/json")
    json.NewEncoder(w).Encode(response)
}

func main() {
    http.HandleFunc("/json", jsonHandler)
    http.ListenAndServe(":8080", nil)
}
```

In this example, the Response struct defines the JSON structure. The jsonHandler function creates an instance of Response and sets the Content-Type header to "application/json". The json.NewEncoder(w).Encode(response) line encodes the response object as JSON and writes it to the response writer.

Using these tools and techniques, you can develop powerful, flexible HTTP applications in Go, taking full advantage of the robust capabilities provided by the net/http package.

10.9 Concurrency: sync and atomic Packages

The concurrency model in Go is a fundamental design feature of the language. This section details two crucial packages in Go's standard library that facilitate concurrent programming: sync and sync/atomic. Together, these packages provide the tools necessary for managing concurrent access to shared resources, ensuring safe and efficient execution of concurrent code.

The sync package provides synchronization primitives such as mutexes, wait groups, and condition variables. These primitives allow the programmer to control the execution of multiple goroutines, ensuring that resources are not accessed simultaneously in ways that cause data races or inconsistencies. The sync/atomic package offers low-level atomic memory primitives useful for managing state shared across goroutines without using locks.

```
package main

import (
    "fmt"
    "sync"
)

var counter int

func increment(wg *sync.WaitGroup) {
    for i := 0; i < 1000; i++ {
        counter++
    }
    wg.Done()
}

func main() {
    var wg sync.WaitGroup
    for i := 0; i < 10; i++ {
        wg.Add(1)
```

```
        go increment(&wg)
    }
    wg.Wait()
    fmt.Println("Final counter value:", counter)
}
```

Listing 10.6: Demonstration of a simple race condition.

In the above example, several goroutines increment a shared variable counter. Lacking synchronization, the final value of counter is inconsistent and shows a race condition. To prevent this, we use synchronization primitives.

Mutexes:

A sync.Mutex provides mutual exclusion, ensuring only one goroutine can access critical sections of code at any one time. By locking and unlocking a mutex, the code can safely manipulate shared resources.

```
package main

import (
    "fmt"
    "sync"
)

var (
    counter int
    mu sync.Mutex
)

func increment(wg *sync.WaitGroup) {
    for i := 0; i < 1000; i++ {
        mu.Lock()
        counter++
        mu.Unlock()
    }
    wg.Done()
}

func main() {
    var wg sync.WaitGroup
    for i := 0; i < 10; i++ {
        wg.Add(1)
        go increment(&wg)
    }
    wg.Wait()
    fmt.Println("Final counter value:", counter)
}
```

Listing 10.7: Example with Mutex to protect a shared variable.

This example ensures the increments to counter are atomic by introducing a sync.Mutex, which we lock before accessing the variable and unlock after accessing it. This way, only one goroutine can increment counter at a time, resulting in a consistent final value.

Sync.WaitGroup:

The sync.WaitGroup is used to wait for a collection of goroutines to finish executing. The code below demonstrates how a WaitGroup can be employed to block the main thread until all goroutines complete their tasks.

```
package main

import (
    "fmt"
    "sync"
    "time"
)

func worker(id int, wg *sync.WaitGroup) {
    defer wg.Done()
    fmt.Printf("Worker %d starting\n", id)
    time.Sleep(time.Second)
    fmt.Printf("Worker %d done\n", id)
}

func main() {
    var wg sync.WaitGroup

    for i := 1; i <= 5; i++ {
        wg.Add(1)
        go worker(i, &wg)
    }

    wg.Wait()
    fmt.Println("All workers completed")
}
```

Listing 10.8: Using WaitGroup to synchronize goroutines.

In this example, each worker function simulates a task that takes one second to complete. The WaitGroup ensures the main goroutine waits until all workers are finished before printing "All workers completed".

Atomic Operations:

For scenarios demanding high performance with shared state, the sync/atomic package offers atomic operations that lock variables at the hardware level, avoiding the overhead associated with mutexes.

```
package main

import (
    "fmt"
    "sync"
    "sync/atomic"
)

var counter int64

func increment(wg *sync.WaitGroup) {
    for i := 0; i < 1000; i++ {
        atomic.AddInt64(&counter, 1)
    }
    wg.Done()
}

func main() {
    var wg sync.WaitGroup

    for i := 0; i < 10; i++ {
        wg.Add(1)
        go increment(&wg)
    }

    wg.Wait()
    fmt.Println("Final counter value using atomic ops:", counter)
}
```

Listing 10.9: Using atomic operations for concurrency.

Here, atomic.AddInt64 performs an atomic addition on counter, ensuring it is done safely and efficiently even when accessed concurrently by multiple goroutines. The final value of counter will be consistent and correct.

Conclusion:

Employing these synchronization techniques, one can effectively manage and control the behavior of concurrent programs, ensuring consistent and error-free execution while leveraging the full potential of Go's concurrency model. By understanding the appropriate use cases for mutexes, wait groups, and atomic operations, programmers can build robust and efficient concurrent applications.

10.10 Parsing JSON: encoding/json Package

The encoding/json package in Go provides functions for encoding and decoding JSON objects. JSON (JavaScript Object Notation) is a lightweight data interchange format that is easy for humans to read and write, and easy for machines to parse and generate. This section explains the primary functionalities of the encoding/json package, including marshaling structures to JSON and unmarshaling JSON into Go structures.

encoding/json includes two primary functions:

- json.Marshal: converts a Go data structure into JSON.
- json.Unmarshal: converts JSON into a Go data structure.

To illustrate the use of these functions, consider the following example where we define a simple Go structure and demonstrate how to marshal and unmarshal this structure.

```
package main

import (
    "encoding/json"
    "fmt"
)

type Person struct {
    Name string `json:"name"`
    Age int `json:"age"`
    Email string `json:"email"`
}

func main() {
    // Initializing a Person struct
    person := Person{Name: "John Doe", Age: 30, Email: "john.doe@example.com
        "}

    // Marshaling the struct to JSON
    personJSON, err := json.Marshal(person)
    if err != nil {
        fmt.Println("Error marshaling JSON:", err)
        return
    }

    // Printing the JSON representation
    fmt.Println(string(personJSON))
```

```
    // Sample JSON string
    jsonString := `{"name": "Jane Doe", "age": 25, "email": "jane.doe@example.
        com"}`

    // Unmarshaling the JSON string into a Person struct
    var newPerson Person
    err = json.Unmarshal([]byte(jsonString), &newPerson)
    if err != nil {
        fmt.Println("Error unmarshaling JSON:", err)
        return
    }

    // Printing the new Person struct
    fmt.Println(newPerson)
}
```

Listing 10.10: Marshaling and Unmarshaling Example

```
{"name":"John Doe","age":30,"email":"john.doe@example.com"}
{Jane Doe 25 jane.doe@example.com}
```

In the example, the Person struct has fields for Name, Age, and Email. The struct tags specify the corresponding JSON keys. During marshaling, the Go struct is converted to a JSON string using json.Marshal. Conversely, during unmarshaling, the JSON string is converted back into a Go struct using json.Unmarshal.

JSON format allows nesting, which means an entity can contain other entities. Below is an example of a more complex structure.

```
package main

import (
    "encoding/json"
    "fmt"
)

type Address struct {
    Street string `json:"street"`
    City string `json:"city"`
    State string `json:"state"`
    Zip string `json:"zip"`
}

type Employee struct {
    Name string `json:"name"`
    Age int `json:"age"`
    Email string `json:"email"`
    Address Address `json:"address"`
}
```

```
func main() {
    // Initializing an Employee struct
    employee := Employee{
        Name: "Alice Smith",
        Age: 28,
        Email: "alice.smith@example.com",
        Address: Address{
            Street: "123 Main St",
            City: "Springfield",
            State: "IL",
            Zip: "62704",
        },
    }

    // Marshaling the struct to JSON
    employeeJSON, err := json.Marshal(employee)
    if err != nil {
        fmt.Println("Error marshaling JSON:", err)
        return
    }

    // Printing the JSON representation
    fmt.Println(string(employeeJSON))

    // Sample JSON string for nested structure
    jsonString := `{"name": "Bob Johnson", "age": 34, "email": "bob.
        johnson@example.com", "address": {"street": "456 Elm St", "city": "
        Metropolis", "state": "NY", "zip": "10001"}}`

    // Unmarshaling the JSON string into an Employee struct
    var newEmployee Employee
    err = json.Unmarshal([]byte(jsonString), &newEmployee)
    if err != nil {
        fmt.Println("Error unmarshaling JSON:", err)
        return
    }

    // Printing the new Employee struct
    fmt.Println(newEmployee)
}
```

Listing 10.11: Nested JSON Example

```
{"name":"Alice Smith","age":28,"email":"alice.smith@example.com","address":{"street":"123 Main
{Bob Johnson 34 bob.johnson@example.com {456 Elm St Metropolis NY 10001}}
```

In this example, the Employee struct contains an Address field, which itself is a struct. This demonstrates how Go can handle nested JSON objects. When marshaled, the nested structs are correctly converted to their respective JSON format, and the reverse occurs during unmarshaling.

Handling JSON data often includes dealing with unknown or dynamic structures, which is efficiently managed using interface{}. Here is an example of processing a JSON object whose structure is not known in advance.

```
package main

import (
    "encoding/json"
    "fmt"
)

func main() {
    // Sample dynamic JSON string
    jsonString := `{"name": "Charlie Brown", "age": 42, "interests": ["music", "
        sports"], "address": {"street": "789 Oak St", "city": "Gotham", "state": "
        NJ", "zip": "07001"}}`

    // Declaring a variable of type map
    var data map[string]interface{}

    // Unmarshaling the JSON string into the map
    err := json.Unmarshal([]byte(jsonString), &data)
    if err != nil {
        fmt.Println("Error unmarshaling JSON:", err)
        return
    }

    // Accessing data from the parsed JSON
    fmt.Println("Name:", data["name"])
    fmt.Println("Age:", data["age"])

    // Type asserting nested data
    address := data["address"].(map[string]interface{})
    fmt.Println("Street:", address["street"])
}
```

Listing 10.12: Dynamic JSON Processing Example

```
Name: Charlie Brown
Age: 42
Street: 789 Oak St
```

In this case, the JSON string is unmarshaled into a map[string]interface{}. The interface{} type allows us to handle various data types. After unmarshaling, we can access and process the data using type assertions.

Understanding the encoding/json package functions and handling dynamic JSON data equips developers with the tools to efficiently process JSON in Go applications.

10.11 Building CLI Applications: flag Package

The flag package in Go is essential for building command-line interface (CLI) applications. It allows developers to define and parse command-line flags, providing a simple means to configure applications through user-supplied inputs. This section delves into the fundamental aspects of using the flag package, covering flag definition, parsing, and typical use cases, detailing various types of flags and error handling mechanisms.

To begin using the flag package, import the package in your Go source file as follows:

```
import "flag"
```

A flag is created with the definition of its name, default value, and a usage message. The flag package supports various types of flags including string, integer, boolean, float64, and duration. Flag variables must be declared with methods corresponding to the flag's type. Below is an example demonstrating the creation and usage of different flag types.

```
package main

import (
    "flag"
    "fmt"
)

func main() {
    // Define flags
    stringFlag := flag.String("name", "defaultName", "a string flag")
    intFlag := flag.Int("age", 25, "an integer flag")
    boolFlag := flag.Bool("married", false, "a boolean flag")
    floatFlag := flag.Float64("gpa", 2.5, "a float64 flag")

    // Parse flags
    flag.Parse()

    // Accessing flag values
    fmt.Println("Name:", *stringFlag)
    fmt.Println("Age:", *intFlag)
    fmt.Println("Married:", *boolFlag)
    fmt.Println("GPA:", *floatFlag)
```

```
}
```

Executing the above program with different flag values would yield:

```
$ go run main.go -name=John -age=30 -married=true -gpa=3.8
Name: John
Age: 30
Married: true
GPA: 3.8
```

Here each flag is set with a default value and a usage message which can be shown by executing the program with the -help or -h flag. This is automatically handled by the flag package.

```
$ go run main.go -help
Usage of /tmp/go-build23412356/b001/exe/main:
  -age int
        an integer flag (default 25)
  -gpa float
        a float64 flag (default 2.5)
  -married
        a boolean flag
  -name string
        a string flag (default "defaultName")
```

In addition to basic flag types, the flag package supports custom flag types through the Var method, which implements the flag.Value interface. This enables greater flexibility for complex flag types.

```
type listFlag []string

// String is to satisfy the flag.Value interface
func (i *listFlag) String() string {
    return fmt.Sprint(*i)
}

// Set is to satisfy the flag.Value interface
func (i *listFlag) Set(value string) error {
    *i = append(*i, value)
    return nil
}

var languages listFlag

func init() {
    flag.Var(&languages, "lang", "a list of programming languages")
}

func main() {
    flag.Parse()
    fmt.Println("List of languages:", languages)
}
```

Running this program with multiple instances of the -lang flag aggregates the values into a slice.

```
$ go run main.go -lang=Go -lang=Python -lang=C++
List of languages: [Go Python C++]
```

Error handling in the flag package is straightforward. If the user provides an invalid format or a non-existent flag, the package will output an error message and the usage help text.

Best practices when using the flag package include defining flags in the init function to ensure they are set up before main runs, providing meaningful default values, and comprehensive usage descriptions to guide users effectively. This concrete approach maximizes utility and clarity in CLI applications designed with Go.

10.12 Creating Temporary Files and Directories: ioutil Package

Go's ioutil package provides various utility functions that simplify common file operations, including facilities for creating temporary files and directories. These capabilities are crucial in scenarios where the application requires scratch space for intermediate data or unique, ephemeral file system locations during its execution.

To create a temporary file in Go, the ioutil.TempFile function is employed. It has the following signature:

```
func TempFile(dir, pattern string) (*os.File, error)
```

The dir parameter specifies the directory in which the file is created. If the dir is empty, the default directory for temporary files, as defined by the operating system, is used. The pattern parameter determines the filename pattern. The string "*" within the pattern is replaced by a random string to ensure the filename's uniqueness. The function returns an os.File pointer and an error value.

An exemplary usage of ioutil.TempFile is as follows:

```
package main

import (
    "fmt"
    "io/ioutil"
    "os"
)

func main() {
```

```
    tempFile, err := ioutil.TempFile("", "example-*.txt")
    if err != nil {
        fmt.Println("Error creating temporary file:", err)
        return
    }
    defer os.Remove(tempFile.Name())

    fmt.Println("Temporary file created:", tempFile.Name())

    if _, err := tempFile.WriteString("This is a temporary file."); err != nil {
        fmt.Println("Error writing to temporary file:", err)
        return
    }

    if err := tempFile.Close(); err != nil {
        fmt.Println("Error closing temporary file:", err)
    }
}
```

In this example, a temporary file with a name matching the pattern example-*.txt is created in the default temporary directory. The os.Remove(tempFile.Name()) function call, deferred to execute at the end of the main function, ensures the temporary file is cleaned up. Writing to and closing the temporary file are performed with straightforward error handling.

To create a temporary directory, the ioutil.TempDir function is utilized. Its signature is as follows:

```
func TempDir(dir, pattern string) (string, error)
```

Similar to ioutil.TempFile, the dir parameter specifies the parent directory, while the pattern parameter provides the directory name pattern. It returns the name of the newly created directory and an error if any.

Here is an example of how to create a temporary directory:

```
package main

import (
    "fmt"
    "io/ioutil"
    "os"
)

func main() {
    tempDir, err := ioutil.TempDir("", "example-dir-")
    if err != nil {
        fmt.Println("Error creating temporary directory:", err)
        return
```

```
    }
    defer os.RemoveAll(tempDir)

    fmt.Println("Temporary directory created:", tempDir)

    tempFile, err := ioutil.TempFile(tempDir, "file-*.txt")
    if err != nil {
        fmt.Println("Error creating file in temporary directory:", err)
        return
    }
    defer os.Remove(tempFile.Name())

    fmt.Println("File created in temporary directory:", tempFile.Name())

    if _, err := tempFile.WriteString("This file is inside a temporary directory.");
        err != nil {
        fmt.Println("Error writing to file in temporary directory:", err)
        return
    }

    if err := tempFile.Close(); err != nil {
        fmt.Println("Error closing file in temporary directory:", err)
    }
}
```

In this example, a temporary directory is created with the pattern example-dir- in the default temporary directory. The result is stored in tempDir. The defer os.RemoveAll(tempDir) call ensures that the entire temporary directory and its contents are removed when the program finishes. A temporary file is then created within this directory, written to, and properly closed, demonstrating nested temporary file management.

Both ioutil.TempFile and ioutil.TempDir are indispensable tools for handling scenarios requiring transient storage. While ioutil package is slated for deprecation in favor of os and io packages, understanding its usage is essential for maintaining legacy Go code.

Chapter 11

Testing in Go

This chapter focuses on testing in Go, starting with writing basic tests using the testing package. It discusses table-driven tests, benchmarking, and profiling, as well as mocking and dependency injection. The chapter also covers testing with examples, running tests, understanding output, and organizing test files. Additionally, it explores code coverage analysis, best practices for testing, and integration and end-to-end testing to ensure software quality and reliability.

11.1 Introduction to Testing in Go

Testing is an essential aspect of software development that ensures the reliability, performance, and correctness of your code. In Go, the `testing` package provides functionality to write and run tests, benchmarks, and example tests.

Fundamentals of Testing in Go

Go's approach to testing is both streamlined and integrated within the language itself, which encourages developers to adopt and maintain robust testing practices. Unlike some other languages where testing frameworks are external libraries, Go includes a dedicated `testing` package in its standard library. This integration means that you need not worry about external dependencies for basic testing functionalities.

Test Files and Conventions

In Go, test files are conventionally named with the _test.go suffix and are placed in the same directory as the code they test. This naming convention allows the Go tool to distinguish test files from regular code files.

For instance, if you have a package named mypackage with a file mypackage.go, your test file would be named mypackage_test.go.

A simple test function has the following structure:

```
package mypackage

import "testing"

func TestFunctionName(t *testing.T) {
    // Test code goes here
}
```

The TestFunctionName function name must start with Test, followed by a name that describes the test. The function takes a single parameter, t, of type *testing.T provided by the testing package. This parameter is used to report test failures.

Running Tests

To run tests, use the go test command:

```
$ go test
```

By default, go test searches for all files matching the pattern *_test.go in the current directory and runs the tests defined in those files. The tool reports whether the tests pass or fail and provides additional information when a test fails.

Writing a Basic Test

Consider a simple function for addition in the mypackage package:

```
package mypackage

func Add(a, b int) int {
    return a + b
}
```

To test this function, create a corresponding test function in mypackage_test.go:

```
package mypackage

import "testing"
```

```
func TestAdd(t *testing.T) {
    result := Add(2, 3)
    expected := 5
    if result != expected {
        t.Errorf("Add(2, 3) = %d; want %d", result, expected)
    }
}
```

This test checks if Add(2, 3) produces the correct result, which should be 5. The t.Errorf method provides formatted output to detail what went wrong if the test fails.

Understanding Testing Functions

The testing package provides several methods to handle test failures:

- t.Error(args ...interface): Reports an error.
- t.Errorf(format string, args ...interface): Reports a formatted error.
- t.Fail(): Marks the function where it was called as having failed but continues execution.
- t.Fatal(args ...interface): Reports an error and stops execution.
- t.Fatalf(format string, args ...interface): Reports a formatted error and stops execution.

Each of these methods allows you to provide informative output that clarifies what went wrong during test execution.

Structuring Tests with Test Functions

Proper test structuring is crucial for maintaining clear and effective test cases. Break down tests into multiple functions when handling complex logic or numerous scenarios. For example, multiple test cases for different inputs:

```
func TestAdd(t *testing.T) {
    tests := []struct {
        a, b, expected int
    }{
        {1, 1, 2},
        {-1, -1, -2},
        {-1, 1, 0},
        {0, 0, 0},
    }
```

```
    for _, tt := range tests {
        result := Add(tt.a, tt.b)
        if result != tt.expected {
            t.Errorf("Add(%d, %d) = %d; want %d", tt.a, tt.b, result, tt.expected)
        }
    }
}
```

This example uses a table-driven approach, where a table of inputs and expected results is created, and the test iterates over them, checking each case. This approach is powerful and scales well with more complex testing scenarios.

Understanding and applying these basic testing principles is foundational to mastering Go programming. Integrating testing into your development workflow significantly enhances code quality and reliability, preparing you for more advanced topics covered in subsequent sections.

11.2 Writing Basic Tests

In this section, we will focus on writing basic tests in Go. Testing is a fundamental practice in ensuring the correctness and reliability of software. Go provides a comprehensive testing framework through the testing package, which facilitates the creation and execution of tests. This package is integrated into the Go toolchain, enabling the easy execution of tests.

To begin with, a basic test in Go is a function that tests a specific piece of functionality in your code. These functions are named with the prefix Test, followed by a descriptive name. The naming convention is crucial as the Go test tool relies on this prefix to identify and execute the test functions.

A minimal test function has the following form:

```
package yourpackage

import "testing"

func TestFunctionName(t *testing.T) {
    // test logic here
}
```

The testing.T parameter provides methods for reporting and logging errors. For instance, it includes methods such as t.Error, t.Errorf, t.Fatal, and t.Fatalf, which are used to signal failure conditions.

Consider an example where we want to test a function that adds two integers:

```
package math

func Add(a, b int) int {
    return a + b
}
```

To test this function, we could write the following test:

```
package math

import "testing"

func TestAdd(t *testing.T) {
    // Arrange
    x := 2
    y := 3
    expected := 5

    // Act
    result := Add(x, y)

    // Assert
    if result != expected {
        t.Errorf("Add(%d, %d) = %d; want %d", x, y, result, expected)
    }
}
```

In this example, the TestAdd function follows a typical structure seen in testing: the Arrange-Act-Assert pattern. First, we arrange our test data; next, we act by calling the function under test; finally, we assert the outcome is as expected.

The t.Errorf method reports an error if the function does not return the expected result. This method takes a format string and arguments similar to fmt.Printf.

When you run this test, you invoke the Go tool with the following command:

```
$ go test
```

This command searches for all tests in the current directory, runs them, and reports their success or failure.

Another useful feature is table-driven tests. They allow you to run the same test logic with different sets of inputs and expected outputs. Here is an example of how we could refactor TestAdd to use table-driven tests:

```
package math

import "testing"

func TestAdd(t *testing.T) {
    tests := []struct {
        x int
        y int
        expected int
    }{
        {1, 1, 2},
        {2, 2, 4},
        {10, 5, 15},
    }

    for _, tt := range tests {
        result := Add(tt.x, tt.y)
        if result != tt.expected {
            t.Errorf("Add(%d, %d) = %d; want %d", tt.x, tt.y, result, tt.expected)
        }
    }
}
```

Here, we define a slice of structs, where each struct holds a test case with inputs x, y, and the expected result. We then iterate over this slice and execute the test logic. This approach is beneficial as it reduces code duplication and makes it easier to add more test cases.

In addition to t.Errorf, Go's testing package also provides methods such as t.Fatal. Unlike t.Errorf, which logs an error and continues executing the test, t.Fatal logs the error and stops the execution of the current test. Use t.Fatal when further execution does not make sense if an error has occurred.

```
func TestAdd_Fatal(t *testing.T) {
    x := 1
    y := 1
    expected := 3

    result := Add(x, y)
    if result != expected {
        t.Fatalf("Add(%d, %d) = %d; want %d", x, y, result, expected)
    }

    t.Log("Test completed") // This line will not be executed if t.Fatalf is invoked.
```

```
}
```

Sometimes, it is important to ensure that resources are properly cleaned up after a test. Go's testing.T provides a method Cleanup that registers a function to be called when the test function returns. It is often leveraged to release resources allocated during the test.

```
func TestWithCleanup(t *testing.T) {
    // Allocate some resource (e.g., open a file or a network connection)
    resource := "allocated resource"

    t.Cleanup(func() {
        // Clean up resource
        resource = "cleaned up"
    })

    // Perform tests using the resource
    if resource != "allocated resource" {
        t.Fatal("expected resource to be allocated")
    }
}
```

Writing basic tests in Go is thus a systematic process of setting up test cases, executing functions with those cases, and verifying that the function behaves as expected. Through the use of tools and patterns provided by the testing package, tests become both robust and maintainable. This solid foundation ensures that developers can confidently evolve and maintain their codebases.

11.3 Using the testing Package

Go provides a comprehensive built-in testing framework with the testing package, which makes it easier to write unit tests for functions and methods. This package is part of Go's standard library and requires minimal setup to start writing and running tests. To utilize the testing package, you need to create a test file that follows the naming convention *_test.go. Test functions must be prefixed with "Test" followed by the name of the function being tested and accept a *testing.T parameter.

Below is a basic example demonstrating the structure and syntax for writing tests using the testing package:

```
package math
```

```
import "testing"

func Add(a, b int) int {
    return a + b
}

func TestAdd(t *testing.T) {
    result := Add(2, 3)
    expected := 5

    if result != expected {
        t.Errorf("Add(2, 3) = %d; want %d", result, expected)
    }
}
```

This example includes a simple Add function and a corresponding TestAdd function. The testing.T type provides several methods for reporting test failures and logging additional information. The t.Errorf method is used to log an error message if the test condition result != expected evaluates to true, indicating the test has failed.

```
=== RUN   TestAdd
--- PASS: TestAdd (0.00s)
PASS
ok      math    0.123s
```

The test output indicates that the TestAdd function ran successfully. The first line === RUN TestAdd signifies the start of the test, while the — PASS: TestAdd (0.00s) line shows the test has passed, taking 0.00 seconds to execute.

Table-Driven Tests

Table-driven tests are a common pattern in Go testing where you define multiple test cases as entries in a table and loop over them, reducing redundancy and improving test coverage. Here is a refactored version of the previous TestAdd function using table-driven tests:

```
func TestAdd(t *testing.T) {
    tests := []struct {
        name string
        a, b int
        expected int
    }{
        {"2+3", 2, 3, 5},
        {"-1+1", -1, 1, 0},
        {"0+0", 0, 0, 0},
        {"-2-3", -2, -3, -5},
    }
```

```
    for _, tt := range tests {
        t.Run(tt.name, func(t *testing.T) {
            result := Add(tt.a, tt.b)
            if result != tt.expected {
                t.Errorf("Add(%d, %d) = %d; want %d", tt.a, tt.b, result, tt.
                    expected)
            }
        })
    }
}
```

This test function defines a slice of anonymous structs, each representing a test case with fields name, a, b, and expected. The t.Run method is used to run each test case, identified by tt.name, which helps in isolating each test case and provides better output when a test fails.

Mocking and HTTP Testing

The testing package can also be used in conjunction with the net/http/httptest package for testing HTTP handlers. Here's an example demonstrating how to test an HTTP handler using these packages:

```
package main

import (
    "net/http"
    "net/http/httptest"
    "testing"
)

func HelloHandler(w http.ResponseWriter, r *http.Request) {
    w.WriteHeader(http.StatusOK)
    w.Write([]byte("Hello, World!"))
}

func TestHelloHandler(t *testing.T) {
    req, err := http.NewRequest("GET", "/", nil)
    if err != nil {
        t.Fatal(err)
    }

    rr := httptest.NewRecorder()
    handler := http.HandlerFunc(HelloHandler)

    handler.ServeHTTP(rr, req)

    if status := rr.Code; status != http.StatusOK {
        t.Errorf("handler returned wrong status code: got %v want %v",
            status, http.StatusOK)
```

```
    }

    expected := "Hello, World!"
    if rr.Body.String() != expected {
        t.Errorf("handler returned unexpected body: got %v want %v",
            rr.Body.String(), expected)
    }
}
```

This example demonstrates the use of httptest.NewRecorder to record HTTP responses and http.NewRequest to create a new HTTP request. The t.Fatal method is used to handle errors that should stop the test immediately, while t.Errorf is used for non-fatal errors to continue test execution.

Running Tests

To run tests in your Go package, you use the go test command. This command automatically finds all files ending with *_test.go and executes the test functions. Here is an example of executing tests:

```
$ go test
PASS
ok      math    0.123s
```

To obtain more verbose output, you can use the -v flag:

```
$ go test -v
=== RUN   TestAdd
--- PASS: TestAdd (0.00s)
PASS
ok      math    0.123s
```

For more in-depth analysis and better debugging, the testing package provides additional flags such as -cover to check test coverage and -bench for benchmarking which will be covered further in subsequent sections.

Error Reporting

Proper error reporting in tests is crucial for diagnosing issues quickly. The testing.T type offers several methods to facilitate error reporting:

- t.Error(args...): Reports an error. The test is marked as failed, but it continues.
- t.Errorf(format string, args...): Reports an error with formatted output. The test is marked as failed, but it continues.

- t.Fatal(args...): Reports an error and stops the test execution immediately.
- t.Fatalf(format string, args...): Reports an error with formatted output and stops the test execution immediately.

```
func TestDivide(t *testing.T) {
    _, err := Divide(1, 0)
    if err == nil {
        t.Fatal("expected an error but got nil")
    }
}
```

In this example, the t.Fatal method is used to stop the test execution immediately if an error is not received as expected, ensuring that subsequent test logic does not run in an invalid state.

Go's testing package provides a robust and flexible framework for writing and running tests. It encourages good testing practices by integrating seamlessly with the language and offering extensive features for error reporting, running tests, and ensuring code correctness. Proper utilization of these tools is critical for maintaining high-quality Go code.

11.4 Table-Driven Tests

Table-driven tests in Go are a methodology used to streamline and organize the testing of multiple scenarios within a concise and easily maintainable format. Instead of writing individual tests for each scenario, a single test function iterates over a slice of test cases. Each test case is a struct containing the input and expected output for a specific test scenario.

A common pattern for defining table-driven tests involves the following components:

- Definition of a struct to represent a single test case.
- Initialization of a slice containing all test cases.
- A loop iterating over the slice, running the test function for each test case, and checking the results.

Here is an example to illustrate table-driven testing in Go.

```
package math

import (
    "testing"
)

// Define the function to be tested
func Add(a, b int) int {
    return a + b
}

// Define the test case struct
type testCase struct {
    inputA int
    inputB int
    expectedOutput int
}

// Define and run the table-driven test
func TestAdd(t *testing.T) {
    // Initialize the test cases
    testCases := []testCase{
        {inputA: 1, inputB: 2, expectedOutput: 3},
        {inputA: -1, inputB: 1, expectedOutput: 0},
        {inputA: -1, inputB: -1, expectedOutput: -2},
        {inputA: 0, inputB: 0, expectedOutput: 0},
    }

    // Iterate over each test case
    for _, tc := range testCases {
        t.Run(fmt.Sprintf("%d+%d", tc.inputA, tc.inputB), func(t *testing.T) {
            result := Add(tc.inputA, tc.inputB)
            if result != tc.expectedOutput {
                t.Errorf("Add(%d, %d) = %d; expected %d", tc.inputA, tc.inputB,
                    result, tc.expectedOutput)
            }
        })
    }
}
```

Listing 11.1: Table-driven Test Example

In this example, the struct testCase encapsulates the inputs and expected output for each scenario. The testCases slice holds multiple instances of the struct, each representing a different test scenario. The loop inside the TestAdd function invokes the Add function for each test case and checks whether the result matches the expected output.

To debug or further investigate a specific test case, it might be helpful to label the sub-tests. In the above example, we use t.Run to create subtests with descriptive names using the fmt.Sprintf function. This labeling helps in identifying which test case fails without referencing the content of the error message.

When dealing with more cases, especially when the number of input parameters increases, table-driven tests offer a succinct alternative to writing separate functions. Additionally, they make it easier to add, delete or modify test cases, as the test logic is not entangled with individual checks.

Let's consider another example where we perform table-driven testing on a function that validates email addresses.

```
package validator

import (
    "testing"
    "regexp"
)

// Function to be tested for email validation
func IsValidEmail(email string) bool {
    var emailRegex = regexp.MustCompile(`^[^@\s]+@[^@\s]+\.[^@\s]+$`)
    return emailRegex.MatchString(email)
}

// Define the test case struct
type emailTestCase struct {
    email string
    expectedOutput bool
}

// Define and run the table-driven test
func TestIsValidEmail(t *testing.T) {
    // Initialize the test cases
    testCases := []emailTestCase{
        {email: "test@example.com", expectedOutput: true},
        {email: "invalid-email", expectedOutput: false},
        {email: "another.test@domain.co", expectedOutput: true},
        {email: "@no-local-part.com", expectedOutput: false},
    }

    // Iterate over each test case
    for _, tc := range testCases {
        t.Run(tc.email, func(t *testing.T) {
            result := IsValidEmail(tc.email)
            if result != tc.expectedOutput {
                t.Errorf("IsValidEmail(%q) = %v; expected %v", tc.email, result,
                    tc.expectedOutput)
            }
        })
    }
```

```
}
```

Listing 11.2: Advanced Table-Driven Test Example

In this example, the function IsValidEmail is tested against various valid and invalid email strings. Each test case clearly specifies what email address is being tested and the expected result, simplifying the understanding of test coverage.

This approach can be extended to handle more complex functions and different types of input by expanding the test case struct to accommodate additional parameters. An effective use of table-driven tests fosters maintainability and readability, especially when the software evolves and new test cases are identified.

Furthermore, combining table-driven tests with other Go testing features like t.Parallel() allows running tests concurrently, leveraging Go's concurrency model, making the testing process more efficient.

In summary, table-driven tests are instrumental in simplifying and organizing test scenarios in Go, promoting robustness and extensibility in the testing suite.

11.5 Benchmarking and Profiling

Benchmarking and profiling are essential techniques for evaluating the performance and identifying bottlenecks in Go programs. These practices are indispensable for fine-tuning the efficiency and responsiveness of software. This section delves into the methodologies for creating benchmarks using Go's built-in testing frameworks, followed by an introduction to profiling tools and techniques.

Benchmarking in Go leverages the testing package, which provides support for writing benchmarks similarly to how it supports writing tests. Benchmarks measure the time and memory consumption of code under various conditions, typically focusing on critical path functions.

```
func BenchmarkExample(b *testing.B) {
    for i := 0; i < b.N; i++ {
        ExampleFunction()
    }
}
```

Listing 11.3: Basic Benchmark Example

In the above example, BenchmarkExample is a benchmark function. Each benchmark function in Go must start with Benchmark followed by the name of the function you are benchmarking. The *testing.B parameter provides methods and attributes that are useful for benchmark management, including the iteration count b.N. The b.N attribute determines how many times the loop will execute to provide a statistically significant sample.

Executing benchmarks is straightforward and can be done through the Go command-line tool:

```
$ go test -bench=.
```

This command runs all benchmarks in the package, providing detailed results for each. The output includes operations per second (ops/s), which is a vital metric for performance comparison.

For more granular control, Go supports benchmarking allocation counts, which can help determine the memory footprint of specific operations.

```
func BenchmarkAllocations(b *testing.B) {
    b.ReportAllocs()
    for i := 0; i < b.N; i++ {
        AllocateMemoryFunction()
    }
}
```

Listing 11.4: Benchmarking Memory Allocations

By calling b.ReportAllocs() within the benchmark function, one can gather detailed information about memory allocations, revealing insights into unnecessary heap allocations that could be optimized.

Profiling, on the other hand, involves collecting data about a program's execution to understand its performance characteristics. The most common types of profiles are CPU, memory, and block profiles. Profiling in Go can be performed using the runtime/pprof package.

Start by importing runtime/pprof and adding code to create and write the profile data into a file.

```
import (
    "os"
    "runtime/pprof"
)

func main() {
    f, err := os.Create("cpu.prof")
```

```
    if err != nil {
        log.Fatal("could not create CPU profile: ", err)
    }
    defer f.Close()
    if err := pprof.StartCPUProfile(f); err != nil {
        log.Fatal("could not start CPU profile: ", err)
    }
    defer pprof.StopCPUProfile()

    // Your program here
}
```

Listing 11.5: CPU Profiling with runtime/pprof

When the profile data is collected, it can be analyzed using command-line tools provided by the Go distribution, such as go tool pprof.

```
$ go tool pprof cpu.prof
```

This command opens an interactive interface for exploring the CPU profile, allowing you to examine various statistics and visualizations, such as top functions consuming the most CPU time.

Memory profiling is conducted similarly, capturing heap allocations rather than CPU activity.

```
f, err := os.Create("mem.prof")
if err != nil {
    log.Fatal("could not create memory profile: ", err)
}
defer f.Close()
runtime.GC() // get up-to-date statistics
if err := pprof.WriteHeapProfile(f); err != nil {
    log.Fatal("could not write memory profile: ", err)
}
```

Listing 11.6: Memory Profiling with runtime/pprof

In this snippet, runtime.GC() is called to ensure that the garbage collector has run and the profile data reflects the most current memory allocations.

Furthermore, block profiling can be used to identify contention in goroutines, highlighting the frequency and duration of blocking operations.

```
runtime.SetBlockProfileRate(1)
defer func() {
    f, err := os.Create("block.prof")
    if err != nil {
        log.Fatal("could not create block profile: ", err)
```

```
    }
    defer f.Close()
    if err := pprof.Lookup("block").WriteTo(f, 0); err != nil {
        log.Fatal("could not write block profile: ", err)
    }
}()
```

Listing 11.7: Block Profiling with runtime/pprof

In this example, the block profiling rate is set to 1, which means every blocking event is recorded. This information is critical for diagnosing issues such as goroutine leaks and synchronization problems.

Through effective benchmarking and profiling, one achieves deeper insights into the performance characteristics of Go programs. These techniques are pivotal for diagnosing inefficiencies and guiding optimization efforts.

11.6 Mocking and Dependency Injection

To address the challenges of creating robust and reliable tests in Go, we need to explore the concepts of mocking and dependency injection. These techniques allow us to isolate components, simulate various scenarios, and verify interactions without relying on actual implementations.

Mocking is the practice of replacing real dependencies in tests with controlled stand-ins known as mocks. This allows for precise control over inputs and outputs, ensuring that the tests are both reliable and repeatable.

Dependency Injection (DI) refers to the technique of providing a component with its dependencies rather than allowing it to create them internally. This makes the component easier to test, as the dependencies can be replaced with mocks or other test doubles.

Using Mocking in Go

Consider a scenario where you have a function that depends on an external service to fetch data. For instance, suppose you have a function, GetUserProfile, which fetches user profile details from an external API. To test GetUserProfile without relying on the actual API, you can use a mock.

Define an interface that encapsulates the behavior of the external service:

```
type UserProfileService interface {
    FetchUserProfile(userID string) (UserProfile, error)
}
```

With the interface defined, you can implement the function GetUserProfile to depend on this interface rather than a concrete type:

```
func GetUserProfile(service UserProfileService, userID string) (UserProfile, error) {

    return service.FetchUserProfile(userID)
}
```

Next, create a mock implementation of the UserProfileService for testing purposes:

```
type MockUserProfileService struct {
}

func (m *MockUserProfileService) FetchUserProfile(userID string) (UserProfile,
    error) {
    return UserProfile{
        ID: userID,
        Name: "John Doe",
        Email: "john.doe@example.com",
    }, nil
}
```

With the mock in place, you can now write tests for GetUserProfile:

```
func TestGetUserProfile(t *testing.T) {
    mockService := &MockUserProfileService{}
    userID := "12345"

    profile, err := GetUserProfile(mockService, userID)
    if err != nil {
        t.Fatalf("expected no error, got %v", err)
    }

    if profile.ID != userID {
        t.Errorf("expected user ID %s, got %s", userID, profile.ID)
    }
}
```

The test verifies that the GetUserProfile function correctly utilizes the mock service and returns the expected results. By adopting this approach, you avoid the need to make actual API calls, making the tests faster and more reliable.

Dependency Injection in Go

Dependency Injection can be achieved in Go using constructor injection, where dependencies are provided through function or method parameters. Consider a scenario where a service depends on a repository to perform database operations. Define an interface for the repository:

```
type UserRepository interface {
    FindUserByID(userID string) (User, error)
}
```

Implement the service to depend on the UserRepository interface:

```
type UserService struct {
    repository UserRepository
}

func NewUserService(repo UserRepository) *UserService {
    return &UserService{repository: repo}
}

func (s *UserService) GetUser(userID string) (User, error) {
    return s.repository.FindUserByID(userID)
}
```

A concrete implementation of the UserRepository might perform actual database operations. For testing, you can create a mock implementation:

```
type MockUserRepository struct {
}

func (m *MockUserRepository) FindUserByID(userID string) (User, error) {
    return User{
        ID: userID,
        Name: "Jane Doe",
        Email: "jane.doe@example.com",
    }, nil
}
```

Tests for the UserService can now be written to use the mock repository:

```
func TestUserService_GetUser(t *testing.T) {
    mockRepo := &MockUserRepository{}
    service := NewUserService(mockRepo)
    userID := "67890"

    user, err := service.GetUser(userID)
    if err != nil {
        t.Fatalf("expected no error, got %v", err)
    }
```

```
    if user.ID != userID {
        t.Errorf("expected user ID %s, got %s", userID, user.ID)
    }
}
```

By injecting the repository dependency into the UserService, you can easily replace it with a mock during tests. This approach ensures that the UserService operates correctly regardless of the actual implementation of the repository.

Practical Tips

When applying mocking and dependency injection, it is beneficial to follow these best practices:

- Define interfaces that precisely encapsulate the behavior required by the dependent component.
- Avoid creating overly generic interfaces; keep them focused on the specific behaviors needed for tests.
- Make use of constructor functions to inject dependencies, ensuring that components are consistently initialized with the required dependencies.
- Leverage Go's type embedding to facilitate the creation of mocks, especially for complex interfaces.
- Use tools like gomock to automatically generate mock implementations, simplifying the mocking process and reducing boilerplate code.

Effective utilization of mocking and dependency injection significantly enhances the maintainability and reliability of your tests by isolating individual components and verifying their behavior in controlled environments. These techniques ensure that changes in one part of the system do not inadvertently affect others, leading to more robust software.

11.7 Testing with Examples

Testing with examples in Go serves a dual purpose: it validates the functionality of your code while simultaneously providing illustrative documentation for future users and maintainers. The go test tool automatically extracts and runs these examples, making them an indispensable part of the testing suite. This section delves into the nuances of writing effective example tests and seamlessly integrates them into the broader testing framework.

Creating Example Tests

Example tests are written as functions that start with the prefix Example followed by the name of the function or method being tested. These functions do not return any value but instead conclude with output that can be compared to expected results. Let us consider a simple function Add that adds two integers.

```
package math

// Add takes two integers and returns their sum
func Add(x, y int) int {
    return x + y
}
```

Listing 11.8: Simple Add Function

The corresponding example test for this function should be written in a manner that both demonstrates its usage and verifies its correctness.

```
package math_test

import (
    "fmt"
    "math"
)

func ExampleAdd() {
    result := math.Add(1, 2)
    fmt.Println(result)
    // Output: 3
}
```

Listing 11.9: Example Test for Add Function

Output Expectations

Comments within the example function specify the output using the format // Output: expected_output. During test execution, go test compares the actual output with this expected output. Any discrepancy results in a test failure. The match is exact, including white spaces and newlines, which demands precise and careful output specification.

Handling Multiple Outputs

Example functions can return multiple outputs if required. Consider modifying the earlier Add function to AddSubtract, which returns both the sum and difference of two integers.

```
package math

// AddSubtract returns the sum and difference of two integers
func AddSubtract(x, y int) (int, int) {
    sum := x + y
    diff := x - y
    return sum, diff
}
```

Listing 11.10: AddSubtract Function with Multiple Outputs

The example test accommodates multiple outputs by specifying each expected output on a new line.

```
package math_test

import (
    "fmt"
    "math"
)

func ExampleAddSubtract() {
    sum, diff := math.AddSubtract(3, 1)
    fmt.Println(sum)
    fmt.Println(diff)
    // Output:
    // 4
    // 2
}
```

Listing 11.11: Example Test for AddSubtract Function

Documenting Edge Cases and Errors

Example tests are also invaluable for documenting how a function handles edge cases or erroneous inputs. Let us extend the Add function to introduce an error if the inputs are negative.

```
package math

import (
    "errors"
)

// Add takes two integers and returns their sum. Returns an error if any input is
    negative.
func Add(x, y int) (int, error) {
    if x < 0 || y < 0 {
```

```
        return 0, errors.New("inputs must be non-negative")
    }
    return x + y, nil
}
```

Listing 11.12: Modified Add Function with Error Handling

The corresponding example test should include scenarios to document both successful and erroneous outcomes.

```
package math_test

import (
    "fmt"
    "math"
)

func ExampleAdd() {
    sum, err := math.Add(1, 2)
    if err != nil {
        fmt.Println("error:", err)
    } else {
        fmt.Println(sum)
    }
    // Output: 3

    sum, err = math.Add(-1, 2)
    if err != nil {
        fmt.Println("error:", err)
    } else {
        fmt.Println(sum)
    }
    // Output: error: inputs must be non-negative
}
```

Listing 11.13: Example Test for Modified Add Function

Package-Level Example Tests

In addition to function-specific example tests, Go allows the creation of package-level examples that demonstrate comprehensive usage scenarios, showcasing how various functions within the package collaborate.

```
package math_test

import (
    "fmt"
    "math"
)

func Example() {
```

```
    sum, _ := math.Add(1, 2)
    diff, _ := math.AddSubtract(5, 3)

    fmt.Printf("Sum: %d, Difference: %d\n", sum, diff)
    // Output: Sum: 3, Difference: 2
}
```

Listing 11.14: Package-Level Example Test

Run Example Tests

To execute the example tests, the command go test can be used in the terminal. This command discovers and runs all example tests within the package and verifies their outputs against the specified expectations.

```
$ go test
ok      math      0.002s
```

Example tests in Go are a powerful instrument in the developers' toolkit, offering a means to validate code functionality while simultaneously educing instructional documentation. Through their strategic incorporation, functions can be demonstrated comprehensively, enabling both verification and elucidation.

11.8 Running Tests and Understanding Output

To ensure the reliability and correctness of your Go code, understanding how to run tests and interpret their output is crucial. This section covers the fundamental commands and practices for executing tests within the Go environment and interpreting the results produced.

Running tests in Go is facilitated by the go test command. It compiles the test binary and executes it, offering clear output that shows the success or failure of tests.

```
$ go test
```

This command automatically discovers and runs all test files in the current directory. A test file is identified by the suffix _test.go. For instance, if you have a file named example_test.go, the go test command will include it.

Detailed Test Execution

In many cases, more detailed output is desired to diagnose issues or gain insights into the testing process. This is where the -v flag becomes useful. When running tests with the -v flag, Go provides verbose output, enumerating each test case along with its pass or fail status.

```
$ go test -v
```

Verbose execution generates output that resembles:

```
=== RUN   TestExampleFunction
--- PASS: TestExampleFunction (0.00s)
PASS
ok      example.com/project/package   0.001s
```

Each test function, prefixed with Test, is listed along with its status (e.g., PASS, FAIL, or SKIP) and the time taken to execute.

Output Interpretation

Understanding the structure of the test output is essential for effective debugging and validation: - === RUN marks the beginning of a test function. - — PASS indicates a successful test. - FAIL indicates an unsuccessful test. - ok signals that all tests within a package have completed and passes. - The time metrics help identify performance bottlenecks, critical for optimizing test execution times.

Consider a scenario where a failing test is encountered:

```
$ go test -v
```

```
=== RUN   TestFailingFunction
--- FAIL: TestFailingFunction (0.00s)
        example_test.go:10: Expected false, but got true
FAIL
exit status 1
FAIL    example.com/project/package   0.001s
```

Here, example_test.go:10 directs the programmer to the line where the error occurred. The message Expected false, but got true gives valuable insight into what went wrong. The line where the test fails often contains a t.Errorf or t.Fatalf call, generating this output.

Additionally, skipping tests is possible when certain conditions are not met. For instance, long-running tests might be skipped based on environmental conditions. This can be achieved using the t.Skip method within a test function.

```
func TestSkippedFunction(t *testing.T) {
    if testing.Short() {
        t.Skip("skipping test in short mode.")
    }
    // test logic...
}
```

Running go test -short will skip tests that call t.Skip under the testing.Short() condition. The output will reflect this:

```
=== RUN   TestSkippedFunction
    example_test.go:5: skipping test in short mode.
--- SKIP: TestSkippedFunction (0.00s)
PASS
ok      example.com/project/package   0.001s
```

SKIP informs the user that the test has been intentionally bypassed.

Running Tests for Specific Functions

It is also possible to run a subset of tests, focusing on specific functions rather than the entire test suite. This can significantly save time and focus efforts on problematic areas. The -run flag takes a regular expression matching the names of tests to be executed.

```
$ go test -run TestSpecificFunction
```

This will execute tests only matching TestSpecificFunction. To match a pattern of test names:

```
$ go test -run 'Test*Function'
```

This pattern matches all tests with names starting with Test and ending with Function, providing flexibility in test execution.

Extended Output Control

For further refining the test execution and report analysis, various flags are available: - -cover to include coverage reports. - -bench to include benchmarks. - -timeout to set a test timeout.

Understanding and utilizing these flags can significantly enhance the depth of test insights and the coverage of test metrics.

Incorporating these advanced techniques and flags empowers developers to perform detailed and streamlined testing operations, leading to greater code reliability and robustness without redundant testing overhead.

11.9 Organizing Test Files and Packages

Effective organization of test files and packages in Go is critical to maintaining a clean and efficient codebase. Proper organization not only enhances readability and maintainability but also facilitates easier execution of tests. This section details best practices for organizing test files and packages in Go, which involves leveraging Go's directory structure conventions, categorizing tests logically, and employing naming conventions.

Directory Structure: Go enforces a strict convention for organizing source files and tests. Test files should typically reside in the same directory as the files they are testing. The test file names follow a specific pattern. For instance, if we have a source file named example.go, the corresponding test file should be named example_test.go.

Example directory structure:

```
myproject/
  main.go
  main_test.go
  utils/
     utils.go
     utils_test.go
  handlers/
     handlers.go
     handlers_test.go
  models/
     models.go
     models_test.go
```

Test File Naming Conventions: Test file names should end with _-test.go. This convention is essential because Go's built-in testing tool, go test, explicitly searches for files ending with _test.go. Inside these test files, test functions should follow the pattern TestFunctionName(t *testing.T) where 'FunctionName' corresponds to the actual function being tested.

Here's an example of a function and its test:

```
package utils
```

```go
// Add adds two integers
func Add(a int, b int) int {
    return a + b
}
```

Listing 11.15: Example function and its test

```go
package utils

import (
    "testing"
)

func TestAdd(t *testing.T) {
    result := Add(2, 3)
    if result != 5 {
        t.Errorf("Expected 5, but got %d", result)
    }
}
```

Listing 11.16: Test for the Add function

Logical Grouping: It is good practice to group tests logically within the same directory as their respective source files. For example, all utility functions and their tests would be placed under the utils directory. This practice ensures that tests are easily discoverable and directly associated with the functionality they validate.

Internal vs. External Tests: In Go, we differentiate between internal and external tests based on whether the tests are part of the same package as the code they are testing. Internal tests are useful for testing unexported functions and methods. These tests reside in the same package as the code and can access unexported members.

External tests, by contrast, are placed in a different package, typically named packagename_test. These tests can only access exported functions and methods but simulate how external users interact with the package. This helps in validating the package's public API and its usability.

Example of internal and external tests:

```go
package handlers

// Internal test in handlers_test.go
func TestInternalFunction(t *testing.T) {
    // Call an unexported function within the package
    result := internalFunction()
    if result != expected {
        t.Errorf("Expected %v, but got %v", expected, result)
```

```
    }
}

// External test in handlers_extern_test.go
package handlers_test

import (
    "testing"
    "handlers"
)

func TestExternalFunction(t *testing.T) {
    result := handlers.ExternalFunction()
    if result != expected {
        t.Errorf("Expected %v, but got %v", expected, result)
    }
}
```

Listing 11.17: Internal and external tests

Using Mocks and Stubs: Organizing test files and packages effectively also involves structuring mocks and stubs appropriately. Mocks simulate the behavior of real objects, whereas stubs provide predefined responses. Both are essential tools in unit testing for isolating the code under test.

Mocks and stubs should reside in the same directory as the tests that use them. For example, if you create a mock for a database interface, ensure that the mock resides within the same directory as the test that utilizes it.

Example of a mock:

```
package handlers

import (
    "github.com/stretchr/testify/mock"
)

// MockDB is a mock of the DB interface
type MockDB struct {
    mock.Mock
}

func (m *MockDB) GetUser(id int) (User, error) {
    args := m.Called(id)
    return args.Get(0).(User), args.Error(1)
}
```

Listing 11.18: Example of a mock implementation

Integrating these organizational practices promotes a structured, maintainable, and efficient testing strategy. Ensuring a uniform layout across the project aids in seamless navigation and quick identification of relevant tests, fostering a better development and testing lifecycle.

11.10 Code Coverage Analysis

Code coverage analysis is a critical component of software testing, offering a quantitative measure of how much of the source code has been tested. In Go, the standard toolchain provides robust support for code coverage analysis through the go test command. This section delves into the methodologies and tools used for measuring code coverage, interpreting coverage reports, and integrating coverage analysis into your development workflow.

To measure code coverage, Go utilizes a combination of instrumentation and the cover tool to collect coverage data. Instrumentation involves inserting special instructions into the code to track execution paths. This process is automated by Go's testing tools.

Listing 11.19: Running Tests with Coverage Analysis

```
go test -cover ./...
```

This command runs the tests in the specified packages and generates a coverage report. The -cover flag instructs go test to collect coverage data. The ./... pattern informs Go to include all subdirectories recursively.

To gain a deeper understanding of the coverage report, you can generate a detailed profile file. This can be achieved by using the -coverprofile flag as shown below.

Listing 11.20: Generating a Coverage Profile

```
go test -coverprofile=coverage.out ./...
```

The output file coverage.out is a plain text file that contains information about which parts of the code were executed during the test run. This file can be further analyzed to generate a human-readable report using the go tool cover command.

To visualize the coverage data, use the following command:

Listing 11.21: Visualizing Coverage Data

```
go tool cover -html=coverage.out
```

This command processes the coverage.out file and opens a web browser displaying an HTML visualization of the code coverage. This visualization highlights the executed and unexecuted lines, helping you identify untested parts of your codebase.

For projects adhering to continuous integration (CI) practices, integrating code coverage analysis into the pipeline ensures that coverage metrics are generated with every build. Here is an example of a CI configuration using GitHub Actions:

Listing 11.22: GitHub Actions CI Configuration for Coverage Analysis

```
name Go

on
  push
    branches [main]
  pull_request
    branches [main]

jobs
  test
    runs-on ubuntu-latest

    steps
    - uses actions/checkout@v2
    - name Set up Go
      uses actions/setup-go@v2
      with
        go-version '^1.16'
    - name Run tests with coverage
      run |
        go test -coverprofile=coverage.out ./...
        go tool cover -func=coverage.out
    - name Upload coverage report
      uses actions/upload-artifact@v2
      with
        name coverage-report
        path coverage.out
```

Analyzing code coverage data involves interpreting the coverage percentage and identifying areas of the code that are not tested. The go tool cover -func=coverage.out command can be used to generate a summary of coverage data for functions in a package, providing insights into which functions require additional testing.

Listing 11.23: Generating Function-Level Coverage Report

```
go tool cover -func=coverage.out
```

```
github.com/example/project/main.go:15:   init        100.0%
github.com/example/project/main.go:25:   main         85.7%
total:                         (statements)    92.5%
```

The report shows the coverage percentage for each function, with an overall summary at the bottom. A high coverage percentage indicates that a significant portion of the code has been tested, while a lower percentage suggests that additional tests are needed to achieve comprehensive test coverage.

Incorporating code coverage analysis into your development workflow can significantly improve code quality by ensuring that all code paths are exercised by your tests. However, it is crucial to recognize that achieving 100

Practices such as writing table-driven tests, employing boundary testing, and creating tests for both common and edge cases are essential to complement code coverage metrics. Additionally, integrating linting tools and static analysis tools into your workflow can further enhance the robustness and reliability of your codebase.

As you advance in Go programming, you will find that combining code coverage analysis with other testing methodologies creates a holistic approach to software quality assurance. This approach ensures that your code is not only well-covered but also well-tested, leading to more resilient and reliable software systems.

11.11 Best Practices for Testing

Testing in Go is essential to ensure the reliability and correctness of your codebase. Adhering to certain best practices can significantly enhance the effectiveness of your tests, making them more maintainable and easier to understand. This section outlines several key best practices for testing in Go.

1. Write Clear and Concise Tests

Clear and concise tests are easier to read, understand, and maintain. Use descriptive names for your test functions to convey their purpose. For instance, instead of naming a function Test1, use a meaningful name like TestCalculateSumWithPositiveNumbers.

```
func TestCalculateSumWithPositiveNumbers(t *testing.T) {
    result := CalculateSum(3, 5)
    if result != 8 {
        t.Errorf("Expected 8, but got %d", result)
    }
}
```

This test clearly specifies that it is testing the CalculateSum function with positive numbers and checks if the result is as expected.

2. Use Table-Driven Tests

Table-driven tests allow for testing multiple scenarios with a single test function. This makes the test code more compact and easier to manage. Define the test cases in a slice and iterate over them.

```
func TestCalculateSum(t *testing.T) {
    tests := []struct {
        name string
        a, b int
        expected int
    }{
        {"positive numbers", 3, 5, 8},
        {"negative numbers", -2, -3, -5},
        {"mixed numbers", -2, 5, 3},
    }

    for _, tt := range tests {
        t.Run(tt.name, func(t *testing.T) {
            result := CalculateSum(tt.a, tt.b)
            if result != tt.expected {
                t.Errorf("Expected %d, but got %d", tt.expected, result)
            }
        })
    }
}
```

Here, t.Run allows naming each sub-test, and if a sub-test fails, it will be easier to identify which case caused the failure.

3. Check for Edge Cases

Edge cases are scenarios that occur at the extreme ends of the input spectrum. Testing edge cases ensures your code handles all possible scenarios gracefully. For example, if you are testing a function that divides numbers, include edge cases such as division by zero.

```
func TestDivide(t *testing.T) {
    tests := []struct {
        name string
```

```
        dividend, divisor, expected float64
        wantErr bool
    }{
        {"divide by non-zero", 10, 2, 5, false},
        {"divide by zero", 10, 0, 0, true},
    }

    for _, tt := range tests {
        t.Run(tt.name, func(t *testing.T) {
            result, err := Divide(tt.dividend, tt.divisor)
            if (err != nil) != tt.wantErr {
                t.Errorf("Expected error: %v, got: %v", tt.wantErr, err)
            }
            if result != tt.expected && !tt.wantErr {
                t.Errorf("Expected %f, but got %f", tt.expected, result)
            }
        })
    }
}
```

In this example, the test verifies that the division function handles division by zero appropriately by checking for an error.

4. Isolate Tests from External Dependencies

Tests should not depend on external systems such as databases, APIs, or file systems, as these dependencies can make tests flaky and slow. Use mocking or dependency injection to isolate your tests.

Consider the following example of testing a function that fetches data from an API:

```
type MockAPIClient struct{}

func (m *MockAPIClient) GetData() (string, error) {
    return "mock data", nil
}

func TestFetchData(t *testing.T) {
    client := &MockAPIClient{}
    data, err := FetchData(client)
    if err != nil {
        t.Fatalf("Expected no error, but got %v", err)
    }
    if data != "mock data" {
        t.Errorf("Expected 'mock data', but got %s", data)
    }
}
```

Here, MockAPIClient mocks the API client, ensuring that the test does not depend on the actual API.

5. Use Setup and Teardown Functions

For tests that require setup or teardown, use the t.Cleanup function to register cleanup functions. This ensures that resources are properly released after each test.

```
func TestWithSetupAndTeardown(t *testing.T) {
    setup := func() {
        // perform setup
    }
    teardown := func() {
        // perform teardown
    }

    t.Cleanup(teardown)
    setup()

    // Test implementation
}
```

This approach ensures that even if a test fails, the teardown function will still be executed.

6. Ensure Tests are Deterministic

Tests should produce the same results every time they run. Avoid using random values or relying on external state. If you must use random values, set a seed using math/rand to ensure reproducibility.

math/rand package example with seed:

```
func TestRandomFunction(t *testing.T) {
    rand.Seed(42) // Use a fixed seed for reproducibility
    val := generateRandomValue()
    if val != 10 { // Expected value based on the seed
        t.Errorf("Expected 10, but got %d", val)
    }
}
```

This ensures that the random value generated is predictable and the test remains deterministic.

7. Test for Performance

Performance tests help identify and address potential bottlenecks. Use Go's benchmarking capabilities to measure performance and compare different implementations.

```
func BenchmarkCalculateSum(b *testing.B) {
    for i := 0; i < b.N; i++ {
        CalculateSum(3, 5)
    }
```

```
}
```

Run benchmarks using the `go test -bench .` command to analyze the performance.

Adhering to these best practices enables the development of robust, reliable, and maintainable tests in Go, contributing to the overall quality and reliability of the software.

11.12 Integration and End-to-End Testing

Integration and end-to-end testing are critical in ensuring that the components of your Go applications work together as intended and that the application behaves as expected from the user's perspective. These testing strategies focus on the interactions between different parts of a system and how the system operates in a production-like environment.

Integration Testing involves testing multiple components or systems together to verify that they interact correctly. The goal is to identify issues that may not surface during unit testing, such as interface mismatches, data format problems, or incorrect assumptions about external systems.

End-to-End Testing goes a step further by testing the entire application flow, starting from user interaction to the backend processes and storage systems, mimicking real-world usage as closely as possible.

Let's look at the critical steps and considerations when performing integration and end-to-end testing in Go.

Setting Up Integration Tests

Start by structuring your tests to isolate the system components. Ensure you have a clear understanding of the interactions that must be tested. Consider the following general steps for setting up integration tests in Go:

- Identify the components to integrate and test.
- Mock or stub external dependencies to control the test environment and scenarios.
- Use Go's `testing.T` framework to run the integration tests.
- Clean up any resources or states that tests may alter.

For instance, suppose we have a web service that interacts with a database. An integration test might ensure that the service correctly writes a record to the database and retrieves it. Here's a sample code snippet demonstrating this integration test:

```
package integration_test

import (
    "testing"
    "net/http"
    "net/http/httptest"
    "database/sql"
    _ "github.com/lib/pq" // PostgreSQL driver
)

func TestCreateAndRetrieveRecord(t *testing.T) {
    db, err := sql.Open("postgres", "user=postgres dbname=test sslmode=disable
        ")
    if err != nil {
        t.Fatal(err)
    }
    defer db.Close()

    // Mock HTTP request to create a record
    req, err := http.NewRequest("POST", "/create", nil)
    if err != nil {
        t.Fatal(err)
    }
    rr := httptest.NewRecorder()
    handler := http.HandlerFunc(CreateRecordHandler)
    handler.ServeHTTP(rr, req)

    // Check if the record creation was successful
    if status := rr.Code; status != http.StatusOK {
        t.Errorf("handler returned wrong status code: got %v want %v", status,
            http.StatusOK)
    }

    // Query the database to retrieve the created record
    var name string
    err = db.QueryRow("SELECT name FROM records WHERE id = $1", 1).
        Scan(&name)
    if err != nil {
        t.Fatal(err)
    }

    // Verify the retrieved record
    if name != "Expected Name" {
        t.Errorf("expected name to be 'Expected Name', got %v", name)
    }
}
```

Listing 11.24: Integration Test for Web Service and Database

End-to-End Testing Considerations

End-to-end tests simulate real user scenarios to ensure that the entire application system works as expected. Key aspects to consider when designing end-to-end tests include the following:

- Simulating realistic user interactions.
- Maintaining a near-production environment, including databases, external APIs, and servers.
- Automating test scenarios to cover various application flows.
- Ensuring test isolation to avoid dependencies between tests.

Using tools like Selenium for web applications or Appium for mobile applications can facilitate end-to-end testing by mimicking user interactions like button clicks, form submissions, and navigation.

Below is an example of an end-to-end test for a web application using the chromedp package in Go, which allows controlling Chrome from Go to simulate user actions:

```
package main

import (
    "context"
    "log"
    "github.com/chromedp/chromedp"
    "github.com/chromedp/chromedp/kb"
    "github.com/chromedp/chromedp/runner"
)

func main() {
    ctx, cancel := chromedp.NewContext(context.Background(), chromedp.
          WithRunnerOptions(runner.Headless))
    defer cancel()

    var res string

    err := chromedp.Run(ctx,
        chromedp.Navigate("http://example.com"),
        chromedp.WaitVisible(`#inputField`, chromedp.ByID),
        chromedp.SendKeys(`#inputField`, "sample text", chromedp.ByID),
        chromedp.Click(`#submitButton`, chromedp.ByID),
        chromedp.WaitVisible(`#result`, chromedp.ByID),
```

```
        chromedp.Text(`#result`, &res, chromedp.ByID),
    )
    if err != nil {
        log.Fatalf("chromedp failed: %v", err)
    }

    log.Printf("Result: %s", res)
}
```

Listing 11.25: End-to-End Test Using chromedp

Best Practices for Integration and End-to-End Testing

When implementing integration and end-to-end tests, adhere to the following best practices:

- **Maintain test environments**: Use containers or virtual machines to replicate your production environment accurately.
- **Automate cleanup**: Ensure that each test cleans up resources to prevent state leakage across tests.
- **Prioritize tests**: Focus on critical paths and high-risk areas of your application.
- **Monitor test performance**: Regularly measure and optimize test performance to avoid slow and flakey tests.
- **Integrate with CI/CD**: Implement integration and end-to-end tests within your Continuous Integration and Continuous Deployment (CI/CD) pipelines for early detection of issues.

Properly implemented integration and end-to-end tests can significantly enhance the reliability and quality of your Go applications by ensuring that all system components work seamlessly together.

Chapter 12

Practical Applications and Projects

This chapter applies Go programming concepts to real-world scenarios by guiding you through various practical applications and projects. It includes building a simple web server, creating a RESTful API, working with databases, and developing a command-line tool. Additional projects cover concurrent data processing, JSON parsing, file automation, and building a real-time chat application. The chapter also addresses implementing middleware, deploying Go applications, optimizing performance, and provides case studies and example projects for hands-on experience.

12.1 Building a Simple Web Server

Building a simple web server in Go is an excellent way to explore the language's strong support for networking and HTTP service development. This section demonstrates setting up a basic web server that responds to HTTP requests. We will cover defining HTTP handlers, routing requests, and running the server.

To begin, we need to import the net/http package, which provides essential HTTP client and server implementations. We write a simple handler function to respond to HTTP requests.

```
package main
```

```
import (
    "fmt"
    "net/http"
)

func handler(w http.ResponseWriter, r *http.Request) {
    fmt.Fprintf(w, "Hello, World!")
}

func main() {
    http.HandleFunc("/", handler)
    http.ListenAndServe(":8080", nil)
}
```

Listing 12.1: Basic Web Server Handler

In the above script, we define a function named handler that takes an http.ResponseWriter and an *http.Request as parameters. The handler function uses fmt.Fprintf to write the string "Hello, World!" to the response.

The main function registers the / route with handler using http.HandleFunc. It then starts the web server listening on port 8080 by calling http.ListenAndServe(":8080", nil). Upon accessing http://localhost:8080 from a web browser, the message "Hello, World!" is displayed.

A more complex web server might have multiple endpoints and need to manage various resources more efficiently. This involves creating multiple handler functions and using a multiplexer to route different paths to these handlers.

```
package main

import (
    "fmt"
    "net/http"
)

func helloHandler(w http.ResponseWriter, r *http.Request) {
    fmt.Fprintf(w, "Hello, World!")
}

func aboutHandler(w http.ResponseWriter, r *http.Request) {
    fmt.Fprintf(w, "This is the About page.")
}

func main() {
    http.HandleFunc("/", helloHandler)
```

```
    http.HandleFunc("/about", aboutHandler)
    http.ListenAndServe(":8080", nil)
}
```

Listing 12.2: Multiple Handlers Example

The helloHandler and aboutHandler functions serve different content based on the URL path specified. The http.HandleFunc function associates these handlers with their respective routes. When users visit /, they see "Hello, World!", and when they visit /about, they see "This is the About page."

For proper structuring, especially in larger applications, it is advisable to use a router like gorilla/mux. The mux router allows for more sophisticated handling of routes and variables.

```
package main

import (
    "fmt"
    "net/http"
    "github.com/gorilla/mux"
)

func helloHandler(w http.ResponseWriter, r *http.Request) {
    fmt.Fprintf(w, "Hello, World!")
}

func aboutHandler(w http.ResponseWriter, r *http.Request) {
    fmt.Fprintf(w, "This is the About page.")
}

func main() {
    r := mux.NewRouter()
    r.HandleFunc("/", helloHandler)
    r.HandleFunc("/about", aboutHandler)
    http.ListenAndServe(":8080", r)
}
```

Listing 12.3: Go Server Using gorilla/mux Router

In this example, we use the github.com/gorilla/mux package, so it must first be installed using the command:

```
go get -u github.com/gorilla/mux
```

We initialize a new router with mux.NewRouter() and define routes using r.HandleFunc. The router is then passed to http.ListenAndServe to handle incoming requests. This setup allows for better organization and scalability.

Additionally, configuring the HTTP server using the http.Server struct allows for more customization, such as setting read/write timeouts and configuring TLS.

```
package main

import (
    "fmt"
    "net/http"
    "time"
)

func handler(w http.ResponseWriter, r *http.Request) {
    fmt.Fprintf(w, "Hello, Secure World!")
}

func main() {
    srv := &http.Server{
        Handler: http.HandlerFunc(handler),
        Addr: ":8080",
        WriteTimeout: 15 * time.Second,
        ReadTimeout: 15 * time.Second,
    }
    srv.ListenAndServe()
}
```

Listing 12.4: Configuring HTTP Server with Custom Settings

Here, the http.Server struct is customized with timeouts for better control over the server's resource management. The Handler field is set using the http.HandlerFunc adapter, converting a function to an http.Handler.

Developers can also respond with JSON by setting the appropriate content type and encoding data using the encoding/json package.

```
package main

import (
    "encoding/json"
    "net/http"
)

type Message struct {
    Text string `json:"text"`
}

func jsonHandler(w http.ResponseWriter, r *http.Request) {
    msg := Message{Text: "Hello, JSON!"}
    w.Header().Set("Content-Type", "application/json")
    json.NewEncoder(w).Encode(msg)
}
```

```
func main() {
    http.HandleFunc("/json", jsonHandler)
    http.ListenAndServe(":8080", nil)
}
```

Listing 12.5: Returning JSON Responses

The Message struct is defined with a single field Text and tagged for JSON encoding. The jsonHandler function creates a Message instance, sets the response content type to application/json, and encodes the message into JSON format.

Building web servers in Go is straightforward and efficient, leveraging the language's robust standard library and its performance-focused design.

12.2 Creating a RESTful API

Representational State Transfer (REST) is an architectural style for designing networked applications. In this section, we will explore how to create a RESTful API using Go programming language. This involves defining routes, handling requests, and sending responses.

To begin, we need to import the necessary packages. We will utilize net/http for HTTP functionality and encoding/json for JSON handling.

```
package main

import (
    "encoding/json"
    "net/http"
    "log"
)
```

Next, we'll define a struct to represent the data that our API will manage. For illustration purposes, consider a simple system managing books in a library.

```
type Book struct {
    ID string `json:"id"`
    Title string `json:"title"`
    Author string `json:"author"`
}

var books []Book
```

We'll also create a helper function to initialize some data for our API.

```
func initializeBooks() {
    books = []Book{
        {ID: "1", Title: "1984", Author: "George Orwell"},
        {ID: "2", Title: "To Kill a Mockingbird", Author: "Harper Lee"},
    }
}
```

Now, let's create the main function which serves as our entry point. This function will initialize the book data and define the HTTP routes.

```
func main() {
    initializeBooks()
    http.HandleFunc("/books", getBooks)
    http.HandleFunc("/books/", getBook)
    log.Fatal(http.ListenAndServe(":8080", nil))
}
```

We need to define the getBooks handler function to respond to requests for the list of books. This function will encode the data as JSON and send it back to the client.

```
func getBooks(w http.ResponseWriter, r *http.Request) {
    w.Header().Set("Content-Type", "application/json")
    json.NewEncoder(w).Encode(books)
}
```

To handle requests for a single book, we'll define the getBook handler function. This function extracts the book ID from the URL, finds the corresponding book in our data, and encodes it as JSON.

```
func getBook(w http.ResponseWriter, r *http.Request) {
    id := r.URL.Path[len("/books/"):]
    for _, book := range books {
        if book.ID == id {
            w.Header().Set("Content-Type", "application/json")
            json.NewEncoder(w).Encode(book)
            return
        }
    }
    http.Error(w, "Book not found", http.StatusNotFound)
}
```

Our API can be further expanded to handle the creation, updating, and deletion of books. Let's start by defining a function to create a new book.

```
func createBook(w http.ResponseWriter, r *http.Request) {
    var book Book
```

```
    err := json.NewDecoder(r.Body).Decode(&book)
    if err != nil {
        http.Error(w, err.Error(), http.StatusBadRequest)
        return
    }
    books = append(books, book)
    w.Header().Set("Content-Type", "application/json")
    json.NewEncoder(w).Encode(book)
}
```

We'll add an HTTP handler for this new route in the main function.

```
http.HandleFunc("/books", createBook)
```

For updating an existing book, we need another function that modifies the book's data.

```
func updateBook(w http.ResponseWriter, r *http.Request) {
    id := r.URL.Path[len("/books/"):]
    var updatedBook Book
    err := json.NewDecoder(r.Body).Decode(&updatedBook)
    if err != nil {
        http.Error(w, err.Error(), http.StatusBadRequest)
        return
    }
    for i, book := range books {
        if book.ID == id {
            books[i] = updatedBook
            w.Header().Set("Content-Type", "application/json")
            json.NewEncoder(w).Encode(updatedBook)
            return
        }
    }
    http.Error(w, "Book not found", http.StatusNotFound)
}
```

Similarly, we'll add an HTTP handler for this route in the main function.

```
http.HandleFunc("/books/", updateBook)
```

Lastly, we need to define a function to delete a book from the library.

```
func deleteBook(w http.ResponseWriter, r *http.Request) {
    id := r.URL.Path[len("/books/"):]
    for i, book := range books {
        if book.ID == id {
            books = append(books[:i], books[i+1:]...)
            w.WriteHeader(http.StatusNoContent)
            return
        }
    }
```

```
    http.Error(w, "Book not found", http.StatusNotFound)
}
```

This route will also be added to the main function.

```
http.HandleFunc("/books/", deleteBook)
```

With these functions and routes, we have a basic RESTful API that can create, read, update, and delete books.

The implementation of these basic CRUD operations provides a solid foundation for building more complex APIs. Users are encouraged to extend the functionalities by adding appropriate error handling, authentication mechanisms, and features such as pagination and filtering. The modular nature of Go makes it suitable for developing scalable and maintainable APIs.

Execution of this RESTful API can be observed with the following commands. First, run the Go server:

```
$ go run main.go
```

To see the list of books via a GET request:

```
$ curl http://localhost:8080/books
```

To add a new book via a POST request:

```
$ curl -X POST -d '{"id": "3", "title": "Brave New World", "author": "Aldous Huxley"}' -
H "Content-Type: application/json" http://localhost:8080/books
```

To retrieve a specific book via GET request:

```
$ curl http://localhost:8080/books/3
```

To update a book via PUT request:

```
$ curl -X PUT -d '{"id": "3", "title": "Brave New World", "author": "Aldous Huxley Updated"}' -
H "Content-Type: application/json" http://localhost:8080/books/3
```

To delete a book via DELETE request:

```
$ curl -X DELETE http://localhost:8080/books/3
```

12.3 Working with Databases

Integrating databases into your Go applications allows you to store, retrieve, and manipulate data effectively. This section covers the essentials of working with databases in Go, including connecting to databases, executing queries, and using an ORM (Object-Relational Mapping) for more complex data interactions. We will focus on using SQLite and PostgreSQL as our main databases, but the principles can be applied to other relational databases as well.

Setting Up SQLite Database

SQLite is a self-contained, serverless SQL database engine. To use SQLite in Go, we need to install the required package. In this case, we will use the github.com/mattn/go-sqlite3 package. First, ensure that you have this package installed:

```
go get github.com/mattn/go-sqlite3
```

Here is an example of how to set up a connection to an SQLite database and perform basic operations:

```
package main

import (
    "database/sql"
    "fmt"
    _ "github.com/mattn/go-sqlite3"
)

func main() {
    db, err := sql.Open("sqlite3", "./foo.db")
    if err != nil {
        fmt.Println(err)
        return
    }
    defer db.Close()

    statement, err := db.Prepare("CREATE TABLE IF NOT EXISTS user (id
         INTEGER PRIMARY KEY, name TEXT)")
    if err != nil {
        fmt.Println(err)
        return
    }
    statement.Exec()

    statement, err = db.Prepare("INSERT INTO user (name) VALUES (?)")
    if err != nil {
        fmt.Println(err)
```

```
        return
    }
    statement.Exec("Alice")

    rows, err := db.Query("SELECT id, name FROM user")
    if err != nil {
        fmt.Println(err)
        return
    }

    var id int
    var name string
    for rows.Next() {
        rows.Scan(&id, &name)
        fmt.Println(id, name)
    }
}
```

In the above code, the sql.Open function establishes a connection to the SQLite database named foo.db. The db.Prepare method prepares a SQL statement for execution, and statement.Exec executes it. The db.Query method retrieves rows from the database, and the rows.Next method iterates through the result set.

Connecting to PostgreSQL Database

PostgreSQL is a powerful, open-source relational database system. To connect to PostgreSQL in Go, we will use the github.com/lib/pq package. Install the package using the following command:

```
go get github.com/lib/pq
```

Here is an example of how to connect to a PostgreSQL database and execute some typical operations:

```
package main

import (
    "database/sql"
    "fmt"
    _ "github.com/lib/pq"
)

const (
    host = "localhost"
    port = 5432
    user = "yourusername"
    password = "yourpassword"
    dbname = "yourdbname"
)
```

```
func main() {
    psqlInfo := fmt.Sprintf("host=%s port=%d user=%s "+
        "password=%s dbname=%s sslmode=disable",
        host, port, user, password, dbname)

    db, err := sql.Open("postgres", psqlInfo)
    if err != nil {
        fmt.Println(err)
        return
    }
    defer db.Close()

    err = db.Ping()
    if err != nil {
        fmt.Println(err)
        return
    }

    fmt.Println("Successfully connected!")

    _, err = db.Exec("CREATE TABLE IF NOT EXISTS person (id SERIAL
        PRIMARY KEY, name VARCHAR(50), age INT)")
    if err != nil {
        fmt.Println(err)
        return
    }

    _, err = db.Exec("INSERT INTO person (name, age) VALUES ($1, $2)", "
        Bob", 30)
    if err != nil {
        fmt.Println(err)
        return
    }

    rows, err := db.Query("SELECT id, name, age FROM person")
    if err != nil {
        fmt.Println(err)
        return
    }

    defer rows.Close()
    for rows.Next() {
        var id int
        var name string
        var age int
        err = rows.Scan(&id, &name, &age)
        if err != nil {
            fmt.Println(err)
            return
        }
        fmt.Println(id, name, age)
    }
}
```

In this script, we define connection parameters like host, port, user, password, and dbname. Using these parameters, we create a connection string and connect to the PostgreSQL database with sql.Open. The db.Ping function checks if the connection to the database is alive. We then execute SQL statements to create a table, insert data, and query data.

Using an ORM: GORM

GORM is an ORM library for Go that simplifies interactions with the database. It supports several databases, including MySQL, PostgreSQL, and SQLite. First, install the GORM package along with the appropriate dialect for your database. For instance, for PostgreSQL, you can use the following commands:

```
go get -u gorm.io/gorm
go get -u gorm.io/driver/postgres
```

Here is an example of how to use GORM with PostgreSQL:

```
package main

import (
    "fmt"
    "gorm.io/driver/postgres"
    "gorm.io/gorm"
)

type Product struct {
    gorm.Model
    Code string
    Price uint
}

func main() {
    dsn := "host=localhost user=yourusername password=yourpassword dbname
        =yourdbname port=5432 sslmode=disable"
    db, err := gorm.Open(postgres.Open(dsn), &gorm.Config{})

    if err != nil {
        fmt.Println(err)
        return
    }

    db.AutoMigrate(&Product{})

    db.Create(&Product{Code: "L1212", Price: 1000})

    var product Product
```

```
    db.First(&product, 1)
    fmt.Println(product)

    product.Price = 2000
    db.Save(&product)

    db.Delete(&product)
}
```

In this example, we define a Product struct to represent a database table. The Model embedded struct provides fields like ID, CreatedAt, UpdatedAt, and DeletedAt. We connect to the PostgreSQL database using GORM's gorm.Open function. The AutoMigrate function creates the Product table if it does not already exist. Basic CRUD operations are then performed using methods like Create, First, Save, and Delete.

Working with databases in Go requires proficiency in connecting to a database, executing SQL queries, and managing transactions. Utilizing ORM libraries like GORM can significantly simplify these operations by providing an abstraction layer over raw SQL queries. These skills are fundamental for building robust, data-driven applications.

12.4 Building a Command-Line Tool

Command-line tools are integral to developers and system administrators for automating tasks and improving productivity. Using the Go programming language, this section elaborates on the steps to construct a simple yet functional command-line application.

Project Overview

We will develop a command-line tool called wordcount, which reads a text file and counts the number of words, lines, and characters in the file. This tool will accept various command-line arguments to customize its behavior.

Setting Up the Environment

First, ensure that you have Go installed on your system. Verify the installation by running:

Listing 12.6: Verify Go Installation

```
$ go version
```

```
go version go1.17.1 linux/amd64
```

Create a new directory for the wordcount project and navigate into it:

Listing 12.7: Creating Project Directory

```
$ mkdir wordcount
$ cd wordcount
```

Writing the Main Program

Create a new Go file named main.go. Here we will define the entry point of our application.

```
package main

import (
    "flag"
    "fmt"
    "io/ioutil"
    "log"
    "strings"
)

func main() {
    filePath := flag.String("file", "", "Path to the text file")
    flag.Parse()

    if *filePath == "" {
        log.Fatal("Please provide a file path using the -file flag.")
    }

    content, err := ioutil.ReadFile(*filePath)
    if err != nil {
        log.Fatalf("Failed to read the file: %v", err)
    }

    text := string(content)
    wordCount := len(strings.Fields(text))
    lineCount := len(strings.Split(text, "\n"))
    charCount := len(text)

    fmt.Printf("Words: %d\n", wordCount)
    fmt.Printf("Lines: %d\n", lineCount)
    fmt.Printf("Characters: %d\n", charCount)
}
```

Listing 12.8: Entry Point - main.go

Breakdown of main.go

1. package main: Defines the package name. The main package is the entry point for a Go program. 2. import: Imports necessary packages. 3. flag.String: Defines a command-line flag named file and associates

it with a string variable filePath. 4. flag.Parse(): Parses command-line flags. 5. If filePath is empty, the program logs an error and exits. 6. ioutil.ReadFile: Reads the contents of the specified file. 7. Handles potential read errors using log.Fatalf. 8. Converts the file's byte content to a string. 9. Counts words, lines, and characters using functions like strings.Fields, strings.Split, and len. 10. Outputs the results.

Running the Tool

After writing the code, build and run the tool:

Listing 12.9: Build and Run

```
$ go build -o wordcount
$ ./wordcount -file=sample.txt
```

```
Words: 100
Lines: 20
Characters: 600
```

Enhancing the Command-Line Tool

We will extend the tool to support additional functionalities:

1. Add flags for counting specific characters. 2. Output results in different formats such as JSON.

Update the main.go as follows:

```
package main

import (
    "encoding/json"
    "flag"
    "fmt"
    "io/ioutil"
    "log"
    "strings"
)

type Counts struct {
    Words int `json:"words"`
    Lines int `json:"lines"`
    Characters int `json:"characters"`
}

func main() {
    filePath := flag.String("file", "", "Path to the text file")
    countChar := flag.String("char", "", "Specific character to count")
    outputJSON := flag.Bool("json", false, "Output in JSON format")
    flag.Parse()
```

```
    if *filePath == "" {
        log.Fatal("Please provide a file path using the -file flag.")
    }

    content, err := ioutil.ReadFile(*filePath)
    if err != nil {
        log.Fatalf("Failed to read the file: %v", err)
    }

    text := string(content)
    wordCount := len(strings.Fields(text))
    lineCount := len(strings.Split(text, "\n"))
    charCount := len(text)

    counts := Counts{
        Words: wordCount,
        Lines: lineCount,
        Characters: charCount,
    }

    if *countChar != "" {
        specificCharCount := strings.Count(text, *countChar)
        fmt.Printf("Occurrences of '%s': %d\n", *countChar, specificCharCount)
    }

    if *outputJSON {
        jsonOutput, err := json.MarshalIndent(counts, "", " ")
        if err != nil {
            log.Fatalf("Failed to generate JSON: %v", err)
        }
        fmt.Println(string(jsonOutput))
    } else {
        fmt.Printf("Words: %d\n", wordCount)
        fmt.Printf("Lines: %d\n", lineCount)
        fmt.Printf("Characters: %d\n", charCount)
    }
}
```

Listing 12.10: Enhanced main.go

Running the Enhanced Tool

Build and run the updated tool with additional flags:

Listing 12.11: Build and Run Enhanced Tool

```
$ go build -o wordcount
$ ./wordcount -file=sample.txt -char=a -json
```

```
Occurrences of 'a': 10
{
  "words": 100,
  "lines": 20,
```

```
    "characters": 600
}
```

This extends our command-line tool's capabilities, making it more versatile. Users can count specific characters and receive output in JSON format. This approach exemplifies how Go's robust standard library can efficiently handle tasks and enhance developer productivity.

12.5 Concurrent Data Processing

Concurrent data processing in Go leverages the language's powerful concurrency primitives: goroutines and channels. These features make Go particularly suited for tasks that can be performed in parallel, thus improving the efficiency and performance of data-intensive applications.

Goroutines are lightweight threads managed by the Go runtime. Channels provide a way for goroutines to communicate with each other and synchronize their execution. The combination of these two features allows for robust concurrent programming.

To illustrate the practical application of concurrent data processing, consider a scenario where multiple data sources need to be processed concurrently and the results combined.

```
package main

import (
    "fmt"
    "sync"
)

func processData(id int, wg *sync.WaitGroup, results chan<- int) {
    defer wg.Done()
    // Simulate data processing
    result := id * 2 // Placeholder for actual data processing logic
    results <- result
}

func main() {
    var wg sync.WaitGroup
    results := make(chan int, 10) // Buffered channel for results
    numDataSources := 10

    for i := 0; i < numDataSources; i++ {
        wg.Add(1)
        go processData(i, &wg, results)
```

```
    }

    wg.Wait()
    close(results)

    finalResults := make([]int, 0, numDataSources)
    for result := range results {
        finalResults = append(finalResults, result)
    }

    fmt.Printf("Processed results: %v\n", finalResults)
}
```

Listing 12.12: Concurrent data processing in Go

In this example, the processData function simulates the processing of data. It accepts an identifier, a pointer to a sync.WaitGroup, and a results channel as arguments. The defer wg.Done() statement ensures that the Done method is called when the processData function completes, thereby decrementing the WaitGroup counter.

The main function initializes a sync.WaitGroup and a buffered channel for holding the results. A loop spawns multiple goroutines to process data concurrently, each increments the WaitGroup counter by calling wg.Add(1).

After launching all goroutines, the wg.Wait() call blocks until the counter is zero, meaning all goroutines have finished their work. The results channel is then closed, and the final results are collected and printed.

Channels allow goroutines to communicate without sharing memory directly, which avoids race conditions. By default, channels are unbuffered, but in this case, a buffered channel is used to accommodate the number of results.

For more complex scenarios, such as processing data with varying lengths or prioritizing certain tasks, Go's concurrency primitives can be extended.

```
package main

import (
    "fmt"
    "sync"
    "time"
)

func processData(id int, priority int, wg *sync.WaitGroup, results chan<- int,
        p_ch chan struct{}) {
    defer wg.Done()
```

```
    select {
    case p_ch <- struct{}{}:
        fmt.Printf("Processing high priority data: %d\n", id)
        time.Sleep(time.Millisecond * 50) // Simulate high priority work
        results <- id * 2
        <-p_ch
    default:
        fmt.Printf("Processing normal data: %d\n", id)
        time.Sleep(time.Millisecond * 100) // Simulate normal priority work
        results <- id * 2
    }
}

func main() {
    var wg sync.WaitGroup
    results := make(chan int, 10)
    p_ch := make(chan struct{}, 2) // Priority channel
    numDataSources := 10

    for i := 0; i < numDataSources; i++ {
        wg.Add(1)
        priority := i % 2 // Assign priority alternately for demonstration
        go processData(i, priority, &wg, results, p_ch)
    }

    wg.Wait()
    close(results)

    finalResults := make([]int, 0, numDataSources)
    for result := range results {
        finalResults = append(finalResults, result)
    }

    fmt.Printf("Processed results: %v\n", finalResults)
}
```

Listing 12.13: Advanced concurrent data processing

This example introduces a priority channel p_ch to allow certain goroutines to process high-priority data first. The select statement is used to attempt sending on the priority channel; if successful, the goroutine processes high-priority data. If not, it defaults to processing normal data. The priority channel is buffered with a size of 2, enabling up to two high-priority tasks concurrently.

Concurrent data processing can be further optimized by employing worker pools to handle tasks. Worker pools limit the number of concurrent goroutines, thereby reducing overhead and potentially improving performance.

```
package main
```

```
import (
    "fmt"
    "sync"
)

func worker(id int, tasks <-chan int, results chan<- int, wg *sync.WaitGroup) {
    defer wg.Done()
    for task := range tasks {
        fmt.Printf("Worker %d processing task %d\n", id, task)
        results <- task * 2 // Simulate task processing
    }
}

func main() {
    var wg sync.WaitGroup
    tasks := make(chan int, 10)
    results := make(chan int, 10)
    numWorkers := 3
    numTasks := 10

    // Start workers
    for i := 0; i < numWorkers; i++ {
        wg.Add(1)
        go worker(i, tasks, results, &wg)
    }

    // Send tasks to workers
    go func() {
        for i := 0; i < numTasks; i++ {
            tasks <- i
        }
        close(tasks)
    }()

    // Wait for workers to finish
    wg.Wait()
    close(results)

    finalResults := make([]int, 0, numTasks)
    for result := range results {
        finalResults = append(finalResults, result)
    }

    fmt.Printf("Processed results: %v\n", finalResults)
}
```

Listing 12.14: Concurrent processing with a worker pool

In this pattern, a number of worker goroutines are created to process tasks from a channel. The workers retrieve tasks from the tasks channel, process them, and send the results to the results channel. The main function sends a fixed number of tasks to the tasks channel and closes it once all tasks are dispatched. Finally, the results are aggregated and printed. Thus, concurrent data processing leverages goroutines and channels to efficiently manage multiple data processing tasks. Employing patterns such as worker pools further enhances flexibility and performance in handling complex tasks.

12.6 Parsing and Handling JSON

JSON (JavaScript Object Notation) serves as a lightweight data-interchange format extensively used to represent structured data. It is easy to read and write for humans and simple to parse and generate for machines. In Go, the standard library provides comprehensive support for encoding and decoding JSON via the encoding/json package.

To work with JSON data in Go, we typically perform two primary operations: encoding Go data structures into JSON format, and decoding JSON data into Go data structures.

Decoding JSON data

Consider an example where we have the following JSON data:

```
{
    "Name": "Alice",
    "Age": 30,
    "Email": "alice@example.com",
    "Active": true
}
```

To decode this JSON data into a Go struct, we first define the corresponding struct type. We then use the Unmarshal function from the encoding/json package to decode the JSON into an instance of the struct.

Here's how to accomplish this:

```
package main

import (
    "encoding/json"
    "fmt"
    "log"
)

// User defines the structure corresponding to the JSON data.
```

```
type User struct {
    Name string `json:"Name"`
    Age int `json:"Age"`
    Email string `json:"Email"`
    Active bool `json:"Active"`
}

func main() {
    // JSON data to be decoded.
    jsonData := `{
        "Name": "Alice",
        "Age": 30,
        "Email": "alice@example.com",
        "Active": true
    }`

    // Creating an instance of User to hold the decoded data.
    var user User

    // Decoding JSON data.
    err := json.Unmarshal([]byte(jsonData), &user)
    if err != nil {
        log.Fatalf("error decoding JSON: %v", err)
    }

    // Printing the decoded struct.
    fmt.Printf("%+v\n", user)
}
```

Listing 12.15: Decoding JSON into a Go struct

```
{Name:Alice Age:30 Email:alice@example.com Active:true}
```

In this code:

- The struct User specifies field tags using the json keyword to map JSON keys to struct fields.
- json.Unmarshal converts JSON data into the struct. It takes a byte slice of JSON data and a pointer to the struct where the data will be stored.

Encoding Go data into JSON

To encode a Go struct into JSON format, we use the Marshal function from the encoding/json package. Consider the following example:

```
package main
```

```
import (
    "encoding/json"
    "fmt"
    "log"
)

// User defines the structure to be encoded into JSON.
type User struct {
    Name string `json:"Name"`
    Age int `json:"Age"`
    Email string `json:"Email"`
    Active bool `json:"Active"`
}

func main() {
    // Creating an instance of User.
    user := User{
        Name: "Bob",
        Age: 25,
        Email: "bob@example.com",
        Active: false,
    }

    // Encoding the struct into JSON data.
    jsonData, err := json.Marshal(user)
    if err != nil {
        log.Fatalf("error encoding JSON: %v", err)
    }

    // Converting JSON byte slice to a string and printing.
    fmt.Println(string(jsonData))
}
```

Listing 12.16: Encoding a Go struct into JSON

```
{"Name":"Bob","Age":25,"Email":"bob@example.com","Active":false}
```

In this code:

- The Marshal function converts the Go struct instance into a JSON-encoded byte slice.
- We then print the byte slice as a string to see the JSON representation.

Handling nested JSON structures

In real-world scenarios, JSON data often contains nested objects or arrays. Consider the following JSON data representing nested user information:

```
{
  "Name": "Alice",
  "Age": 30,
  "Email": "alice@example.com",
  "Active": true,
  "Address": {
    "Street": "123 Main St",
    "City": "Metropolis",
    "Zip": "12345"
  }
}
```


We can define Go structs to reflect this nested structure:

```
package main

import (
    "encoding/json"
    "fmt"
    "log"
)

// Address defines the structure of the nested Address object.
type Address struct {
    Street string `json:"Street"`
    City string `json:"City"`
    Zip string `json:"Zip"`
}

// User defines the structure with a nested Address object.
type User struct {
    Name string `json:"Name"`
    Age int `json:"Age"`
    Email string `json:"Email"`
    Active bool `json:"Active"`
    Address Address `json:"Address"`
}

func main() {
    // JSON data with nested object.
    jsonData := `{
        "Name": "Alice",
        "Age": 30,
        "Email": "alice@example.com",
        "Active": true,
        "Address": {
            "Street": "123 Main St",
            "City": "Metropolis",
            "Zip": "12345"
        }
    }`

    // Creating an instance of User to hold the decoded data.
    var user User
```

```
    // Decoding JSON data.
    err := json.Unmarshal([]byte(jsonData), &user)
    if err != nil {
        log.Fatalf("error decoding JSON: %v", err)
    }

    // Printing the decoded struct.
    fmt.Printf("%+v\n", user)
}
```

Listing 12.17: Handling nested JSON structures in Go

```
{Name:Alice Age:30 Email:alice@example.com Active:true Address:{Street:123 Main St City:Metropoli
```

This approach can be extended to handle arrays within JSON data. For example, if the user has multiple addresses:

```
{
    "Name": "Alice",
    "Age": 30,
    "Email": "alice@example.com",
    "Active": true,
    "Addresses": [
        {
            "Street": "123 Main St",
            "City": "Metropolis",
            "Zip": "12345"
        },
        {
            "Street": "456 Side St",
            "City": "Gotham",
            "Zip": "67890"
        }
    ]
}
```

The corresponding Go structs would be:

```
package main

import (
    "encoding/json"
    "fmt"
    "log"
)

// Address defines the structure of address objects.
type Address struct {
    Street string `json:"Street"`
    City string `json:"City"`
    Zip string `json:"Zip"`
}
```

```
// User defines the structure with an array of Address objects.
type User struct {
    Name string `json:"Name"`
    Age int `json:"Age"`
    Email string `json:"Email"`
    Active bool `json:"Active"`
    Addresses []Address `json:"Addresses"`
}

func main() {
    // JSON data with nested array.
    jsonData := `{
        "Name": "Alice",
        "Age": 30,
        "Email": "alice@example.com",
        "Active": true,
        "Addresses": [
            {
                "Street": "123 Main St",
                "City": "Metropolis",
                "Zip": "12345"
            },
            {
                "Street": "456 Side St",
                "City": "Gotham",
                "Zip": "67890"
            }
        ]
    }`

    // Creating an instance of User to hold the decoded data.
    var user User

    // Decoding JSON data.
    err := json.Unmarshal([]byte(jsonData), &user)
    if err != nil {
        log.Fatalf("error decoding JSON: %v", err)
    }

    // Printing the decoded struct.
    fmt.Printf("%+v\n", user)
}
```

Listing 12.18: Handling JSON arrays in Go

```
{Name:Alice Age:30 Email:alice@example.com Active:true Addresses:[{Street:123 Main St City:Metro
```

Handling unknown or dynamic JSON fields

Sometimes we encounter JSON data where the structure is unknown or varies. Go provides a way to handle such JSON data using map structures or empty interfaces.

Suppose we receive JSON data with arbitrary fields:

```
{
  "Name": "Eve",
  "Attributes": {
    "Height": "5.7ft",
    "Weight": "68kg",
    "Hobbies": ["reading", "traveling"]
  }
}
```

We can use a map to handle this dynamic data:

```
package main

import (
    "encoding/json"
    "fmt"
    "log"
)

func main() {
    // JSON data with dynamic fields.
    jsonData := `{
        "Name": "Eve",
        "Attributes": {
            "Height": "5.7ft",
            "Weight": "68kg",
            "Hobbies": [
                "reading",
                "traveling"
            ]
        }
    }`

    // Creating a map to hold the decoded data.
    var data map[string]interface{}

    // Decoding JSON data.
    err := json.Unmarshal([]byte(jsonData), &data)
    if err != nil {
        log.Fatalf("error decoding JSON: %v", err)
    }

    // Printing the decoded map.
    fmt.Printf("%+v\n", data)
}
```

Listing 12.19: Handling dynamic JSON fields in Go

map[Attributes:map[Height:5.7ft Hobbies:[reading traveling] Weight:68kg] Name:Eve]

12.7 File Processing and Automation

In Go, file processing and automation entail manipulating and managing files programmatically. These operations include reading from files, writing to files, searching within files, and automating repetitive file-based tasks. The standard library in Go provides robust support for file I/O through the os, io, and bufio packages. This section explores these capabilities by demonstrating practical examples and explaining key concepts to enhance your understanding.

Reading Files

Reading from a file in Go involves opening the file and using various methods provided by the os package. Below is an example of reading a file's contents and printing it to the standard output:

```
package main

import (
    "fmt"
    "io/ioutil"
    "log"
    "os"
)

func main() {
    fileName := "sample.txt"

    // Open the file for reading
    file, err := os.Open(fileName)
    if err != nil {
        log.Fatalf("Failed to open file: %v", err)
    }
    defer file.Close() // Ensure the file will be closed after reading

    // Read the file's content
    content, err := ioutil.ReadAll(file)
    if err != nil {
        log.Fatalf("Failed to read file: %v", err)
    }

    // Print the file content
    fmt.Println(string(content))
}
```

In this example, the os.Open function is used to open the file, and ioutil.ReadAll reads the entire content of the file into memory. The defer statement ensures the file is closed once the reading operation is complete. The content is then converted to a string and printed.

Writing Files

Writing to a file involves creating or opening the file with appropriate permissions and then writing the desired content. Below is an example demonstrating how to write a string to a file:

```
package main

import (
    "log"
    "os"
)

func main() {
    fileName := "output.txt"
    content := "Hello, World!"

    // Create or open the file for writing
    file, err := os.Create(fileName)
    if err != nil {
        log.Fatalf("Failed to create file: %v", err)
    }
    defer file.Close() // Ensure the file is closed after writing

    // Write content to the file
    _, err = file.WriteString(content)
    if err != nil {
        log.Fatalf("Failed to write to file: %v", err)
    }

    log.Println("File written successfully")
}
```

Here, os.Create opens the file in write mode, creating it if it does not exist. The file.WriteString function writes the string to the file. The defer statement ensures the file is closed after the operation, and logging is used to indicate successful file writing.

Buffered File Operations

For more efficient file processing, especially when dealing with large files, buffered I/O can be used. The bufio package provides buffered readers and writers to optimize read and write operations:

```
package main

import (
    "bufio"
    "log"
    "os"
)

func main() {
    fileName := "largefile.txt"

    // Open the large file
    file, err := os.Open(fileName)
    if err != nil {
        log.Fatalf("Failed to open file: %v", err)
    }
    defer file.Close() // Ensure the file is closed after reading

    // Create a buffered reader
    reader := bufio.NewReader(file)

    // Read the file line by line
    for {
        line, err := reader.ReadString('\n')
        if err != nil {
            if err.Error() == "EOF" {
                break
            }
            log.Fatalf("Failed to read file: %v", err)
        }
        // Process the line
        log.Print(line)
    }
}
```

In this code snippet, bufio.NewReader creates a buffered reader for the given file. The ReadString method reads the file line by line until reaching the end of the file. This approach is particularly useful for processing files that do not fit into memory.

Automating File Processing Tasks

Automation often involves combining file reading and writing tasks with logic to process the data. The following example shows how to read a file line by line, process each line, and write the processed lines to another file:

```
package main

import (
    "bufio"
    "log"
    "os"
    "strings"
)

func main() {
    inputFileName := "input.txt"
    outputFileName := "output.txt"

    // Open the input file
    inputFile, err := os.Open(inputFileName)
    if err != nil {
        log.Fatalf("Failed to open input file: %v", err)
    }
    defer inputFile.Close()

    // Create the output file
    outputFile, err := os.Create(outputFileName)
    if err != nil {
        log.Fatalf("Failed to create output file: %v", err)
    }
    defer outputFile.Close()

    // Create buffered readers and writers
    reader := bufio.NewReader(inputFile)
    writer := bufio.NewWriter(outputFile)

    // Process the file line by line
    for {
        line, err := reader.ReadString('\n')
        if err != nil {
            if err.Error() == "EOF" {
                break
            }
            log.Fatalf("Failed to read from input file: %v", err)
        }

        // Process the line (example: convert to uppercase)
        processedLine := strings.ToUpper(line)

        // Write the processed line to the output file
```

```
        _, err = writer.WriteString(processedLine)
        if err != nil {
            log.Fatalf("Failed to write to output file: %v", err)
        }
    }

    // Ensure all buffered operations are applied
    err = writer.Flush()
    if err != nil {
        log.Fatalf("Failed to flush writer buffer: %v", err)
    }

    log.Println("File processing and automation completed successfully")
}
```

In this comprehensive example, the input file is read line by line, each line is processed (converted to uppercase), and the processed line is written to the output file. Buffered I/O is used to optimize the read and write operations.

Utilizing File Info

Additional file information can be accessed and used within your program. The os package offers the Stat function to retrieve metadata about a file:

```
package main

import (
    "fmt"
    "log"
    "os"
)

func main() {
    fileName := "sample.txt"

    // Retrieve file information
    fileInfo, err := os.Stat(fileName)
    if err != nil {
        log.Fatalf("Failed to get file info: %v", err)
    }

    // Display file information
    fmt.Printf("File Name: %s\n", fileInfo.Name())
    fmt.Printf("Size: %d bytes\n", fileInfo.Size())
    fmt.Printf("Permissions: %s\n", fileInfo.Mode())
    fmt.Printf("Last Modified: %s\n", fileInfo.ModTime())
    fmt.Printf("Is Directory: %v\n", fileInfo.IsDir())
```

```
}
```

In this example, os.Stat is used to obtain information about the file, such as its name, size, permissions, modification time, and whether it is a directory. This metadata can be useful for logging, condition-based processing, or performing file checks before operations.

Using these techniques and examples, you can efficiently process files and automate file-related tasks in Go. Each method provides fundamental building blocks that can be expanded into more complex applications involving file manipulation and automation.

12.8 Building a Real-Time Chat Application

To demonstrate the capabilities of Go in handling concurrent data streams and real-time applications, we will build a real-time chat application. This section will guide you through the development of a fully functional chat server using Go's standard libraries and web technologies such as WebSockets.

Setting Up the Project

Create a new directory for your project and initialize a new Go module:

```
$ mkdir chatapp
$ cd chatapp
$ go mod init chatapp
```

Dependencies

For this project, we will use the Gorilla WebSocket package, which simplifies the handling of WebSocket connections in Go. Add this package to your project:

```
$ go get github.com/gorilla/websocket
```

Chat Server Structure

We will organize our server with the following structure:

- main.go: Entry point of the application.
- client.go: Handles individual client connections.
- hub.go: Manages all active connections and broadcasts messages.

Creating the Hub

The hub will manage our WebSocket connections and broadcast messages to all connected clients. Create a new file, hub.go, and define the hub structure and methods:

```
package main

type Hub struct {
    clients map[*Client]bool
    broadcast chan []byte
    register chan *Client
    unregister chan *Client
}

func newHub() *Hub {
    return &Hub{
        clients: make(map[*Client]bool),
        broadcast: make(chan []byte),
        register: make(chan *Client),
        unregister: make(chan *Client),
    }
}

func (h *Hub) run() {
    for {
        select {
        case client := <-h.register:
            h.clients[client] = true
        case client := <-h.unregister:
            if _, ok := h.clients[client]; ok {
                delete(h.clients, client)
                close(client.send)
            }
        case message := <-h.broadcast:
            for client := range h.clients {
                select {
                case client.send <- message:
                default:
                    close(client.send)
                    delete(h.clients, client)
                }
            }
        }
    }
}
```

Handling Client Connections

Next, we will create a client.go file to manage individual client connections. The Client structure will reference the hub and handle incoming and outgoing messages:

```
package main

import (
    "github.com/gorilla/websocket"
)

type Client struct {
    hub *Hub
    conn *websocket.Conn
    send chan []byte
}

func (c *Client) readPump() {
    defer func() {
        c.hub.unregister <- c
        c.conn.Close()
    }()
    for {
        _, message, err := c.conn.ReadMessage()
        if err != nil {
            break
        }
        c.hub.broadcast <- message
    }
}

func (c *Client) writePump() {
    defer func() {
        c.conn.Close()
    }()
    for {
        select {
        case message, ok := <-c.send:
            if !ok {
                c.conn.WriteMessage(websocket.CloseMessage, []byte{})
                return
            }
            c.conn.WriteMessage(websocket.TextMessage, message)
        }
    }
}
```

Upgrading HTTP to WebSocket

We need to handle the HTTP upgrade to WebSocket protocol in our main file. Create main.go and set up the HTTP server and WebSocket handler:

```
package main

import (
```

```
    "net/http"
    "github.com/gorilla/websocket"
)

var upgrader = websocket.Upgrader{
    ReadBufferSize: 1024,
    WriteBufferSize: 1024,
}

func serveWs(hub *Hub, w http.ResponseWriter, r *http.Request) {
    conn, err := upgrader.Upgrade(w, r, nil)
    if err != nil {
        return
    }
    client := &Client{hub: hub, conn: conn, send: make(chan []byte, 256)}
    client.hub.register <- client

    go client.writePump()
    client.readPump()
}

func main() {
    hub := newHub()
    go hub.run()
    http.HandleFunc("/ws", func(w http.ResponseWriter, r *http.Request) {
        serveWs(hub, w, r)
    })
    err := http.ListenAndServe(":8080", nil)
    if err != nil {
        panic("Error: " + err.Error())
    }
}
```

This code sets up an HTTP server that listens on port 8080, upgrades HTTP requests at the /ws endpoint to WebSocket connections, and handles the client interactions through the hub.

Client-Side Integration

To interact with our WebSocket server, you need a simple HTML client. Create an index.html file:

```
<!DOCTYPE html>
<html>
<head>
    <title>Chat Application</title>
</head>
<body>
    <textarea id="chatLog" cols="100" rows="20" readonly></textarea><br/>
    <input type="text" id="messageInput" size="50" />
    <button onclick="sendMessage()">Send</button>

    <script>
        const ws = new WebSocket("ws://localhost:8080/ws");
```

```
        ws.onmessage = function(event) {
            const chatLog = document.getElementById("chatLog");
            chatLog.value += event.data + "\n";
        };

        function sendMessage() {
            const messageInput = document.getElementById("messageInput");
            ws.send(messageInput.value);
            messageInput.value = "";
        }
    </script>
</body>
</html>
```

This simple HTML document contains a text area to display chat messages, an input field to type new messages, and a button to send messages. The JavaScript code establishes a WebSocket connection to the server and handles incoming messages by appending them to the text area. The sendMessage function sends the content of the input field to the server.

Launch the server by running the go run command, and open index.html in your web browser to start chatting.

```
$ go run main.go
```

Handling Errors and Cleanup

It's crucial to handle errors and close connections properly to avoid memory leaks and ensure application stability. The existing code partially addresses this, but we should ensure every resource is cleaned up correctly.

hub.go and client.go already include basic cleanup code in defer statements, but make sure to add any additional cleanup procedures if your implementation demands so.

To observe the application's execution, run the server and open multiple browsers pointing to your chat application's index.html. Start sending messages and observe how they are broadcast to other connected clients in real-time.

12.9 Implementing Middleware

Middleware plays a vital role in managing HTTP requests and responses in web applications. In Go, middleware is a function that wraps around another HTTP handler to extend its functionality, such as logging, authentication, session management, or data compression.

Middleware functions are typically implemented as higher-order functions that take an http.Handler as input and return a new http.Handler. This design allows multiple middleware layers to be composed together, each adding its own layer of functionality.

To create middleware in Go, you can define a function that accepts an http.Handler and returns an http.Handler. Here is an example of a simple logging middleware:

```
package main

import (
    "log"
    "net/http"
    "time"
)

// LoggingMiddleware logs the details of each request and how long it took to
    process.
func LoggingMiddleware(next http.Handler) http.Handler {
    return http.HandlerFunc(func(w http.ResponseWriter, r *http.Request) {
        start := time.Now()
        next.ServeHTTP(w, r)
        log.Printf("%s %s %s", r.Method, r.RequestURI, time.Since(start))
    })
}

func main() {
    finalHandler := http.HandlerFunc(func(w http.ResponseWriter, r *http.
        Request) {
        w.Write([]byte("Hello, World!"))
    })

    http.Handle("/", LoggingMiddleware(finalHandler))
    http.ListenAndServe(":8080", nil)
}
```

Listing 12.20: Logging Middleware

In this example, the LoggingMiddleware function takes an http.Handler called next and returns an http.HandlerFunc. Inside this function, it captures the start time of the request, delegates the request to the next handler, and then logs the method, URI, and duration of the request.

Middleware can also be used to perform authentication. Here is an example of an authentication middleware that checks for a valid API key:

```
package main
```

```
import (
    "net/http"
)

// AuthMiddleware ensures requests have a valid API key.
func AuthMiddleware(next http.Handler) http.Handler {
    return http.HandlerFunc(func(w http.ResponseWriter, r *http.Request) {
        apiKey := r.Header.Get("X-API-KEY")
        if apiKey != "EXPECTED_API_KEY" {
            http.Error(w, "Forbidden", http.StatusForbidden)
            return
        }
        next.ServeHTTP(w, r)
    })
}

func main() {
    handler := http.HandlerFunc(func(w http.ResponseWriter, r *http.Request) {
        w.Write([]byte("Authenticated request"))
    })

    http.Handle("/secure", AuthMiddleware(handler))
    http.ListenAndServe(":8080", nil)
}
```

Listing 12.21: Authentication Middleware

Here, AuthMiddleware intercepts the HTTP request, checks for the required API key, and either proceeds with the request or returns a 403 Forbidden error.

Middleware can be chained together to build more complex behavior. Go's http.ServeMux allows the composition of multiple middleware layers. For example, you can use both logging and authentication middleware together:

```
package main

import (
    "log"
    "net/http"
    "time"
)

func LoggingMiddleware(next http.Handler) http.Handler {
    return http.HandlerFunc(func(w http.ResponseWriter, r *http.Request) {
        start := time.Now()
        next.ServeHTTP(w, r)
        log.Printf("%s %s %s", r.Method, r.RequestURI, time.Since(start))
    })
}
```

```
func AuthMiddleware(next http.Handler) http.Handler {
    return http.HandlerFunc(func(w http.ResponseWriter, r *http.Request) {
        apiKey := r.Header.Get("X-API-KEY")
        if apiKey != "EXPECTED_API_KEY" {
            http.Error(w, "Forbidden", http.StatusForbidden)
            return
        }
        next.ServeHTTP(w, r)
    })
}

func main() {
    finalHandler := http.HandlerFunc(func(w http.ResponseWriter, r *http.
        Request) {
        w.Write([]byte("Authenticated and logged request"))
    })

    chainedHandler := LoggingMiddleware(AuthMiddleware(finalHandler))

    http.Handle("/secure", chainedHandler)
    http.ListenAndServe(":8080", nil)
}
```

Listing 12.22: Chaining Middleware

In this example, the middleware functions are composed by passing the output of one middleware function as the input to the next. The LoggingMiddleware wraps around AuthMiddleware, ensuring that requests are first authenticated and then logged.

Implementing middleware is a powerful technique to enhance functionality and maintain code modularity in Go web applications. By wrapping core handlers with additional logic, middleware enables developers to enforce cross-cutting concerns in a clean and manageable way.

12.10 Deploying Go Applications

Deploying Go applications efficiently involves understanding the build process, cross-compilation, containerization, hosting options, and distribution strategies. This section will explore each of these aspects to ensure that you can deploy your Go applications in a robust and scalable manner.

Go Build Process

The go build command is integral to the Go deployment process. This command compiles the Go source code into an executable binary. The basic syntax for building a Go application is:

```
go build -o output_binary_name source_file.go
```

The -o flag specifies the output binary name. If omitted, the default executable will be named after the source file.

Cross-Compilation

One of Go's strengths is its ability to cross-compile applications to run on different operating systems and architecture platforms. Setting the GOOS and GOARCH environment variables serves this purpose. For example, to build a Windows 64-bit executable from a Unix-based system:

```
GOOS=windows GOARCH=amd64 go build -o output_binary_name.exe source_file.
    go
```

The available values for GOOS include darwin, linux, windows, etc., while GOARCH options include amd64, 386, arm, etc.

Containerization with Docker

Using Docker to containerize Go applications provides an isolated environment that packages the application along with its dependencies. A basic Dockerfile for a Go application could look like this:

```
# Start with a base Go image
FROM golang:1.16-alpine as builder

# Set the current working directory
WORKDIR /app

# Copy the Go source files
COPY . .

# Build the Go application
RUN go build -o myapp

# Create a new image for the runtime
FROM alpine:latest
WORKDIR /root/
COPY --from=builder /app/myapp .

# Run the Go binary
CMD ["./myapp"]
```

To build and run the Docker container:

```
docker build -t my-go-app .
docker run -d -p 8080:8080 my-go-app
```

Here, the first docker build command constructs the Docker image, and the docker run command starts a container from the image.

Hosting Options

There are various platforms available for hosting Go applications, ranging from traditional virtual private servers (VPS) to more advanced solutions like managed Kubernetes and serverless platforms.

- **Virtual Private Servers (VPS)**: Services such as AWS EC2, DigitalOcean, or Linode provide scalable VPS options. You can deploy your Go application binary directly on a VPS by uploading it and configuring it to run as a service.
- **Managed Kubernetes**: Platforms like Google Kubernetes Engine (GKE), Amazon EKS, and Azure AKS offer managed Kubernetes clusters for deploying containerized Go applications. You create Kubernetes deployment and service definitions in YAML format to orchestrate your application.
- **Serverless Platforms**: AWS Lambda, Google Cloud Functions, and Azure Functions provide serverless hosting environments where you can run functions triggered by events. Package your Go application as a handler and deploy it in these environments for responsive, event-driven operations.

Distribution Strategies

Ensuring the reliability and scalability of your Go application involves using effective distribution and versioning strategies. Tools such as dep, Go Modules, and CI/CD pipelines are pivotal to this process.

- **Go Modules**: Go Modules streamline dependency management and versioning. Initialize a module in your project with:

  ```
  go mod init your_module_name
  ```

  This creates a go.mod file, where dependencies and their versions are tracked.
- **Continuous Integration/Continuous Deployment (CI/CD)**: Implementing CI/CD pipelines automates the build, test, and deployment processes. Tools like Jenkins, GitHub Actions, and GitLab CI/CD can be configured to integrate with repositories and execute defined pipelines. A simple GitHub Actions workflow for deploying a Go application might look like:

```
name: Go CI

on: [push]

jobs:
  build:
    runs-on: ubuntu-latest
    steps:
    - uses: actions/checkout@v2
    - name: Set up Go
      uses: actions/setup-go@v2
      with:
        go-version: 1.16
    - name: Build
      run: go build -v ./...
    - name: Test
      run: go test -v ./...
```

This workflow checks out the code, sets up the Go environment, builds the application, and runs tests upon every push to the repository.

Different deployment strategies provide the flexibility to choose the right mix of tools and platforms suited to the application requirements and organizational infrastructure.

12.11 Optimizing Performance

Efficient performance is a critical component in software development, particularly when working with systems designed for high load and concurrency. This section explores various methods and techniques to optimize the performance of Go applications.

Performance optimization generally begins with identifying bottlenecks using profiling tools. The primary tool for profiling Go applications is 'pprof', which provides insights into CPU and memory usage. To start profiling, one must import the 'net/http/pprof' package in their Go application and set up a pprof HTTP handler.

```
package main

import (
    "net/http"
    _ "net/http/pprof"
)

func main() {
    go func() {
```

```
        log.Println(http.ListenAndServe("localhost:6060", nil))
    }()
    // Your application logic here
}
```

Listing 12.23: Adding pprof to a Go application

Once the application is running, the profiler data can be accessed at 'http://localhost:6060/debug/pprof/'. After identifying the performance bottlenecks, optimization strategies can be applied in the following areas: memory management, CPU utilization, and efficient concurrency patterns.

Memory management can be improved by minimizing garbage collection overhead. Go's garbage collector (GC) is efficient, but it can still consume significant CPU time and affect performance. To reduce this overhead, consider the following practices:

- Minimize allocation: Reuse objects instead of repeatedly allocating new ones. Object pools can be managed using the 'sync.Pool' type.

```
var pool = sync.Pool{
    New: func() interface{} {
        return new(MyStruct)
    },
}

func getMyStruct() *MyStruct {
    return pool.Get().(*MyStruct)
}

func releaseMyStruct(obj *MyStruct) {
    pool.Put(obj)
}
```

Listing 12.24: Using sync.Pool to manage object reuse

- Reduce pointer chasing: Use value types instead of pointers when possible, which may also improve cache locality.

For CPU utilization improvements, ensure that computationally expensive operations are optimized. Profiling can reveal hot spots in the code where most of the CPU time is being spent. Common strategies include:

- Algorithmic improvements: Optimize algorithms to reduce their time complexity. Utilize efficient data structures and practices, such as memoization or dynamic programming.

```
var cache = make(map[int]int)

func fib(n int) int {
    if n <= 1 {
        return n
    }
    if val, found := cache[n]; found {
        return val
    }
    result := fib(n-1) + fib(n-2)
    cache[n] = result
    return result
}
```

Listing 12.25: Optimizing an algorithm via memoization

- Parallel processing: Utilize goroutines effectively, balancing concurrency with overhead constraints. Remember that excessive use of goroutines may lead to increased context switching.

```
func compute(nums []int) int {
    ch := make(chan int)
    for _, num := range nums {
        go func(n int) {
            ch <- expensiveComputation(n)
        }(num)
    }
    sum := 0
    for range nums {
        sum += <-ch
    }
    return sum
}

func expensiveComputation(n int) int {
    // Simulating a time-consuming computation
    time.Sleep(1 * time.Second)
    return n * n
}
```

Listing 12.26: Using goroutines for parallel processing

Efficient concurrency patterns involve more than just using goroutines. It includes managing shared data with proper synchronization mechanisms to avoid race conditions and ensuring that the number of goroutines does not exceed the resources available. The 'sync' package provides several synchronization primitives like 'Mutex' and 'WaitGroup'.

```
var (
    mu sync.Mutex
    counter int
)

func increment() {
    mu.Lock()
    defer mu.Unlock()
    counter++
}

func main() {
    var wg sync.WaitGroup
    for i := 0; i < 1000; i++ {
        wg.Add(1)
        go func() {
            defer wg.Done()
            increment()
        }()
    }
    wg.Wait()
    fmt.Println("Final counter value:", counter)
}
```

Listing 12.27: Using sync.Mutex for data synchronization

Another important aspect is avoiding the creation of temporary objects that increase memory pressure, which can be alleviated by optimizing the handling of slices and strings.

- Efficient slice handling: Preallocate slices when the final size is known to avoid repeated allocations.

```
func generateNumbers(n int) []int {
    numbers := make([]int, 0, n)
    for i := 0; i < n; i++ {
        numbers = append(numbers, i)
    }
    return numbers
}
```

Listing 12.28: Preallocating slices to avoid repeated allocations

- String operations: Minimize concatenations and consider using 'strings.Builder' for constructing large strings efficiently.

```
var builder strings.Builder
builder.WriteString("This is a test string. ")
builder.WriteString("Appending another string segment.")
result := builder.String()
```

Listing 12.29: Using strings.Builder for efficient string concatenation

Profiling to track and measure the impact of these optimizations ensures that changes positively influence performance. A methodical approach combining profiling insights and applying the discussed strategies will lead to substantial performance improvements in Go applications.

12.12 Case Studies and Example Projects

Case Study: Building a Blogging Platform

To begin with, we will develop a simple blogging platform, illustrating how the various components such as web servers, databases, and web APIs come together in a cohesive application. This platform will allow users to create, read, update, and delete blog posts.

main.go:

```
package main

import (
    "net/http"
    "github.com/gorilla/mux"
)

func main() {
    r := mux.NewRouter()
    r.HandleFunc("/posts", createPost).Methods("POST")
    r.HandleFunc("/posts", getPosts).Methods("GET")
    r.HandleFunc("/posts/{id}", getPost).Methods("GET")
    r.HandleFunc("/posts/{id}", updatePost).Methods("PUT")
    r.HandleFunc("/posts/{id}", deletePost).Methods("DELETE")

    http.ListenAndServe(":8000", r)
}
```

Listing 12.30: Main application entry point

handlers.go:

```
package main
```

```
import (
    "encoding/json"
    "net/http"
    "github.com/gorilla/mux"
)

type Post struct {
    ID string `json:"id"`
    Title string `json:"title"`
    Content string `json:"content"`
}

var posts []Post

func createPost(w http.ResponseWriter, r *http.Request) {
    var post Post
    json.NewDecoder(r.Body).Decode(&post)
    post.ID = "1" // This would be replaced by a unique ID generator in a real
        app
    posts = append(posts, post)
    json.NewEncoder(w).Encode(post)
}

func getPosts(w http.ResponseWriter, r *http.Request) {
    json.NewEncoder(w).Encode(posts)
}

func getPost(w http.ResponseWriter, r *http.Request) {
    params := mux.Vars(r)
    for _, post := range posts {
        if post.ID == params["id"] {
            json.NewEncoder(w).Encode(post)
            return
        }
    }
    http.NotFound(w, r)
}

func updatePost(w http.ResponseWriter, r *http.Request) {
    params := mux.Vars(r)
    for i, post := range posts {
        if post.ID == params["id"] {
            posts = append(posts[:i], posts[i+1:]...)
            var updatedPost Post
            json.NewDecoder(r.Body).Decode(&updatedPost)
            updatedPost.ID = params["id"]
            posts = append(posts, updatedPost)
            json.NewEncoder(w).Encode(updatedPost)
            return
        }
    }
    http.NotFound(w, r)
}
```

```
func deletePost(w http.ResponseWriter, r *http.Request) {
    params := mux.Vars(r)
    for i, post := range posts {
        if post.ID == params["id"] {
            posts = append(posts[:i], posts[i+1:]...)
            break
        }
    }
    json.NewEncoder(w).Encode(posts)
}
```

Listing 12.31: HTTP handlers for the blogging platform

This example demonstrates setting up routes for handling CRUD operations on blog posts, with each functionality encapsulated in appropriate handler functions.

Case Study: Creating a RESTful API for Library Management System

Next, we will design a RESTful API for a library management system. This will involve managing books and users – supporting functionalities such as listing available books, lending books to users, and adding new books.

library.go:

```
package main

import (
    "net/http"
    "github.com/gorilla/mux"
)

func main() {
    r := mux.NewRouter()
    r.HandleFunc("/books", addBook).Methods("POST")
    r.HandleFunc("/books", getBooks).Methods("GET")
    r.HandleFunc("/books/{id}", getBook).Methods("GET")
    r.HandleFunc("/books/{id}", lendBook).Methods("PUT")
    r.HandleFunc("/books/{id}", deleteBook).Methods("DELETE")

    http.ListenAndServe(":8000", r)
}
```

Listing 12.32: Library management system initialization

handlers.go:

```
package main
```

```
import (
    "encoding/json"
    "net/http"
    "github.com/gorilla/mux"
)

type Book struct {
    ID string `json:"id"`
    Title string `json:"title"`
    Author string `json:"author"`
    Status string `json:"status"` // "available" or "lent"
}

var books []Book

func addBook(w http.ResponseWriter, r *http.Request) {
    var book Book
    json.NewDecoder(r.Body).Decode(&book)
    book.ID = "1" // This would be replaced by a unique ID generator in a real
        app
    book.Status = "available"
    books = append(books, book)
    json.NewEncoder(w).Encode(book)
}

func getBooks(w http.ResponseWriter, r *http.Request) {
    json.NewEncoder(w).Encode(books)
}

func getBook(w http.ResponseWriter, r *http.Request) {
    params := mux.Vars(r)
    for _, book := range books {
        if book.ID == params["id"] {
            json.NewEncoder(w).Encode(book)
            return
        }
    }
    http.NotFound(w, r)
}

func lendBook(w http.ResponseWriter, r *http.Request) {
    params := mux.Vars(r)
    for i, book := range books {
        if book.ID == params["id"] {
            books[i].Status = "lent"
            json.NewEncoder(w).Encode(books[i])
            return
        }
    }
    http.NotFound(w, r)
}

func deleteBook(w http.ResponseWriter, r *http.Request) {
```

```
    params := mux.Vars(r)
    for i, book := range books {
        if book.ID == params["id"] {
            books = append(books[:i], books[i+1:]...)
            break
        }
    }
    json.NewEncoder(w).Encode(books)
}
```

Listing 12.33: HTTP handlers for managing books

The system manages books' status, indicating if they are available or lent out, by modifying the Book struct and adding corresponding handler functions.

Example Project: Concurrent Data Processing Pipeline

The following example demonstrates using Go's concurrency features to create a data processing pipeline that can process multiple data streams concurrently.

pipeline.go:

```
package main

import (
    "fmt"
    "time"
)

func generateData(channel chan int) {
    for i := 1; i <= 10; i++ {
        channel <- i
        time.Sleep(time.Second)
    }
    close(channel)
}

func processData(channel chan int, results chan int) {
    for data := range channel {
        results <- data * 2
    }
    close(results)
}

func main() {
    dataChan := make(chan int)
    resultsChan := make(chan int)

    go generateData(dataChan)
    go processData(dataChan, resultsChan)
```

```
    for result := range resultsChan {
        fmt.Println(result)
    }
}
```

Listing 12.34: Concurrent data processing pipeline

Output:

```
2
4
6
8
10
12
14
16
18
20
```

This project outlines how to create and handle channels, demonstrating the transmission of data values and concurrent processing using goroutines.

Example Project: JSON Parsing and Validation Utility

This project describes the implementation of a tool for parsing and validating JSON data. This utility reads a JSON file, parses it into a Go struct, validates the structure, and handles any errors appropriately.

jsonutil.go:

```
package main

import (
    "encoding/json"
    "fmt"
    "io/ioutil"
    "os"
)

type Person struct {
    Name string `json:"name"`
    Age int `json:"age"`
    Email string `json:"email"`
}

func main() {
    file, err := os.Open("data.json")
    if err != nil {
        fmt.Println("Error opening file:", err)
        return
```

```
    }
    defer file.Close()

    byteValue, _ := ioutil.ReadAll(file)

    var person Person
    json.Unmarshal(byteValue, &person)

    if person.Name == "" || person.Email == "" {
        fmt.Println("Invalid JSON format!")
        return
    }

    fmt.Println("Name:", person.Name)
    fmt.Println("Age:", person.Age)
    fmt.Println("Email:", person.Email)
}
```

Listing 12.35: JSON parsing and validation utility

This utility ensures that the input JSON is valid and correctly structured, providing valuable feedback in case of inconsistencies.

The case studies and example projects detailed herein illustrate a range of Go's capabilities, from web development to concurrent programming and data handling, thereby equipping you to leverage Go effectively for diverse real-world applications.

Made in United States
Orlando, FL
04 November 2026

90207064R00236